Why Women Wear What They Wear

MATERIALIZING CULTURE

. . . .

Why Women Wear What They Wear

Sophie Woodward

Oxford • New York

English edition

First published in 2007 by
Berg
Editorial offices:
First Floor, Angel Court, 81 St Clements Street, Oxford, OX4 1AW, UK
175 Fifth Avenue, New York, NY 10010, USA

Berg is the imprint of Oxford International Publishers Ltd.

Library of Congress Cataloging-in-Publication Data

Woodward, Sophie.
Why women wear what they wear / Sophie Woodward.
p. cm.
Includes bibliographical references and index.
ISBN-13: 978-1-84520-698-7 (cloth)
ISBN-10: 1-84520-698-3 (cloth)
ISBN-13: 978-1-84520-699-4 (pbk.)
ISBN-10: 1-84520-699-1 (pbk.)
1. Clothing and dress. 2. Clothing and dress—Social aspects.
3. Clothing and dress—Psychological aspects. I. Title.
TT507.W65 2007
646'.34—dc22
2007037812

British Library Cataloguing-in-Publication Data

A catalogue record for this book is available from the British Library.

ISBN 978 1 84520 698 7 (Cloth)
ISBN 978 1 84520 699 4 (Paper)

Typeset by Apex Publishing, LLC, Madison, WI, USA.
Printed in the United Kingdom by Biddles Ltd, King's Lynn

www.bergpublishers.com

For Kath and Steve
In memory of Sue Benson

Contents

Acknowledgements

This book owes a great deal to all of those who have supported me throughout the time it took to research and write. Because this book arose out of the ethnography for my PhD thesis, I would like to thank the Economic and Social Research Council for funding it; I am extremely grateful to Daniel Miller for his fantastic ideas and continued support throughout my research. I would also like to thank Joanne Entwistle and Emma Tarlo for useful comments on the original thesis, and those at Berg Publishers for their patience and help in turning the manuscript into a book.

I would especially like to thank my parents Kath and Steve for their constant belief in me; Kath, for her incredible insights and editing, and Steve, for his grasp of language and grammar. I would also like to remember Sue Benson, who died whilst I was writing this book but who was inspirational to me from the beginning. This book would also not have been possible without non-academic support, so thank-you to the rest of my family, Richard, Tamsin, Jack, Cleo and Eppy. For keeping me sane, thank-you to Bede, Joe, Paul, Philippa, Sarah, Cath, Zanna, Katy, Cristina, Colly, Craig, Emanuela and Vicky. For teaching me the fun side of academic life, I thank Dan, Rhoda, Shaila and Michelle.

Finally, and most importantly, I owe a debt of gratitude to all of the women who let me into their homes and bedrooms. Their participation made the fieldwork on which this book was based a pleasure to carry out, and it is because of their candidness in sharing their clothing triumphs and disasters with me that makes this book what it is.

Introduction

Wearing only her pale pink silk camisole and shorts, Sadie gazes uninspired at the clothes in her open wardrobe; she is going to her friend's leaving party the following day straight after work, and is attempting to select an outfit before she goes to bed. She stands in front of the wardrobe hoping her imagination will be roused by something she sees hanging before her. Ordinarily she selects her outfit just before going out, when the anticipation of the event galvanizes her into action. However, unsure as to what the weather will be like or what frame of mind she will be in the following day, she is unable to decide as her excitement is cast into shadow by the prospect of an eight-hour working day. She becomes despondent after a while and decides to select her shoes first, which she displays on a shelf in her bedroom. She tries on her favourite pair: pink ballet-style shoes with high metallic pink heels, which she only wears when she sporadically decides to try them on in her flat. She is so enthralled with the shoes that every outfit she has tried them on with before has failed to live up to their allure. Sadie is determined to wear them on this occasion, as she stands in front of the mirror, twisting her feet round so that they become visible from every angle, admiring the unusual shade of pink and the sculptural effect of the heels. Basking in the imagined admiration of her friends, she decides resolutely that she must wear the shoes.

She now has to resolve the problem of what to wear with them the following evening, and returns to the wardrobe. As she cannot afford anything new, she frantically looks along her rails for anything that will 'go' with the shoes, and happens upon her cream cord mini-skirt. On trying it on with the shoes she is delighted at the complementarity of the colours. The skirt, being quite neutral, draws attention to the shoes. As the outfit is now two-thirds complete, she is determined not to be thwarted by a lack of a suitable top. As she goes through the piles of tops in the bottom of her wardrobe nothing seems appropriate. She clutches a pile of potentials in her arms, and holds each one in front of her body as she considers it: her cream top is too pale, making the top and skirt blend into one, and all her black, colourful or patterned tops are too dark for the outfit, drawing attention away from the shoes. In her frustration, she flings the clothes on the floor. She stands looking at shoes again in mirror; she is now wearing the cord skirt, and still happens to have her pale pink pyjama top on. On being confronted by her reflection, she makes the fortuitous realization that the whole outfit 'goes'. She holds up her feet to examine the shoes, twisting them so they shimmer slightly: "The top's the same colour as the shoes when they catch the light!!" Sadie exclaims in delight. Initially unsure as to whether she can wear her nightwear on a night out in the West End of London, she decides no one will notice. She then chooses some underwear to go with the outfit, and ends up selecting a mint green bra with a pink trim: "then there'll be a flash of matching colours" when the top of the bra peeps out at the top of the camisole.

On this particular occasion, Sadie is trying to create an outfit that will be appropriate to the social occasion, yet as she goes out with the same group of friends each weekend she still wants to look different and unique. As she chooses what to wear, she has to negotiate a balance between fitting in, dressing appropriately and looking and feeling like herself. The act of dressing is therefore the moment where social expectations and personal preferences conjoin, as Sadie has to consider wider aspects of her social existence: her status as a young woman, her sexuality, relationships with friends and men she wants to impress. The occasion she is dressing for requires her to assemble a new outfit, and so the moment becomes anguished because she cannot just fall back on an 'easy' or 'safe' item of clothing. This concern is exacerbated by the perceived splendour of the shoes, as she worries nothing will be able to live up to them. Sadie has such a clear sense of 'what goes' that she looks at the whole range of her clothing in the wardrobe and exclaims in despair that she has 'nothing to wear', before serendipitously discovering that her nightwear 'goes' with the shoes.

The account of how Sadie puts together an outfit described above is taken from my fieldwork and exemplifies many of the negotiations women make when choosing what to wear. This act of getting dressed takes place at least once a day and as such is ubiquitous and experienced by all women irrespective of age, occupation, sexuality, religion, ethnicity or interest in clothing. It is the occasion when women have to negotiate their bodies, respectability, style, status, and their self-perception and is therefore a crucial moment in understanding why women choose to wear what they wear. The opening description of Sadie's wardrobe dilemma was an occasion at which I was present, as part of the wider ethnography upon which this book is based. The ethnography involved observing women as they choose what to wear in their bedrooms, and discussing these choices with the women themselves. It thereby occupies one of the most important and largely missing elements in the study of clothing and fashion, which is the choices made not while shopping but in the private act of creating ones public appearance. As the example of Sadie's clothing dilemma highlights, the items that women reject when dressing are just as important as the items of clothing that are worn. This book therefore offers a crucial 'back-stage' understanding of the publicly presented dressed body, as women always have in mind this 'seen' context when choosing what to wear. Kaiser (2003) has discussed the impact of social interactions upon how women construct their identities through clothing, as a balance between how women appear to others and how they see their own appearance. This book follows Kaiser's theory to its logical empirical conclusions by looking at the relationship between how women look and how they feel in the moment of dressing. The gaze of others is refracted through women's memories of particular occasions and their imagined projections of how others might see them.

The importance of looking at the act of getting dressed was recognized in Tarlo's seminal account (1996) of the dilemmas over dressing in the context of an Indian village. Her research shows that, far from being prescribed by social categories such as caste, clothing is in fact extremely contested, and the locus for multiple social and personal identities. My book is the first comprehensive attempt to understand the practice of dressing in a Western context. The literature on dress and identity is based primarily upon the public presentation of the self, whether the focus is upon embodiment (Entwistle, 2000), particular sub-cultural identities (Hodkinson, 2002), or looking at the practice of selecting clothing (Hansen, 2000). This publicly presented self is always created in private, which is why this book presents an account of the private act of getting dressed. This 'wardrobe moment', which is experienced at least once a day, mediates clothing as appearance management and public display and the private, intimate domain of the bedroom and wardrobe. When the outfit is worn, unless it proves to be a failure, all of these anxieties are concealed; it is in the unseen domain of the bedroom where the anguished moments occur. As women choose outfits from their wardrobe, they stand looking at their reflection and wonder about whether they have 'got it right' for a particular occasion, for someone their age; they may also worry whether their bum looks too big, their legs too short, or their skin too sallow. By looking at these intimate processes of selection and rejection of outfits, it is possible to shed light on issues that are seen as important at a macro-level in the fashion context, such as issues of individuality and conformity (Simmel, 1971), ambivalence (Wilson, 1985), body image (Wolf, 1990, Bordo, 1995), the fashionable ideal (Thesander, 1997) and anxiety (Arnold, 2001, Clarke and Miller, 2002). These are experienced, in the moment of dressing as an internal ambivalence for the individual.

This book discusses these internal dilemmas as they are exteriorized both through the material form of clothing, as women look at items of clothing and wonder 'is this me', and also through the reflected image of the dressed body in the mirror. Clothing materializes questions of identity in a particularly intimate way, as women's relationship to their clothing arises out of the sensual experiences of wearing items on their bodies. The relationship clothing has to the body is pivotal in how women decide what to wear both in terms of a material, embodied relationship of how clothing feels on the skin and allows the body to move, and also in terms of the ways in which clothing affects the appearance of the body. As women look at their dressed bodies in the mirror, they do so in the context of omnipresent images of fashionable bodies in various media, which construct and perpetuate normative ideals of beauty and femininity (Gunter and Wykes, 2005). The impact these images have upon how women see their own body shapes is a hot topic in current public discourse. The potentially damaging effect of having size zero models is being discussed in political arenas as much as in celebrity gossip magazines. These debates speculate endlessly upon the possible impact of these images which idealize extreme thinness. In looking at how women make clothing choices, it is possible to address this same debate, yet in a manner which moves beyond speculation to see to what extent, if at all, women actually do measure up their bodies against these publicly presented ideals. The relationship between these images and how women see their own bodies cannot be assumed, but rather this book will consider instead how women's self-image is particular for the specific occasion they are dressing for. Cultural norms and social expectations are important depending upon what a woman's 'project' (de Beauvoir, 1997, Moi, 2002) is, and so women's relationship to beauty ideals depend upon the specific occasion women are dressing for.

In order to access these intimate concerns women have over their own body images, I had to be present when women were making their clothing choices. I carried out an in-depth ethnography over fifteen months in both London and Nottingham, which took place primarily in bedrooms. As this moment is so private, it was necessary to be present so often that my presence was no longer alien and intimidating. Unlike much of the research into clothing and identity, these women were not selected from any pre-determined social categories or identities, such as social class or a particular ethnicity or sexuality, as these often assume a primary point of identification, around which the clothing coheres. Instead, I worked with women who were grouped by their connection to each other through social networks (friendship groups, families, work colleagues). This approach allows my research to investigate the multiple intersecting identities of gender, class, ethnicity, occupation, religion (Anthias, 1997). In looking at the whole spectrum of clothing women own, and what they choose to wear, or reject, this book arrives at a comprehensive account of the multiple, ambivalent aspects of women's selves, some of which are actualized through the final outfit that is selected and 'seen', as other aspects lie unworn in the wardrobe. Dependent upon the social context women are dressing for, different identities emerge as salient. Therefore, in this book, social categories such as class, gender, ethnicity and sexuality are discussed as they frame women's clothing choices, but are not seen to determine them.

The chapters move from a focus upon the individual, her biography and aesthetic to the larger context, both social and commercial, that impinges upon them. Starting with the wardrobe, as a personal collection, the book moves through to the considerations of the gaze of others, to external influences, such as fashion. Much of the material presented in the book is lead by intimate, in depth discussions of specific women and how they choose outfits for particular occasions. The issues that are discussed and theorized in this book therefore arise from the concerns that women actually have when they get dressed. These case studies are used to explore issues such as: whose opinions are important when women choose outfits, how women use their 'past' to construct a current outfit, what impact normative dress codes actually have, and why women with wardrobes full of clothing so often state they have 'nothing to wear'.

Chapter 1 'Understanding Women and their Wardrobes' outlines my approach to the topic. As an act that is so everyday and seemingly ordinary, the act of choosing what to wear is notably absent from the literature on fashion, and as such this chapter sets out a way of understanding and theorizing it, and outlines how it can contribute to current literature on dress and identity. Following Tarlo's example of an ethnography women's clothing in India (1996), the act of choosing what to wear is discussed as a practice of identity construction, from the resources in the wardrobe, which I discuss as a form of 'distributed personhood' (Gell, 1998), as clothing forms a literal and metaphorical extension of the self. The concerns that women have when choosing what to wear relate to both how the clothing makes them 'feel' and how it makes them 'look'. Therefore this chapter introduces positions which help understand the materiality of clothing, from anthropology (Miller, 1987, Barnes and Eicher, 1993, Weiner and Schneider, 1989) and costume history (Taylor, 2004). The way clothing makes women feel is also importantly a question of the body, and so I introduce phenomenological approaches to clothing as an embodied practice (Moi, 2002, Young, 2004). This is linked to how women 'look' through the social psychological theories of Mead (1982) and Kaiser (2003), in terms of how women see their own body image through their imagined and remembered opinions of others. These discussions are finally considered in light of the particular context of contemporary Britain, in terms of the social parameters of identity, definitions of what is in 'fashion', as potential concerns which influence women's clothing choices.

Chapter 2 'Hanging out in the Home and the Bedroom' makes the case for carrying out an urban ethnography. The majority of the ethnography took place in women's homes, and bedrooms, and in this chapter I discuss the issues which arise from carrying out research in such an intimate domain. As a precursor to the detailed case studies in the following chapters, here I offer an overview of the context of research; in terms of place, the geographical locations of London and Nottingham, space, the micro-context of the bedroom, and people: the networks of women with whom I worked, and the background of each woman. A crucial part of offering context for the detailed case studies is the contents of the wardrobe itself, and so here I also outline the general trends of how women organize their clothing, how many items they own and how many items they actually wear.

Chapter 3 'But What Were You Wearing? Clothes and Memories' is the first of two chapters which consider the wardrobe as a personal collection, in particular here the focus is upon how women's memories may be stored in clothing. Taking specific case studies, I discuss how clothing, through its sensuality and tactility as it holds the shape of the body, materializes personal narratives and biographies. Items women keep, but no longer wear, can be seen to embody former aspects of the self (Banim and Guy, 2001). By looking at biography as it exists in the material form of clothing, rather than through conventional verbal narratives, this chapter seeks to challenge and question the idea that personal narratives are linear and coherent (such as Giddens, 1991). Instead, I consider examples of when 'former' items are reworn as part of a contemporary identity as the 'past' is made present in the act of dressing.

Chapter 4, 'Looking Good, Feeling Right: The Aesthetics of Getting Dressed' explores the aesthetics of the wardrobe through the key concern women have when choosing what to wear: 'does this go'? Through looking at the links between 'how I look' and 'how I feel' this chapter address the issue of what it means to feel 'comfortable' in an outfit, as comfort is considered both in terms of appearance and how it feels on the body. This addresses the issues of whether items 'go' together in terms of fabrics, colours and styles, and also whether the clothing is 'really me'. This 'me' involves balancing personal style with external sartorial expectations and media constructions of body ideals (Gunter and Wykes, 2005). The wardrobe is discussed as a personal aesthetic (Gell, 1998), as a balance between the personal and the generic as this 'me' has to incorporate 'place' and social context.

In Chapter 5 'Looking in the Mirror: Seeing and Being Seen' focuses in particular at the position mirrors have in the act of choosing an outfit, as women dress through the imagined opinions and 'gaze' of others. Making up and dressing the self are therefore seen as acts of self-construction. The chapter considers theoretical discussions of 'the gaze' (Bonner et al, 1992) through the empirical examples of women engaging with their own mirror image to look at the multiple layers this involves: as women dress for other men, for other women and also importantly for themselves. In this chapter I address the extent to which women are influenced by wider cultural influence of body ideals (Thesander, 1997). Mead's (1982) theories are developed to incorporate how women look at their own bodies in front of the material mirror, as they remember and imagine the 'gaze' of others. Particular attention is given in this chapter to notions of 'artifice' and how women spend hours constructing how they 'really' look.

Chapter 6 'Mothers, Daughters, Friends: Dressing in Relationships' moves beyond the imagined gaze of others to look at the concrete ways in which actual social networks impact upon dressing. This chapter focuses upon all the clothing women own that was given to them by someone else; it draws from anthropological theories of the gift (Godelier, 1999, Mauss, 1992, Osteen, 2002) to look at how particular relationships are embedded in items of clothing. I discuss cases of gifted clothing between mothers and daughters, and clothes swapping amongst young women. Applying Weiner's discussion of exchange practices in Melanesia (1992) to my example, I look at how short-term and long-term exchanges of clothing are crucial in creating and redefining particular relationships. I use the examples of women's clothes swapping to reflect upon the ambivalences and paradoxes of British kinship (MacFarlane, 1987, Strathern, 1992), as clothing allows women to both assert their individuality and autonomy, and to simultaneously define themselves through their relationships to others. This chapter raises the idea that women are 'dressing the self' in relationships.

Chapter 7 'Fashion: Breaking and Making the rules' discusses how women negotiate being fashionable as one of the many concerns they have when choosing what to wear. I discuss how much the 'external' fashion context influences women's decisions, both in terms of women's understanding of what is 'in' fashion, and the extent to which swiftly changing fashions (Vinken, 2004) produce uncertainty. In understanding how women's wardrobes relate to the wider fashion context, I also discuss a couple of instances of how women choose outfits from the shops. I look at how women negotiate potential wardrobe and shopping panics, as women have rules for 'what goes', which are both defined externally, through fashion magazines and television programmes, and internally, through women's own sense of what goes. These 'rules' are also discussed as a potential domain for innovation, as women break the rules to create new looks.

Chapter 8, 'Dressing up and Dressing Down: can you wear jeans?' considers the underlying dynamic of all wardrobes and acts of dressing. This is discussed in terms of what I define as 'habitual' and 'non-habitual': clothing which is 'safe' and clothing which transforms. This highlights that dressing involves the balance and negotiation between being creative and individual, yet simultaneously conforming to the expectations of others, and indeed of themselves. Whilst many facets of identity may be ordinarily un-thought out and naturalized, such as gender (Young, 2005), I consider here how particular social occasions (such as a ball) leads to a self-reflexive engagement with these. On such occasions women consider how to conform to normative expectations of femininity, or class-specific notions of respectability (Skeggs, 1997). Given the ubiquity of the fabric denim in women's wardrobes, I discuss this fabric as it raises these interlinking issues of conformity and individuality. The data is discussed in light of Goffman's theories of social roles (1971), and the ways in which social occasions call for the mobilization of certain aspects of the self.

The conclusion outlines the implications of an approach to dress and identity that focuses upon the process through which women choose what to wear. In seeing choosing what to wear as an act of rejection and selection, or success and failure to construct an identity, I argue that a theory of dress and identity needs to be a theory of ambivalence. The ambivalences that writers such as Simmel and Wilson have seen as central to the macro-level for fashion are discussed as a micro-dilemma for women as they choose what to wear. In situating these fashion ambivalences in the wider, situated and specific concerns women have when getting dressed, I use this to reflect upon how women relate to 'fashion' and to the media representations of body images. The section concludes with a rethinking of how getting dressed can be theorized as an act of identity construction, as choosing what to wear is an act of 'surfacing', 'presenting' and drawing in aspects of the self and relationships.

Understanding Women and Their Wardrobes

Accounts on fashion, dress and identity proliferate, bearing testament to the centrality of questions of identity at both the macro level, as fashion is seen to encapsulate
the ambivalences and contradictions of capitalism and modernity (Arnold, 2001,
Breward and Evans, 2005, Wilson, 1985), and at the micro level, as fashion is involved in individual constructions of selfhood. The practice of identity construction
by individuals in their bedrooms and the development of the urban forms of modernity at first glance appear to be disparate concerns. However, in each instance,
considerations of fashion and identity hang upon common themes pointing to the
ambivalences of identity: the artifice or authenticity of appearance, conformity or
innovation, anxiety or possibility. The tension between conformity and individuality can be a motor for change at the level of the fashion system (Simmel, 1971)
and a means for women to create an innovative look from their wardrobes as they
deliberate over looking different and fitting in. An understanding of why women
wear what they wear needs to be as much a consideration of the intimate as of these
wider dilemmas of sartorial normativity, as women balance the 'fashionable ideal'
(Thesander, 1997) with their own flawed bodies. How women manage and construct
their appearances involves the consideration of specific social situations, as well as
the wider social and cultural context (Kaiser, 2003: 58) The broad context of social
expectations are refracted through individual style preferences, social networks and
women's unique biographies.

The factors women deal with when they assemble their appearance are multiple
and wide ranging; this book attempts to see how these many considerations articulate together in women's clothing choices. I will therefore be drawing upon different
perspectives to shed light on the concerns that women have when they get dressed.
Because the act of choosing what to wear starts with the wardrobe, this chapter starts
with 'Understanding Wardrobes' as the toolkit (Levi-Strauss, 1966) from which
women can create identities through clothing. The contention of this book is that, in
order to understand *why* women wear particular outfits, it is necessary to look at *how*
they make selections; in considering what they reject as much as what they select,
the ambivalences of anxiety and individuality become apparent. I discuss this process in 'Understanding Getting Dressed' as a material, embodied practice. Miller's
theory of objectification offers a way of understanding this process, as women look
at items of clothing in the wardrobe and ask 'is this me'? I draw on theories of social

psychology (Mead, 1982) and theories of the gaze to discuss how dressing involves women seeing themselves through the eyes of other people.

When women are getting dressed, they are asking questions such as 'is this me?' or 'could this be me?' or whether something is 'really me'; and so, in the next section, 'Understanding the Self', I outline what I mean by the 'self', both as a discourse, something women are expected to 'have', and as a practice, something that women 'do'. In each case, the self is discussed as gendered (Eicher, 2001) and embodied (Entwistle, 2000); this, in turn, is seen in the context of factors such as class (Skeggs, 1997), ethnicity (Anthias, 2005, Hall, 2000) and occupation, as factors which may be important in framing how women choose their clothing. Given that women ask these identity questions through their clothing, in the fourth section, 'Understanding Clothing', I link the discussion of the self specifically to an understanding of clothing as a form of material culture. I draw from the anthropological literature and the literature of costume history to discuss how the material properties of clothing (worn on the body, as it ages, it is soft) are crucial to the meanings woven within items of clothing. The final section, 'Fashion and the Ambivalences of Identity', discusses how clothing choices are affected by the specific fashion context of contemporary Britain and how the anxieties and ambivalences this produces may impact upon how women choose what to wear.

Understanding Wardrobes

Does this Go?

The wardrobe is both an architectural structure which houses clothing and the totality of clothing a person owns. Once purchased, clothing spends most of its time either at rest in the wardrobe (Cwerner, 2001) or at some point within the household as part of domestic consumption practices (Gregson and Beale, 2004), as clothing spills out of the wardrobe onto a chair at the end of the bed, linen baskets, under the bed and into the wardrobes of children, partners and friends. Like the bricoleur's toolkit (Levi-Strauss, 1966), the wardrobe is a collection of items accumulated from previous occasions. Yet, when women choose from the wardrobe, they are rarely, if ever, selecting from the whole range of items they own. Instead, they are choosing from the various 'orders' of the wardrobe, which may be based upon social roles (such as work clothing), functionality (such as gym clothing), type of clothing (such as trousers or shirts), colours, textures or even categories such as fun clothing. These orders help women to organize their lives and make the act of choosing what to wear easier.

One of the pivotal questions women ask as they stand in front of the wardrobe is: do these items go together, as each item of clothing acquires its meaning in relation to other items (Sahlins, 1976). When a woman's trusty old cream and red floral shirt is combined with a new blue denim skirt, the usually un-thought-about shirt has to be reconsidered as part of the new assemblage. Textures, patterns and colours acquire a different tone and vividness dependent upon which colour they are placed next to (Gage, 1993). As items are recombined, they acquire different meanings: the floral shirt that looks dowdy worn with flat sensible shoes can appear funky when worn with jeans and the right accessories. However, when women ask 'does this go?', they are not only questioning whether the colours and patterns are complementary, but also whether the outfit is appropriate for a particular social occasion. Even if a top is the perfect colour to go with a new skirt, if it is a work top, it may have to be rejected as inappropriate for going out clubbing with friends. The orders of the wardrobe therefore overlap.

Organizing the wardrobe into these orders allows women to avoid spending hours deciding what to wear each morning because they know what items can be worn together. Even though a strong sense of what goes with what can resolve these daily wardrobe quandaries, this type of thinking can also be restrictive. When a woman buys a new top, she tries to find something that will go with it from her wardrobe, yet arrives at the all-too-frequent conclusion that she has nothing to wear. On occasion, women are tyrannized by their perception of what can be worn together, and in this example, the new makes everything else they own appear inadequate. McCracken (1988) points out that the implication of such 'complementary goods' may prevent any purchases which are out of synch with a particular sense of order. McCracken cites the example of Diderot, who was given a scarlet dressing robe as a gift. Once he possessed this, everything else appeared shoddy and inadequate so that he feels compelled to replace all of his belongings. Often, what cannot be worn together is more powerful than what can, as women end up buying and wearing the same types of clothing all the time.

Is this Skirt Me?

The question 'does this go?' invariably involves the twin question 'is this me?', as the particular styles, colours and textures come to form part of a woman's sense of who she is and who she can be through clothing. Although the items are usually bought in the mass market, the particular range of items in the wardrobe is always unique, as the mass-produced items sit alongside the dress borrowed from a friend or gifted by an auntie. Furthermore, as women wear particular items of clothing, they come to hold memories and personal meanings. It is this act of possession and wearing of clothing over time that serves to singularize what is usually a former commodity (Kopytoff, 1986: 61). The histories of wearing each garment and the ways in which items are combined make a wardrobe unique. The wardrobe is a woman's individual aesthetic; this aesthetic is not only the colours and styles she favours but is also 'personhood in aesthetic form' (Gell, 1998: 157). Women are able to see aspects of themselves in the external form of clothing. Ranging from former selves to fantasy selves to work personas, the diverse aspects of the self are 'distributed' (Gell, 1998: 21) through the array of items of clothing in the wardrobe.

The wardrobe can therefore be seen as a personal aesthetic from which women assemble outfits daily. In dressing, the daily creation of such 'art works' becomes a means through which women attempt to convince others that they are a particular kind of person. They wear the black leather skirt in an attempt to persuade their friends that they are sexy and chic. When they are successful, the item of clothing becomes an extension of the person, as the body, clothing and person are fused. Writing on art collectors, Baudrillard (1981: 118) has pointed out that the art lover has to believe 'he is the equal of the canvas itself'. In the case of clothing, when a woman chooses to wear a funky top, she not only has to believe that she is a funky fashionable person, but moreover when she actually wears the top, she has to both look and act in an appropriate manner. This acquires a particular poignancy as clothing is displayed on the body, because women have to measure whether their bodies live up to the clothing. A woman who desires to be fashionable not only has to wear the right pair of skinny grey drainpipe jeans, she also has to have the skinny thighs that go in them.

Women's sense of what goes together emerges from both an awareness of external factors such as fashions and social expectations and also from the 'fossilised evidence of the history of an individual' (Levi-Strauss, 1966: 22). A woman's personal aesthetic is formed throughout her life, through socialization and the continuing development of personal preferences. Whilst it often seems extremely entrenched, this aesthetic is also open to change. As women's tastes—and indeed lifestyles—shift, the items that they no longer wear yet remain hanging in the wardrobe allow women to remember who they used to be (Banim and Guy, 2001) or to question whether they could be that person again. Evolving tastes leads to the acquisition of new items as much as the redundancy of others; the ensuing wardrobe sort-out, as women throw items away or choose to keep others they no longer wear, often becomes an occasion on which women reflect upon their memories and biography through their clothing. As bad memories through clothing are thrown out and successful former selves are retained and continue to hang in the wardrobe, sorting out the wardrobe is an occasion upon which women are able to engage with and be active in constructing their biography through their clothing. Giddens (1991) has suggested that the construction of personal narratives is a key means through which individuals are able to establish stability in their identities in the face of the potentially disordering aspects of everyday life. The implication of this is that when women are ordering their clothing, they may also be ordering their lives and their biographies in order to make sense of their current identity.

In Giddens's account, this process of ordering a personal biography involves a clear chronological progression, with a clearly terminated past, a present and an aspired-to future. This has resonance for understanding the process of sorting out the wardrobe, yet a consideration of how clothing externalizes memory is far more complex than a straightforward chronology. Cherished items of clothing may be so frayed through over-wearing that they have to be thrown out, as the clothing's propensity to age thwarts our desire to remember. It is through the tactility and sensuality of fabrics that clothing is able to carry memories and former selves; as women touch the item of clothing, the feel of the fabric on her skin allows her to remember and resituate herself in the past. On occasion, the wardrobe sort-out can result in the rediscovery of an item of clothing women didn't know they had. A woman may decide to reactivate these items of clothing and wear the item from an earlier period of their life in combination with a newer item of clothing. In these instances of re-wearing older items of clothing, it is evident that the past is not terminated as it is in conventional biographies (Giddens, 1991); instead, it is made present as the clothing is recombined to help construct a contemporary identity.

Understanding Getting Dressed

Hansen (2004b) has discussed how the act of selecting second-hand goods in a market is an act of inscribing meaning in items of clothing. Items are not seen as being defined by their pre-existing biographies and narratives, but when the people in her ethnography select items, they are active in creating their own personal clothing identities. Clothing is not defined by what it has been in the past, but what it can be in the future, as people imagine themselves wearing the clothing. So, too, when women choose clothing from the wardrobe, as Tarlo (1996) notes, the personal narratives that are already present in items of clothing do not fix the meanings within the clothing. Previous histories of wearing may impact upon what women would consider wearing the item with, or where they would wear it to, but do not in themselves determine the future trajectory of the clothing. Dependent upon how they combine the clothing, or the occasion for which they are selecting items, women are still active in the process of utilizing clothing to deliberate over their identities.

What Tarlo (1996) and Tranberg-Hansen's accounts (2004) highlight is that the relationship between identity and clothing is not fixed and predetermined; instead, identities are constructed in a process of both choosing and wearing clothing. In this process, women are not considering their identities in an abstract sense nor philosophizing over 'who I am' through grandiose theory, but are defining their identities through specific items of clothing. They may question their femininity through the softness of angora or wonder 'is this me?' through the stripes on a sweater or the length of some cropped trousers. Women engage with these questions of identity in a concrete material way. These questions involve women seeing themselves in the items of clothing in their wardrobe; that is, seeing the self in an external form. Miller's concept of objectification (1987), derived from Hegel, offers a particularly useful way of understanding getting dressed as a process of self-construction which involves seeing the self in an external material form. This external form for Hegel can happen at the level of ideas and thoughts, yet for Miller this happens through material objects, such as clothing. For Hegel, objectification is part of the process of the development of self-consciousness, when the subject becomes aware of itself as an 'other', an object. As the subject becomes aware of this process, the subsequent dissatisfaction with the self-as-object in turn leads to the reintegration of this externalization within the self, which is in turn changed. Objectification is therefore a 'a dual process by means of which a subject externalizes itself in a creative act of differentiation, and in turn re-appropriates this externalization through an act which Hegel terms sublation' (Miller, 1987: 28). Miller makes Hegel's theory material by pointing to ways in which this moment of the externalization of the self may happen through objects.

In Hegel's theory, the person only becomes aware that he or she has a self by positing the self as an object. If clothing is considered as an external form of the self, it is evident that women can use clothing to help create their sense of themselves and who they are. Clothing becomes a particular medium through which the self may be discovered and indeed created, as women use clothing to ask 'could this be me?' Outfits are not therefore necessarily being selected to express a pre-existing self (as is often assumed), but rather the self is being constituted and tried on in this process. Women ask the question 'is this me?' through both the items hanging in the wardrobe and as they look at their reflection in the mirror. Looking in the mirror involves seeing the self as an object. In Miller's sense, women are seeing themselves as external, and so when women are looking outwards at the mirror or at the item of clothing, they are simultaneously looking inwards to see whether it 'is me' or whether 'I can be that person'. This moment of seeing the self as an other is often seen through the imagined gaze of other people, either in terms of a generic gaze (Edholm, 1992) as women see themselves as an object to be looked at (Young, 2005: 43) or through the specific gaze of individuals.

As such, women's identities are always relational, and means of looking are often inter-subjective. Mead argues that consciousness of the self emerges as an 'an awareness of the self in relation to others' (1982: 46). Through observations of how others respond to language and gestures, the self is set up as an object seen in the third person. When the self is looking upon itself as an object, Mead has suggested that the 'I' tries to see the 'me' (1982: 102) as others see it. Kaiser has applied these ideas to examine how women choose clothing from retail outlets, as there is a 'dialogue between the I and the me every-time women shop' (2003: 152). When women are choosing what to wear from their wardrobes, there is a similar dialogue between the self-as-object and the self-as-observer: as women look at their reflection in the mirror, they try to imagine how others see them. The trying on of different outfits involves seeing each one through the constructions of different imagined gazes.

The final stage of dressing involves the outfit being worn on the body and can be understood through the final stage of Miller's theory of objectification, wherein the self-as-object is then reintegrated within the self. When this is successful, as the woman realizes that the outfit is 'me', there is no distance between the wearer and the clothing and she feels comfortable in the clothing. There is a fit between who the woman wanted to become and the final outfit on her body, as she both looks and feels right in what she is wearing. However, given that a fundamental part of the process of objectification is the separation of subject from object, there is still the possibility for failure—that the person cannot live up to the items of clothing or that the item will betray the wearer. A woman may buy a backless top to make herself look elegant, yet she may be too self-conscious about wearing it and will fail to be the graceful, chic person she had imagined. The potential for failure is immense; when coupled with the burdens on successfully expressing one's self, there is little wonder the act of dressing becomes such an anxious act. This experience of failure occurs not only in public, but often getting dressed involves the trying on of a succession of failed outfits as women think they know themselves, who they are and how they can look. They then look at themselves in the mirror only to see themselves as deluded, as this is not 'me' at all, as they measure their reflection up against the idealized version of themselves they picture in their mind. At the moment in front of the mirror women certainly do not feel they are simply expressing themselves as they wish; on the contrary, they are going through a long list of failed attempts to find themselves.

Understanding the Self

The self has so far been discussed in terms of how it is engaged with the act of choosing what to wear. In this book, the self is therefore understood not as a universal psychological entity that is simply expressed through clothing, but as something women question, try on and construct through a material, embodied practice. This practice is always particular to individual women, as their sense of self is refracted through their social positioning, such as their occupation, ethnicity or religion. However, such practices do not occur in a vacuum; how women engage with their identities through clothing occurs in the context of a historically and culturally specific Western discourse of the self. In this section, I will outline the Western conception of the self and then consider the implications this has for the practice of constructing the self through clothing.

The problematic relationship between the self and one's appearance can be traced back to the Greek origins of the word for person, meaning 'mask' (Mauss, 1985); as Mauss points out, the word also carried connotations of the dramatic part, person and frame and that the Latin *persona* has similar implications. Mauss also notes that the Romans developed a distinct notion of personnage, defined as a mask of trickery, which comes to stand in opposition to the self. In his discussion of masks, Napier (1985) points out that the distinction between this outer mask and the 'real person' began in Roman times. However, the current ontological separation between an internal authentic essence of the person as opposed to transient and 'false' appearances becomes increasingly concrete from mediaeval times (tracing back to St Augustine), as the mask merely becomes an appendage with no connection to the inner being (Napier, 1985: 14). One of the key implications of this ontological shift is that the surface becomes equated with lack of importance. The real authentic self is seen in metaphysical terms, and accordingly issues surrounding appearance and the body come to be seen as inconsequential.

Such perceptions are historically entrenched and, along with post-Enlightenment dichotomies of rationality-irrationality and body-mind, became tied into the moralizing debates surrounding the rise of consumer society in inextricably gendered ways. The fickle ephemerality of fashion as a feminized phenomenon emerged as part of the emergent Western capitalist market exchange system. De Grazia and Furlough (1996) point to how a particular pattern of consumption emerged in the early eighteenth century, developing around the bourgeois household, with middle-class women's lack of participation in wage labour being a central factor in defining the family. Continuing through into the nineteenth century, women were compelled to invest their time in adorning themselves and the home (Auslander, 1996). From the nineteenth century onwards, wage labour comes to be seen as irrevocably male, with wages being calculated upon the assumption that only men provided for children, obscuring women's role in providing for and socializing the child. Such an obfuscation also entailed calculating a wage based upon subsistence, lest women squandered wages (De Grazia and Furlough, 1996) as there was no arena to theorize the household or consumption. This invisibility of the domestic sphere was exacerbated by the emergence of the public sphere as separate from work or the household, resulting in the latter being seen as particularized or private interests. This division of labour becomes even more firmly entrenched in the early twentieth century, with the invention of the male bread-winner (De Grazia and Furlough, 1996). This coincides with an emphasis on the 'art of being a woman' (Wilson, 1985: 123). In such a climate, women become valorized through their capacity to appear, in opposition to men, who are positioned as primary viewers (Berger, 1972). Rather than such a process being a leisure activity or play, in fact these practices were 'gruelling work' (Wilson, 1985: 122).

Emergent consumer society comes to be seen as feminized, in opposition to production, wherein value is alleged to lie; this dichotomy is tagged onto other oppositions in the ensuing moralizing debates. In particular, feminist critiques of fashion and make-up were centred on the need to reject the 'false' mask of femininity (Daly, 1979) to get to 'real women's values', as if there is a deep 'reality of the female self' as opposed to 'patriarchally imposed, self-denying masks' (Daly, 1979: 27). As Hollows (2000) points out, this assumes that there can be an authentic self outside of culture; given that humans are largely characterized by their existence in 'culture', the intrinsic paradox of invocations to a return to 'nature' in the domain of fashion and make-up becomes apparent. Strathern (1979) similarly suggests that such condemnation assumes that, because all that is being made up is the body, processes of making up do not concern the self.

The Embodied Self

In this Western discourse, the self is disembodied and immaterial. Phenomenological approaches (Merleau-Ponty, 1974) have critiqued the separation of the body and the mind by positioning the body as the existential ground of perception, culture and self-awareness. The importance of the body is paramount in any consideration of clothing; given that it is worn on the body, clothing needs to be understood as a 'situated bodily practice' (Entwistle, 2000: 4), as part of Maussian techniques of the body. Concerns over the body are central to how women choose what to wear, as women consider how the clothing feels on the body through the softness of a top or the warmth of a jacket. The embodied relationship women have to their clothing affects how women are able to move their bodies. Getting dressed and wearing clothes are embodied competences (Entwistle and Wilson, 2001), and so the new and unfamiliar statuesque heels force women to totter awkwardly. The tactile relationship clothing has to women's skin and how they are able to move their bodies affect the identities women are able to construct, as the aforementioned high heels could make a woman accustomed to wearing them feel feminine or powerful. This embodied self-perception arises from how women feel in their own bodies, as their legs feel longer, their backs are straightened; this is also based upon how the body looks. The smirk from passers-by can shatter the confidence of the woman who had been assertively striding forth in high heels. This encounter with how their bodies look is also faced alone in front of the mirror, as women are wondering not only whether they like their new skirt, but whether it makes their legs look too short or their bottom look too big.

That women may judge their own bodies so critically is hardly surprising given the current proliferation of television programmes, magazines and advertisements which promote the increasingly unrealistic ideal body. The expectation on women to 'appear' (Berger, 1972) involves not only having the right outfit, but also having the right body underneath it. Cultural norms of femininity and beauty construct and define what the ideal body should look like and also show women how to attain these bodies. Much contemporary feminism is characterized by paradigms pointing to the performativity of gender (largely influenced by Butler, 1990, 1993) which occurs in the context of normative expectations regarding gender roles. Clothes are part of the way, in Butler's sense, gender is performed. This performance takes place in a climate of social expectations regarding correct dress codes, and when women conform to these they both cite the norms and reinforce them. In terms of women's identities, in Butler's model, individuals are both 'subjected' to the expectations of femininity and are 'subjectivated' (Butler, 1993: 535) by them, as these norms are also the potential domain for agency.

Iris Marion Young (2005) extends Butler's arguments to look at how these norms are lived out by women as a daily embodied practice. She takes the example of 'throwing like a girl' to show how women live and enact expectations of femininity through how women move their bodies. Looking at an ordinary embodied practice, she shows how women internalize gender norms as they come to see their own 'frag-ile' bodies at a distance, as something to be looked at (Young, 2005). In my ethnog-raphy, social norms and images of the ideal body affect the micro-practices of the body: as women are expected to diet, dress themselves, walk and move in accordance with these norms of femininity. The constantly repeated and ubiquitous images of the feminine ideal homogenize and normalize (Bordo, 2003: 24–5) the youthful, slender body. The uniform sameness of this ideal belies the diversity of actual body shapes, and for most women, there is a discrepancy between the ideal and the real body.

However, even if this idealized fashionable body is homogenized and uniform (Bordo, 2003, Thesander, 1997), the impact these images have on women will not necessarily be similarly uniform. Every woman does not always see her body as inadequate in relation to beauty ideals. The body is not merely a passive object on which social norms are imposed, but, as de Beauvoir (1997) has argued, the body is a 'situation' which incorporates women's embodied intentions and agency and also the social norms and constraints in the world. As Moi explains, 'Just as the world constantly makes me, I constantly make myself the woman I am' (2005: 74). The body-as-situation is 'the way the facts of embodiment, social and physical environ-ment, appear in light of the projects a person has. She finds that her movements are awkward in relation to her desire to dance' (Young, 2005: 16). Even though social norms may be a constraint, they are also the 'conditions in which that freedom finds itself' (Moi, 2005: 74).

The implication is that beauty norms may be constraining or enabling, dependent upon what a woman's 'project' is. On the occasion of a woman settling down to read a novel alone on a Sunday morning, she is most likely not considering herself as inadequate in relation to an idealized beauty. However, when the same woman is trying to get a job at a fashion magazine or to bag a footballer as a husband, then, in light of this 'project', a woman may look in the mirror and see her bottom is too flat, her walk is too clumsy in her new heels and her skin is too wrinkled. Whether women are measuring their bodies in relation to beauty norms therefore depends on their 'project', in de Beauvoir's terms.

Situating the Self

If the body is a 'situation', de Beauvoir has also argued that the body in turn is 'situated' in other social parameters such as class (Skeggs, 1997), ethnicity (Kahn,

1993), family position (Hollows, 2000), occupation (Entwistle, 1997), gender and sexuality. These categories intersect, as 'if one "is" a woman, that is surely not all one is' (Butler, 1990: 3). Skeggs (1997) has argued that class, ethnicity and gender are all parameters of identity which intersect, channeling access to resources and as ways of being. Using Bourdieu's multi-faceted notion of capital (economic, educational resources and cultural knowledges), Skeggs asserts that all such categories are 'relations in which capitals come to be organised and valued' (1997: 9). In her study of white working-class women in North West Britain, Skeggs (1997) highlights that these women are not striving for individuality, but instead for fitting in and being respectable; they are not free, autonomous and independent selves, but 'live at the surface, in public, because their subjectivity is produced from and for public knowledge' (1997: 163). Their subjectivity is visible and constructed through relationships to others and duties. Notions of a self are differentially dependent upon gender, class, occupation and family status and are not necessarily produced by Giddens's bourgeois project of the self (1991).

As Skeggs argues (1997, 2004), class is a key structuring factor in considering women's identities and how they intersect with others. Considering the way different identity positions intersect is crucial in challenging essentialist notions of identity, which reduce identity to one core aspect, such as class or ethnicity (Hall, 2005) or sexuality. On the occasion of going out to a club, a lesbian may choose to make visible her sexuality by fitting her own clothing into shared style groupings (Holliday, 2001, Munt, 2001). However, this same woman is situated in other identities, such as her occupation and family upbringing, and her identity cannot be discerned from what she wears on one occasion. Even when multiple social positions are taken into account, Anthias (2005) has argued that you still cannot 'read off' someone's identity. Identity positions are specific to particular locations and to a specific moment in time and space (Anthias, 2005: 43). Women's dispositions are structured by social divisions and family position, yet these come to matter on certain occasions. Kaiser defines identity as the set of individual characteristics and traits that come to define the self in a particular context (Kaiser, 2003: 186), and so clothing is a means through which women are able to construct an occasion-specific identity. A British-Asian woman, on the occasion of a family wedding, may choose to dress in a sari as she makes visible her ethnicity, status and family standing through her clothing. The next day, as she goes out to lunch with a work colleague, she may not choose to identify herself in the same manner. Identity is therefore both structured by social positions and simultaneously structured by women's clothing choices.

Social Individuals

My argument about the historical construction of gendered selves indicates that the origins of the person and of the self are not psychological, innate categories, but arise in particular social contexts. Even though concerns over the person and having a 'sense of self' are culturally ubiquitous (Carrithers, 1985), the self takes on a particular form in historical and social contexts. Recognition of these social constructions does not mean that the social is assumed to exist a priori to the self or individual. Anthropology which positions individuals as representations of particular social categories or roles within a social structure (Leach, 1970, Levi-Strauss, 1969) leaves no room for acts of individual self-constructions. Individuals exist only as instances of particular cultural categories. Yet, in looking at individual women and their clothing choices, this does not signify the opposite tendency wherein the psychological individual and subjectivities are seen to exist prior to cultural constructs and categories. My research addresses the relationship between the individual and the social context through which the relational self comes to be constructed through clothing choices. Social contexts are structuring, but not determining. Tarlo (1996) demonstrates this in her ethnography of clothing dilemmas in the context of clearly demarcated caste divisions of rural India; she shows how the relationship between caste and clothing is contested. The ways individuals recombine items entails the casting aside and rediscovery of new identities. Caste status is not the only consideration; deciding what to wear is also informed by factors such as age, marital status and where one is from (as part of an urban elite or not). Clothing choices are constrained by particular social expectations, and yet still, through the act of dressing and assemblage, there is space for contestation and individual agency.

Even when the focus is on the individual self and her biography, as the last section highlighted, through socialization individuals acquire certain structural dispositions. The social only exists as it is actualized through the practices and agency of individuals; the individual does not exist outside culture. The balance between individual agency and social structures is highlighted in Bourdieu's concept of 'habitus' (1977), as a balance between structure and agency. Habitus is a 'system of lasting transposable dispositions, which, integrating past experiences, functions at every moment as a matrix of perceptions, appreciations and actions' (Bourdieu, 1977: 83). This notion of habitus is tied to social positioning, constituted through different fields, such as education, home and economic position. The structured dispositions are mediated through family upbringing. In this way, women may have particular orientations to clothing and preferences, yet these same structured dispositions are open to change, as women are able to assemble new outfits or make new clothing purchases.

The individual and social intersect through practices of socialization in terms of both the dispositions and tastes that are inculcated into women and also in the actual act of dressing, as women balance normative ideals of femininity with their individual preferences and body shape. Dressing involves considerations of whether clothing is socially suitable for the occasion and the age, status and occupation of a woman; in turn, these considerations must be balanced with whether a woman feels an item 'is her'. Dressing involves the construction of the self through socially acceptable modes of dressing. As such, notions of roles and expectations are negotiated with items that touch the body, and it is impossible for such concerns to remain entirely social. The concerns over social expectations are largely engaged with in terms of how the body looks, as women see themselves through the eyes of others. Choosing what to wear becomes the act of constructing the 'social individual' (Mead, 1982: 102). The 'I' takes the position of how both specified and generic others will see the 'me'; as such, women are always relational in positioning themselves as viewers of themselves. The 'I' is a social self, as it is constructed through the gaze of others and learnt, internalized social expectations. This notion of internalization helps to account for many acts of dressing which are non-reflexive.

Still Mead contends that no two people constitute the social in the same way; as the 'I' can never be known (in being known it becomes a 'me'), it is also the domain of spontaneity and individuality. The 'social' is a unique intersection of different social positions, such as class, occupation, location, gender and marital status. The relationship between the social and individual is integrative; there is no separate re-ality prior to, or distinct from, social expectations or roles. Social expectations exist through individual enactments, as everyday reality and conduct 'is an imitation of the proprieties, a gesture at the exemplary forms and the primal realization of these ideals belongs more to make believe than to reality' (Goffman, 1974: 562). Cultural standards are an integral part of everyday reality. There is no real self that is separate from or prior to anything else, but it is created and performed through unique cultural enactments. Goffman defines the self as 'a changeable formula for managing oneself during events' (1974: 573).

Understanding Clothing

If the self is neither an entirely social construction, nor a unique pre-social indi-vidual, the question this book focuses upon is how women are able to use clothing to change and engage with the self. The material propensities of clothing enable women to construct themselves in particular ways, and therefore women do not just use clothing to straightforwardly 'communicate' (Barthes, 1985, Craik, 1993) to other people. Nor does clothing simply express a real, inner self. A similar argument I am making for clothing has been made in relationship to architecture and the paradox of the white wall (Wigley, 1995), which is often perceived as being transparent and neu-tral, in turn allowing the 'real' structure to show though. Wigley (1995) argues that when Le Corbusier wanted to create a fundamental architectural change in develop-ing modernist architecture, he did so by focusing upon how the walls were painted, before even attempting to address the internal structure. Here the surface and the outer image are a central part of the object and how it is transformed. So, too, for clothing: rather than just allowing women to express their inner selves, the particular item of clothing enacts an internal and behavioural change in the woman: wearing the tailored suit helps create a powerful, confident and in-control woman.

Implicit within the possibility to transform oneself through clothing is that the clothing does not have the desired effect. As Wigley (1995) comments, the white paint started to chip off Le Corbusier's walls, and the illusion of technological modernism peeled away with it. Similarly with clothes, the heel of a shoe may fall off and the elegant identity the individual wishes to project comes tumbling down. Clothes do not just express any identity an individual desires. There is a well-documented recognition of economic and social restraints over our ability to freely express our identity (Bourdieu, 1977), yet this takes the notion of constraint to another level, issuing a clear challenge to post-modern emphases upon 'everyone can be anyone' (cited in Featherstone, 1991: 82). Clothing has the potential to betray the wearer, as the heels that were supposed to make the woman feel powerful rub and chafe her feet.

In the instances when the outfit doesn't work and there is an aesthetic disjuncture between the wearer's sense of self and the final outfit, the clothing comes to feel external to the wearer. In such cases, women develop a self-conscious relationship to the clothing. Objectification, in Miller's sense, is incomplete. However, when an outfit of clothing is successful, there is a fusion between the wearer and the clothing, as, in Gell's (1998) sense, the self can be extended through the items of clothing. The lack of distinction between objects and persons is evidenced cross-culturally. La Fontaine (1985) takes the example of four territorially diverse societies (in Ghana, Uganda, Kenya and Highland New Guinea), which are all characterized by their conceptualization of humans as 'composite creations ... composed of material and immaterial components' (1985: 126). For example, the Gahuku-Gama of Highland New Guinea, the 'material' (incorporating biological aspects and material objects) is central to the human personality. The skin is seen as the locus for the incorporation of social roles and as the location of an individual's characteristics. So, too, in Strathern's work (1979) on self-decoration in Mount Hagen in Melanesia that examines the body decorations employed by men on formal ritual occasions. Strathern makes the point that such elaborate make-up is not disguise in our sense of concealing the identity, but rather this is seen to be where the self is displayed: 'bringing things outside' (Strathern, 1979: 249). Attributes of personality are displayed and draped around the body; on normal occasions when the self is not being presented thus, these attributes are hidden, 'within the skin, a person's basic capacities' (Strathern, 1979: 249). The implication of Strathern's example is that clothing in my ethnography can be a material means through which women bring to the surface aspects of the self.

This can take place through the processes of layering items (Young, 2001) and assembling items in different combinations. Analogous to the layered composition of human skin, with one layer—the dermis—being defined as the 'true' layer, clothes are similarly layered. The pink top a woman wears under her work suit may be the item she sees as 'really' me. Through this process of layering and making different combinations, it is possible to mobilize different facets of the self through a single outfit, because the outfit allows a work persona who is both in control and powerful yet who is still feminine and sexy. The self through clothing may be contradictory. Napier makes an explicit contrast between Christian-influenced perceptions and pantheistic cultures which have a 'polythetic view of personality' (1985: 28). Multiple personalities are not seen as destructive; rather the masks exploit diverse psychological states, facets of personalities and spiritual forces. Taking the specific example of Hinduism and the wearing of masks in Bali, Napier shows how these are linked to ambivalent forces within an individual which are tested out in ritual contexts by the wearing of different masks. In the Western context, such a process would be taken as suggesting multiple personalities rather than as struggles to contain an ambivalence that is foundational. The application of such capacities of masks to clothing usefully highlights the ambivalence between the possibility of the self being expressed through clothing, yet simultaneously being concealed. Masks, being 'transparent and opaque' (Brilliant, 1991: 113), point to the equivocation between surface and depth, and one may 'reveal by concealing' (Warwick and Cavallero, 1998: 133). This raises the possibility that items of clothing may be layered and assembled in particular ways to mobilize different personality traits.

Material Culture and the Anthropology of Clothing

Women can use clothing to bring out aspects of the self through its specific material propensities: how it holds the body in, reveals or conceals flesh, how it catches the light and how it feels on the skin. These material sensibilities are central to understanding how clothing is part of identity construction, yet are not given a central place in many considerations of fashion and identity. Attention to the material detailing of clothing is a founding principle of costume history since its emergence as a sub-set of art history studies in the Renaissance/Early Modern period (Taylor, 2004). However, such analyses have, until recently, remained excluded from academic treatises of clothing. In what Taylor terms the 'Great Divide' (2004: 279) between established academic accounts and costume history, the material expertise of dress museum curators has been largely denigrated as merely descriptive (Fine and Leopold, 1993). It is certainly true that until the mid-twentieth century the history of dress rarely moves beyond the material charting of styles. In fact, such descriptive rather than analytic tendencies are still apparent in more recent seminal works (Boucher, 1967, Laver, 1995).

Rather than condemn approaches which focus upon material documentation and description, there is a great deal to discover from such expertise when these object-based approaches (Taylor, 2002) are situated in wider social and cultural contexts and are seen as worn and lived material objects (such as Summers, 2001, on the corset). Tarrant (1994) stresses the need for an in-depth understanding of cut and construction as a crucial counterweight to purely academic approaches which are 'contorted to some theory without a basic understanding of the properties of cloth and the structure of clothes' (1994: 12). In a similar vein, Breward (2003) highlights the absence of the physical form and structure of the clothing product from writings about the fashion system; instead, the focus is upon the fleeting meanings that briefly reside in items of clothing.

It is the aim of this book to look at clothing as material culture, where a crucial part of this materiality is that it is lived and embodied; the material relationship between women's bodies and the items of clothing they wear must always be considered as specific to social contexts. This emphasis upon the materiality of clothing in cultural contexts proliferates within anthropological accounts on clothing, such as Weiner and Schneider's edited volume (1989), which is based upon an in-depth understanding of the properties of cloth and how these encode, reproduce and reveal or conceal social relationships and identities. All the articles in the book are based upon an understanding of how the particularities of cloth—such as its porosity and as something worn by individuals next to the body—lend themselves to certain cultural categories and identities. Emphasis falls upon the magical properties of clothing: as spiritual values become woven into the cloth in Indonesia (Hoskins, 1989) or as in India, when people wear clothing with perceived magical qualities they are transformed when they wear it (Bayly, 1986). Cohn (1989) writes of certain items of clothing as literally embodying authority. Such a possibility of clothing having magical or transformatory potential is absent from the literature of Western clothing and raises the need to interrogate such folk beliefs pertaining to clothing and the possibility that clothing may have magical properties. Such clothes might be the 'lucky' interview suit which makes a woman feel confident and successful, the top that always perks up a woman's mood or the hoody that makes her feel safe and cosy. The emotional states that clothing can induce may be due to fabric, style or colour. In India, Bayly (1986) notes that, arising out of the particular cultural aesthetic in India, certain colours can lead to enhanced states; so, too, in Britain, where the cultural aesthetic is that the colour red connotes eroticism and makes the wearer feel sexier.

Throughout Weiner and Schneider's book, it is clothing's materiality that enables it to enact a change in the wearer. This applies to the colours and textures of clothing and, in more recent accounts, even to the fibres of cloth (Colchester, 2003, Kuechler and Miller, 2005, Kuechler and Were, 2004). Because cloth is porous and woven, in India, Bayly (1986) shows how the properties of the previous owner will be retained, dependent upon the coarseness of the fabric and the size of the knots. As items are worn over time, they become associated with the wearer for that particular period of his or her life; this is often so marked that people are able to tell their life stories through the clothing they wore. Bean (1989) demonstrates this notion by tracing the biography and changing political affiliations of Gandhi through a history of his clothing choices. This is as true in the case of the conscious political clothing choices of Gandhi as it is for ordinary people on a daily basis. Because clothing is worn habitually over a period of time, it comes to define a person during a particular period of one's life; physically, clothing ages and has its own life span and cultural biography (Hendrickson, 1995, Renne, 1995).

Clothing may age and die before we wish to relinquish our attachment to it; often it is when the clothing has softened and become threadbare that we develop such a connection with it, as it carries within it the material histories of our embodied acts of wearing it. Through being worn, clothing becomes intimately connected to the wearer and carries the 'histories of past relationships, making the cloth itself into a material archive' (Weiner, 1989: 52). Items that are passed from mothers to daughters may be preserved as revered heirlooms, or they may be worn again by the daughter and create a bond between mother and daughter. Clothing acquires its significance as worn on the body, as it is fundamental in both constituting appearance and the 'sensual experience of wearing' (Barnes and Eicher, 1993: 3). Such a focus is evident in Banerjee and Miller's account of the sari (2003) not as a static category of clothing, but as a lived, contested, sensual item of clothing. This account attests to the possibilities within fusing the experiential, tactile facets of clothing with understandings of the material propensities of clothing.

What these anthropological accounts demonstrate is that clothing is always situated in particular social, economic and political contexts, and through its material propensities, it articulates social categories such as gender (Barnes and Eicher, 1993) and ethnicity (Femenias, 2004). However, when clothing is considered in the context of contemporary Britain, it is often seen solely in relation to the fashion context, rather than in the wider social and cultural contexts. Even Weiner and Schneider's account directly contrasts Western fashion's mass production and high turnover with small-scale societies (1989: 16). Such a characterization of traditional cloth as carrying depth and value involves here seeing Western clothing as superficial and transient. It is as if as soon as it enters the context of Western fashion, clothing loses its sociality and materiality. Invariably, such accounts—as do many others, such as Barnes and Eicher (1993)—focus upon gender and social relations of production and weaving; whilst valid, such social relations in small-scale societies should not mean that by implication participation through clothing as consumers entails relationships of ephemerality and superficiality. Weiner and Schneider's book, as is symptomatic of many other accounts, neglects that clothing in industrial societies is amenable to the same sorts of understanding as cloth is in the anthropological record.

As Sennett's (1971) historical analysis makes clear, fashion, clothing and appearance are comprehensible not solely as a self-referential system, but should rather be situated in broader social shifts in notions of appearance and selfhood. Such a rooted and contextualized analysis is a unifying feature of much of the cross-cultural literature. In discussions as wide ranging as contestations over gender and sexuality in Zambia (Hansen, 2004a,b) and local identities through the cultural biography of *traje* amongst the Maya people of Guatemala (Hendrickson, 1995), clothing is seen as helping materialize and constitute cultural categories and social structures. Such an emphasis on cultural contexts and materiality is crucial to looking at clothing in a British context. Previous attempts to apply an anthropological approach to clothing in Britain have involved looking at 'a community' or the clothing of a defined sub-culture. Whilst such approaches have resonance in certain cases, they do not account for the core relationship to clothing that most women have, which is more one of ambivalence and anxiety than of coherence. At a global level, anthropological accounts of clothing point more towards the trans-national passages and flows of clothing (such as the globalization of Asian dress, Niessen, Leshkowich and Jones, 2003, or circuits of African fashion through Dakar, Nairobi and Los Angeles, Rabine, 2002). Considerations of small-scale societies are always situated in these shifting contexts, as even localized identities are seen in turn as contested and changing. So, too, my small-scale research is situated within the wider fashion system, which is both ephemeral and shifting in terms of what is 'in', yet also promotes particular defined notions of what is acceptable wear.

Fashion and the Ambivalences of Identity

This book aims to bring both the situated and contextualized approach of anthropology and an understanding of clothing as material culture to women's wardrobes in London and Nottingham. As such, part of contextualizing clothing involves a consideration of fashion as one of the many factors which impacts women's decisions about what to wear. An understanding of clothing in terms of its materiality goes against the grain of the majority of writings on fashion in the context of the Western fashion system. Given the multiple forms through which fashion is mediated—catwalk shows, magazines, celebrity photographs, television and film—it is hardly surprising that much of the literature focuses upon the images of fashion. This is a significant legacy of Barthes's (1985) analysis of the fashion system as an overarching system of signification, from which individual items derive their meaning. Barthes sees magazines as constitutive of fashion: there are no 'real' clothes which precede the discourse of fashion. The language of the magazines creates images and meanings which 'veil' (1985: xi) the object: here fashion is the reality of the image as constructed in the magazines. Barthes's account, which accords primacy to the visual and the images of fashion, attempted to understand the entire system of fashion as a language and grammar. His legacy has, however, been largely empirical. In the wake of Barthes, most accounts are dominated by a paradigm of semiotic decoding, seen in the many textual analyses of magazines which abound within the literature (Buckley and Gundle, 2000, Evans, 2000, Evans and Thornton, 1989, Winship, 1987).

The plethora of fashion magazines, and the spectacular nature of fashion shows, attests to the importance of understanding the image within fashion. However, far more problematic is when items of clothing are theorized within cultural studies as a form of communication (Lurie, 1992), where fashion is seen as a language, with clothing being the 'words' used to describe yourself. Reducing clothing to its visual properties ignores the crucial tactile and sensual aspects of clothing as worn by people. Given the focus of cultural studies upon popular culture and the everyday, the critique of the emphasis in costume history on the creative genius of the designer (Breward, 2000) is hardly surprising. However, rejecting the emphasis upon the individual object within costume history is tantamount to throwing the baby out with the bath water, because the clothes as material objects are discarded in favour of textual analyses.

The textual analyses of fashion focus upon how, in Barthes's terms, these images 'signify'—that is, how they produce meaning. One of Barthes's important contributions was in emphasizing how the images relate to each other. This is particularly applicable to an understanding of how normative ideals of body image are created, as the multiple images of the fashionable ideal produce meaning in relationship to each other. Gunter and Wykes demonstrate that women's magazines 'repetitively' and 'systematically' construct a hegemonic version of femininity that is body-conscious (Gunter and Wykes, 2005: 95). Their analysis marks a departure from most accounts in that they suggest a link between how magazines produce meanings about the ideal body and how women relate to their own bodies. The presentation of a 'fashionable ideal' (Thesander, 1997) is important as a signifying context, which in turn may impact upon how women see their own image in the mirror: a woman's own reflection is placed within the broader signifying context of the ideal body of magazines.

The fashionable ideal aligns the ideal body with the well-dressed body. Getting it right is not as straightforward as simply following whatever the current fashion is dictated to be. Conformity is often seen as the easier, unimaginative relation to dressing in an individual manner. However, in the current fashion climate, with any number of things being 'in' at the same time, fashionability is defined as an individual's capacity to assemble his or her own outfit (usually involving the mix-and-match aesthetic of charity shops, high street and designer). The onus therefore falls upon the individual to get it right. This occurs in the context of fashion, which is far from systemic in its presentation of styles. The notion of a biannual turnover of homogeneous styles in the context of a trickle-down fashion system is no longer applicable. Academic accounts of fashion have shifted away from taking the abstract workings of the system as their basis, as pioneered by Simmel (1971) and Veblen (1899), where women are positioned as the unreflexive cogs in the machinery of the fashion system. With the rise of cultural studies and emphases on the construction and contestation of meaning, such top-down homogeneous models have come under question; in their studies of sub-cultural style, writers such as McRobbie (1994) and Hebdige (1987) suggest that creativity and innovation come as much from street style as from design houses. These trends identified by McRobbie are now even more accentuated. The multiple domains for the production of knowledge about fashion—magazines, television, fashion designers and celebrities (Entwistle, 2000, White and Griffiths, 2000)—allied with the ubiquity of fashion within all arenas of contemporary life place the burden on individuals to be sartorially aware, yet simultaneously the basis for making these claims is shifting and insecure.

In such a context, a move away from broad-based analyses of the overarching system to the level of an internal dilemma of the individual is pertinent. Simmel (1971) discussed fashion as involving the essential tension between individuality and conformity. Although he explicated this tension as the underpinning for the entire fashion system, Wilson (1985) translates this issue from the abstract workings of a system to an internal dilemma and ambivalence for the individual. The ambiguity lies in the opportunity fashion presents to the individual to be linked to a social group yet at the same time offering a means of expressing individuality. The self is offered, yet is simultaneously undermined. As women choose what to wear, they have to consider looking 'individual', fitting in, specific social occasions and roles and also what is 'in'. As such, a central experience of dressing, in balancing all of these at times contradictory concerns, is anxiety (Clarke and Miller, 2002).

The anxieties fashion produces are only one factor women have to consider when choosing what to wear: they also might have to worry about 'getting it right' for a woman their age or for a new social situation. Participation in fashion is predicated upon requisite knowledges and the 'knowingness' (Gregson, Brooks and Crewe, 2001: 12) that allows women to experiment with new looks and styles. These anxieties and knowledges are complex and multi-layered, as dressing also involves fundamental cultural competences (Craik, 1993, Entwistle 2001, Goffman, 1971a and Mauss, 1973). It also involves the expectation that women will dress appropriately at home, for taking children to school and in the workplace. The images of the fashionable body in magazines are, therefore, always situated in wider cultural norms and expectations over, for example, what is acceptable for older women to wear or what to wear for a first date.

Given the multiple roles women are called upon to occupy, and such evidences of ambiguities and anxiety, getting dressed involves considerations of all of these. My book therefore looks at how women construct and engage with diverse and often contradictory possibilities of the self. Within the cultural studies literature on fashion there is currently an abundance of treatises of sub-cultural style. By focusing upon a particular sub-group, aspects which denote membership to others are the focus of analysis. Such accounts flourish in the literature and include Cole (2000), chapters in Johnson and Lennon (1999) and Brydon and Niessen (1998). All look at one particular group of people or particular primary social identity through clothing, around which other identities are expected to cohere. For example, Keenan (2001) looks at different identities through clothes, such as the Muslim schoolgirl or a ballerina, assuming a particular identity as primary and foundational around which coheres a socially shared identity. Whilst such accounts clearly have validity, in offering a comprehensive account of why women wear what they wear, I look at the diversity of identities women are, formerly were or aspire to being and how these are actualized in the moment of assemblage in front of the wardrobe.

Conclusions

This chapter has provided a theoretical and contextual framework for understanding why women wear what they wear. The framework draws from a range of disciplines and schools of thought, which is a product not only of the interdisciplinary field of fashion and clothing studies, but also arises out of the particular problems and issues that arise in trying to understand women's clothing choices. When women choose what to wear, their considerations range from social roles, their femininity, whether they look fashionable, their sense of self, their relationships and family. Thus, to arrive at a comprehensive understanding of the multiple overlapping concerns that are being negotiated, it is necessary to draw from ideas within a similarly wide range of disciplines. For instance, some key ideas to consider are how women see themselves in the eyes of others (social psychology), how the materiality of clothing allows women to construct their identities (costume history, anthropology), how clothing feels on their bodies (sociology), and the importance of wider cultural contexts (anthropology).

This first chapter has mapped out these issues and set up a framework for the subsequent ethnographic chapters. In the detailed discussion of case studies that ensues, these debates will be reflected upon in light of the empirical material I have gathered. Of particular relevance to my discussion are the wider academic debates over the ideal body as represented in the media and the impact this has upon women, the fragmentation and lack of certainty in fashion and how and why fashions change at the level of the consumer. There has been a great deal written about how fashion is now a fragmented and contested domain, and indeed the creation of distorted and unrealistic beauty ideals has been the subject of much concern, both academic and in the popular press. In looking at how women actually experience these concerns as they choose what to wear in their bedrooms, it is possible to offer novel insights through looking not only at the level of representation nor at the level of the abstract system of fashion, but at the actual level of practice.

These wider concerns over fashion, age and normative beauty ideals are considered by women in the intimate domain of the bedroom, as they stand in front of the mirror. It is therefore only through looking at how women choose their clothing at home that it is possible to access an empirical working out of these macro debates, media images, through seeing the intimate relationship women have with their own bodies and to their clothing. How women choose what to wear is a pivotal moment in how their identities are constructed, and this is the reason that this book focuses upon it. Identity through clothing is a process of construction through the materiality of clothing; it is also the moment at which the individual and the social and the ideal and the actual come together. In looking at what women reject, what they choose to put on, what they always wear and what they never wear, it is possible to arrive at a comprehensive understanding of why women wear what they wear. The next chapter outlines the practicalities of how this is possible.

–2–

Hanging Out in the Home and the Bedroom

To offer a comprehensive account of why women wear what they wear, this book goes behind the scenes and looks at the processes of selection and rejection in the bedroom. Because getting dressed typically occurs when one is alone and is an intensely private moment at which strangers are not present, it poses particular problems of access for an academic researcher. I managed to gain access to this moment through the long-term approach of ethnography: over a period of fifteen months of formal and informal interviews, as I started 'hanging out' with informants, I gradually developed a familiarity with the women I worked with. In many cases, this familiarity meant that I was not only spending time in women's homes, but also in their bedrooms, as women shared their clothing anxieties and successes with me. By hanging out with women, I was able to understand these clothing choices in the wider context of their relationships, jobs and social lives. True to the anthropological tradition of ethnography (Oakley, 1976), although my primary topic of interest is that of clothing, I situated clothing in other aspects of women's personal lives and wider cultural and social contexts (Hendrickson, 1995, Tarlo, 1996). I was therefore able to arrive at an in-depth understanding of the multiple and often contradictory issues and identities that are articulated through the material culture of clothing.

An ethnography that consists of sitting on women's bedroom floors in various homes in London and Nottingham, discussing which top is sexier or which jeans are more slimming, seems far removed from the traditional practice of anthropological fieldwork, where the researcher goes into the field to study a territorially bound community. This lack of boundedness of the research field and participants is in part a product of context. Traditional ethnography was established as a methodology in the first half of the twentieth century as it was carried out in societies where most political, economic and social activities were conducted in public, in a community (Evans-Pritchard, 1940, Malinowski, 1922). The task of the ethnographer in these situations was to situate her- or himself in that one place, observe all activities that occur and later write about them in an anthropological monograph. In contrast, in contemporary British society aside from much paid work, many activities take place behind closed doors, within the home. Even the outside world is appropriated through the Internet and the television within the home (Miller, 2001), and so the home is a key route into understanding contemporary British society.

Early anthropological research that took place within the home focused upon finding the equivalent of the anthropological tribe, with a particular focus upon bounded communities. In studies of clothing, this translated to an attention to a defined community or sub-cultural style (Cole, 2000, Hebdige, 1987). More recently, there has been a shift away from empirical accounts of unified social groupings through clothing, as even accounts of sub-cultures start to question whether such groups are always coherent (Hodkinson, 2002, Holland, 2004, Muggleton, 2000). Anthropological (Hansen, 2000) and geographical (Gregson and Crewe, 2003) accounts have converged in questioning the fixed values within clothing and look more at the movement of clothing through markets (Hansen, 2000), second-hand shops (Gregson and Crewe, 2003) and even within the home (Gregson and Beale, 2004). The wardrobe is a fulcrum for general domestic processes of tidying and sorting, which are grounded in the context of domestic arrangements and relationships. As clothing moves from the shop to the home, to being worn, to being borrowed by a friend, the meanings and values attributed to the clothing are also in flux. The lack of fixity of meaning and the move away from coherent, certain identities is discussed in Clarke and Miller's work (2002), where fashion is experienced by the individual as a source of anxiety. This anxiety is a product not only of fashion, but also of the multiple overlapping roles women are called upon to assume. In choosing what to wear, they are faced with many possibilities, which may range from being chic, sexy or funky, which have to be married with the women's position in life, such as being middle-aged, a grandmother and not having the body she used to have. These ambivalences, anxieties and indeed constraints are all part of the concerns women have to negotiate on a daily basis as they choose what to wear. They are amenable to analysis through looking at the whole array of clothing women own and, therefore, the multiplicity of overlapping identities or roles that women aspire to, have formerly been or enact in their daily lives.

The methodological orientation is ethnographic, yet within this I incorporated a variety of methods: a detailed documentation of every item in the wardrobe (including narratives and memories attached to each item), semi-structured interviews, life histories, clothes diaries and the observation of how women select clothes from the wardrobe and how they are worn. On some occasions, I actually watched how women choose outfits, which involved seeing how they looked at their image in the mirror and asking them questions throughout the process. Documenting the clothing in the wardrobe involved recording the items as material object through noting (and photographing) the details of the material, style and wear and tear of the clothing. I also made a record of women's own comments on their clothing, as this was pivotal to how women made clothing choices, in terms of how it feels on the skin, how it allows the body to move and how the colours contrast and complement each other, bringing out the colour of a woman's eyes or hair. The sensuality, tactility and aesthetics of clothing are crucial to understanding why women choose what to wear. This sensual relationship to items of clothing means that often women are unable to verbalize why it is that they love an item of clothing so much. Because taste preferences are cultivated over a long period of time, women's attachment to particular items is an embodied material relationship of wearing. Women may no longer know the underlying reasons for their particular emotional relationship to items of clothing or can no longer verbalize them as preferences are 'history turned into nature' (Bourdieu, 1977: 78)—eventually, 'what goes' comes to appear obvious and natural.

My research incorporates the 'pathological' approach (Breward, 2003: 64) of costume history, which intricately documents the material details of cut and construction, searching for evidence of wear and tear and the material traces of usage (Ginzburg, 1988). The tears and rips tell the tale of the trousers that have been worn until they fall apart, the still-attached price-tag identifies the cocktail dress a woman had neither the occasion nor the confidence to wear. Costume history focuses attention upon collections in museums, yet these methods have clear resonance for studies of contemporary fashion, and they form an important redress to the lack of engagement with the material form in other academic accounts. The expertise of objects within costume history comes from museum curators, who often only have the material artefacts upon which to base their conclusions. However, in analyses of contemporary clothing, when there is access to images and verbal accounts, it is as if the clothing ceases to exist as a material object. In contrast, my research aims to reconcile this understanding of the materiality of clothing with the focus upon practices of wearing within wider relational and social contexts.

Ethnographic Sites

The fieldwork was carried out in two urban sites in Britain—London and Nottingham—over a period of fifteen months. There are clear differences in the two sites in terms of scale and population, with London's population exceeding seven million and Nottingham's being only 266,988 (2001 Census data). Both locations possess ethnically diverse populations, with the whole gamut of financial resources, yet this is more marked in London, as there is a far greater mobility in the population, not only in terms of immigration, but also migration of people from other cities to London. London is also one of the 'fashion capitals' (Breward and Gilbert, 2006), as it hosts one of the major biannual fashion weeks. In an imagined sense, London is mythologized as the locus of quirky, innovative style arising out of the multiple street markets, such as Camden and Portobello. However, my ethnography made clear that, at the level of how ordinary women select their outfits daily, the commonalities between the two sites are more important than the differences. There are clear continuities between Nottingham and London: each possesses a high street of core chain stores (present in every city and town in Britain), and each is part of the same media context. Women living in Nottingham, as in London, have access to the same mainstream resources on fashion (magazines, television programmes). Both locations are part of the same production of fashion knowledges and sartorial normativity.

The beauty ideals perpetuated in magazines and on television programmes are concerns for women in both locations.

London and Nottingham are understood in this book both as physical locations and constellations of knowledges—that is, as particular sites in which multiple media influences and fashions come together. These are in turn refracted through social structures and positions such as ethnicity and family upbringing. How women interpret these images of beauty ideals and sartorial normativity is in turn mediated through their social networks and friendship groups. The influence of factors such as location, class, ethnicity and gender upon women's clothing choices is complex. As Anthias has argued, you cannot 'read off' someone's identity, simply because they are, for example, white and middle class (2005: 37). Instead, how these social structures impact upon individual identities are always particular in terms of how these structures intersect. Anthias argues that people are both positioned through social structures, in terms of where they live, their ethnicity and class, but also as people have agency, they position themselves (2005: 44). Even though women have certain dispositions and tastes through their class and gender-specific upbringing, on specific occasions of dressing, women may choose to make certain facets of identity visible. This choice depends upon the specific occasion women are dressing for. When women consider location when they choose what to wear, it is not London or Nottingham in the sense of the total city. Instead, it is the micro-sites, such as a particular restaurant or club, within the city that women imagine and dress for. This is as true for gender, class and ethnicity as it is for sexuality. A heterosexual woman may be on an occasion of going out 'on the pull' explicitly considering herself as she will appear attractive to men, yet on another occasion may dress more to be admired for her fashion sense on a shopping trip with her girlfriends. This same shopping trip for one woman may be a cause of immense excitement and pleasure at showing off her new clothes, yet for another may be a cause of anxiety as she does not 'do' femininity in the same ways. As such, place is invoked in specific and shifting ways through dressing and is refracted through an individual's social status and occupation.

Although my research took place in two cities, the actual locus for the majority of this research was the micro-site of women's bedrooms and their wardrobes. As such, this is not an ethnography 'of' a place in the conventional anthropological sense, yet it is still an ethnography 'in' a place as women in both Nottingham and London are drawing upon the same social expectations over what women should wear. Initially, the sole location for fieldwork was London, yet to address the possibility that the specificities of London as a global fashion city (Breward, Conekin and Cox, 2002) might skew my results, I decided to carry out fieldwork in another urban site, Nottingham. Because the networks of women I looked at developed organically, the composition of the women I looked at in each site was different in terms of numbers, age range and ethnicities; as such, it is not a comparative ethnography. The emphasis is upon continuities. Through using a second location I was able to build upon the possibilities of my first fieldwork. Contact in Nottingham was through a former high street fashion designer, and the women I accessed were all former fashion or fine art MA students. The main networks in my London sample were family relations or close-knit friendship groups; the Nottingham women are conjoined by shared knowledges and educational position about fashion. Given that involvement in fashion depends upon the requisite knowledge of both what is fashionable and how items should be worn together, looking at such a group offered the possibility to consider the impacts such knowledges might have. Through my second ethnography, I was able to extend upon the ideas about fashion, innovation and knowledge that emerged from my London fieldwork.

Selecting Informants: Networks

In selecting women to work with, one of my primary concerns was being able to get the ethnographic depth that I needed, and therefore I required women who would be willing to spend significant amounts of time with me. Given the intimate nature of my enquiries, taking place initially within the bedroom, the issue of access was particularly pertinent. In a pilot project, I tried a variety of sites to access the women, all of which proved problematic (such as high street shops, mother and baby groups, women's exercise classes, community centres) as women were reluctant to allow a stranger into their wardrobe. Methods that have proved successful for other researchers in gaining access to the home (such as an ethnography of a street (Miller, 1998)) were not open to me because I was a young woman researching alone. This issue was resolved by using my own diverse social networks within London and Nottingham to access women through personal contacts. Once one woman was secured for fieldwork, she often acted as a gatekeeper by introducing me to her close female acquaintances. This method also meant that I was looking at networks of women, friendship groups, work colleagues and families, which allowed me to understand how the identities women constructed through clothing were always refracted through their friendships and familial relationships (Stanley, 1992).

Contacting women through snowball sampling also made establishing relationships with women easier. A central concern of this research is to establish sufficient familiarity with women to enable them to feel comfortable telling me about, and even allowing me to witness, their anxieties over no longer being able to fit into their jeans. I therefore chose to work with a small number of women yet in some instances spending a great deal of time with them to arrive at this point of intimacy. In Wallman's pioneering (1984) study of London households, her research is based upon the empirical study of eight homes in order to delineate various household practices, rather than forming a representative picture of British society.

Similarly, my research does not offer a comprehensive picture of all women's relationships to clothing, but rather, through in-depth analysis, aims to outline the nuanced and deeply personal relationships these women have to their bodies, clothing and self-identity.

As a consequence of needing to arrive at the point where women were comfortable talking about their dressing concerns, I carried out an in-depth ethnography, and wardrobe interviews, with twenty-seven women in total. My ethnography often involved talking to other people in women's lives—usually friends or partners or family members—and so the number of people talked to and interviewed is greater. The total of twenty-seven women was not pre-planned, but rather emerged as the networks terminated. Of these, fifteen were based in London and twelve in Nottingham. Not all of the women accessed were connected with each other, as in some instances I carried out an initial wardrobe interview with someone, and whilst they themselves were keen to participate, for various reasons I never acquired further contacts through them. However, even these women still existed in relationships to others (Wallman, 1984), and in most instances I talked to other people in their lives in order to ascertain the kind of perceptions and expectations these people have and how these impact upon what women chose to wear. The participation between me and the informants was similarly inclusive and rigorous. In the Nottingham samples, only one participant was not connected to any others (Faye); there were two other networks: one of five women and the other of six. Both groups were connected through being either former fashion students (Alice, Emanuela, Helen, Louise, Anna, Gemma) and the other as having done a similar creative MA (Akane, Nom, Rosanna, Clare, Lydia). The commonalities and unities here are based upon shared knowledges and potential fashion and aesthetic orientations.

In the London sample, six of the wardrobes were of unconnected women (Sadie, Marie, Sarah, Joanna, Margaret, Sonya), and the others were involved within two networks. The two networks are represented below. Figure 2.1 shows a small network of interviewees: two sisters and their sister-in-law. This network was particularly important in explicating close-knit familial relationships. The other London network, represented in Figure 2.2, involved six women. This network incorporated

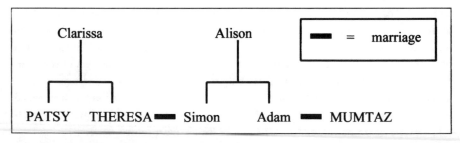

Figure 2.1 London network 1.

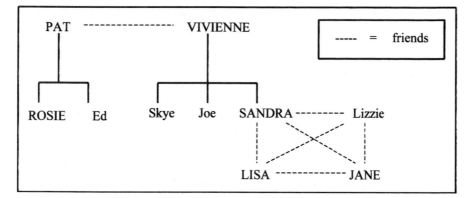

Figure 2.2 London network 2.

mother-daughter relationships, individual friendships and a friendship group of four women who lived together. This network incorporates family, life-long friendship of older women and a group of close-knit contemporaries.

The women I worked with were diverse in terms of their age; the youngest participant was nineteen, the oldest participants were in their late fifties and most were in their twenties or thirties. The majority of women lived with friends or with a partner, with only two of the women living alone; for most women, they either were, or had been, in relationships with men. A quarter of the women I worked with had children of all ages, ranging from new babies to daughters in their thirties. Women's economic backgrounds and occupations ranged from those who seriously struggled financially, lived in rented accommodation, and did not have a job to home owners in lucrative city jobs. The women were of various ethnicities; although most were born in Britain, I worked with many Asian and Jewish women. Over half of the women were white, yet these women were similarly diverse with family routes extending to Italy, Ireland, Scotland and Eastern Europe. Perhaps characteristic of inhabitants in a city such as London, many women cannot be straightforwardly categorized by their ethnicity. However, despite this diversity, my research does not cover every possible variable which could affect clothing choices, and so the findings in this book do not represent all women. For example, all of the women I worked with were able-bodied, and so the extent to which disability affects women's clothing choices could not be addressed in this book. Factors such as ethnicity, sexuality or social class were not the explicit focus of my research, but where they emerged as salient, I discussed them. Therefore, I am not attempting to categorize each woman according to her class, ethnicity or other pre-defined sociological variables, but rather, as I discuss the case studies, the relevant contextual information will be drawn on. The factors which emerge as particularly important in understanding women's clothing choices were working status, financial resources, living situation, relationship status and ethnicity (this was only important in some instances). Whether these come to matter depends upon the specific occasion women are dressing for.

Research Interactions

Underpinning and guiding the overall ethnographic process is the dynamic between researcher and informant; because ethnography is an interactional process wherein information and knowledge is produced through a series of negotiated relationships, an awareness of the position of the researcher is crucial (Silverman, 1997). In fact, the fundamental challenge levelled at naturalist ethnography (such as Duneier, 1992) is the failure to recognize that an ethnographer is not merely recording reality, but is in fact involved in its creation (Clifford and Marcus, 1986). The relations between representation and 'reality' are elided, as they are seen as part of the same process (Lyotard, 1984: xxiv). Two factors of which I was acutely aware when carrying out my research were that I carried out research in Britain (my native country) and that I was looking at women (and am myself a woman). I am not assuming that there is a single category 'woman' or that there is a homogeneous entity 'British society', but rather a set of shifting positionalities and contexts. Because I am in some ways an 'insider' anthropologist, this clearly impacts upon my research and the implicit cultural understandings I possess (Rapport, 2002). Given the heterogeneity of cultural forms and arrangements, my position as an insider is contingent upon each encounter with any particular informant. Furthermore, in pointing to the significance of gender, I am not assuming that there is a commonality amongst all women which overrides all other differences.

In the practice of research, different facets emerge as important at different moments in the encounters. For example, sometimes ethnicity comes to the fore, as one woman I encountered—a Ugandan Asian who also formerly lived in India—has an entire wardrobe of Indian clothing: saris, shalwar kamiz and several Rajasthani outfits. In this instance, there were no shared cultural knowledges between informant and researcher. These women are also positioned in terms of ethnicity, occupation, nationality, religion and familial relationships. Shared expectations and cultural knowledges are contingent. The post-modern critiques levelled at naturalism focus upon the negative influence of the researcher. However, the presence of the researcher can also be utilized in a positive way. Knowledge is acquired in everyday life through interaction between positioned individuals (Hammersley and Atkinson, 1995). Therefore, shared knowledges are also something that can be utilized to elicit information and to build a relationship (Stanley and Wise, 1993). This is particularly important given the intimate nature of my enquiries. For example, many women, whilst willing to show me their hanging clothing, were far more reticent when it came to discussing underwear. My tactic became to share some anecdote of my own, which more often than not served to acquire information in return and established an intimacy.

As a researcher, I used clothing as a means of fitting in to the research encounter and as a way of creating a relationship with informants. My clothing came to matter not only in shared stories, but also as I had to dress the part for each interview. As I anxiously anticipated my first meeting with a woman, I tried to imagine, from what I had been told about her or from our initial phone conversation, how she would dress. In turn, I tried to anticipate what would be the best way for me to dress to generate a rapport. There were numerous occasions when I got it wrong, such as when I first went to visit Alice, who loves prints and bright colours, and I wore my 'safe' outfit of jeans and a black top. On another occasion, when I went to see Vivienne, a woman who rarely wore make-up and deemed excess concern with clothing to be superficial, I was experimenting with wearing false nails. My unprofessional attempt to glue the plastic nails onto my real nails resulted in a lost nail mid-interview. Her withering look as I scrambled on the floor to find it told me just how badly I had anticipated this research encounter.

Because ethnography develops organically, many of the stages of research I had planned did not go as I had wished (a facet of research that is well documented, for example, in Stanley and Wise, 1993). The process of my fieldwork was therefore opposite to the usual trajectory of gradually acquiring access to the intimate domain. Instead, I was starting in this domain of intimacy; in most cases, this worked extremely well as it usually enabled an instant rapport. As I went through women's wardrobes, the intimate stories that emerged meant that getting to know women's clothing was the starting point for developing a more personal relationship with the women. However, in some instances I never moved beyond a few interviews (Hammersley and Atkinson, 1995, Rapport, 2002), as the relationship between myself and informant failed to develop. Even carrying out a couple of interviews with accompanying photographs was extremely useful; such interviews are still embedded in experience (Kvale, 1996) and ensured access to both the home and within the bedroom.

Wardrobe Overview

Given the depth of involvement this methodology entails, much of the chapters that follow will be based upon case studies. To provide a context for these case studies, the rest of this chapter provides an overview of the various clothing in participants' wardrobes, looking at how many items women have, how they store them and how often they wear them. This section considers how the physical structure of the wardrobe impacts both upon how women store their clothing and how women choose what to wear. Most women possessed at least one conventional wardrobe, which consists of a wooden rectangular box structure with two doors, behind which there is a metal rail running horizontally along the top, enabling clothing to be hung on hangers. At the bottom is a drawer which usually houses folded clothes. Some wardrobes also contain open shelves, running from the top of the wardrobe to the bottom, next to the clothing rail. This conventional wardrobe style was possessed by the majority of women, with three exceptions. Two women had alcoves built into the structure of their bedrooms, with a curtain shutting the clothing off, neither liking the feel of a wooden box in their bedroom. The third exception was Rosanna, a woman in her late twenties, who had a walk-in wardrobe. Having finished her degree, she is currently making ends meet by working in a bar in Nottingham, she lives in a council flat on her own and has decorated the entire flat in bright fuchsia and terracotta paint. Her wardrobe forms part of the overall décor of the flat, as it is enclosed by a purple drape, with brightly coloured clothing within it. On walking in to the wardrobe, on both sides there are rails to hang her clothing on, with shelves above; and so, in front of her, and on either side, she is surrounded by clothing. Unlike women with a conventional box wardrobe, her relationship to the clothing is tactile and visual, as the narrowness of the wardrobe means that the clothing touches her as she stands deciding what to wear.

The spatial organization of all wardrobes—with a shelf area and a rail—delimits and enables the dual practices of folding and hanging. Items which are ordinarily worn on the body sit in a piled piece of fabric or hang limp on a hanger, and only the edge of each item of clothing is visible. As a woman stands looking at her wardrobe, the relationship is primarily visual, entailed by the physical distance, as the rail positions all clothing as potential items from which she might select. Only the colours are visible, and to see the shape of the item and how it hangs, the woman has to touch and lift it as part of the process of selection. In dressing, women moreover have to translate the clothing on the hanger to how they imagine they would look in it. Women have to reconnect the totality of the edges of their clothing contained within a piece of furniture at which they can look, with an assembled outfit which looks good on their body. More often than not, women resolve this distance through wearing items they know will work or through the often lengthy processes of trying on multiple items.

Choosing what to wear starts when women open the wardrobe doors or pull back the drapes. All wardrobes I looked at had some form of covering for the clothing, which both functionally prevents clothing damage through exposure to sunlight and dust, and also has the effect of shutting off the clothing in a private, distinct area that is only visible when opened. In almost all cases, clothing is primarily stored in the bedroom; the only exceptions were when clothing was kept in a spare bedroom. The wardrobe is a waking presence, kept in a secluded part of the house, only to be seen by the woman herself, with the exception of women who lived with their partners or husbands and so often shared a wardrobe. The privacy engendered by the wardrobe's presence in the bedroom is heightened by the covering of each wardrobe, which has to be opened to reveal the clothing within. Like Russian dolls which contain ever-increasing inaccessible levels of privacy, within the enclosed, private domain of the home is the bedroom, and the innermost enclave within this is the wardrobe.

In all cases, clothing spills out throughout the whole house and is not just confined within the wardrobe. The different locations of clothing in the house relate to how often it is worn, whether it is about to be disposed of or whether it is in part of clothing's ordinary household cycle of laundering. For transitional clothing (which was about to be thrown out or clothing that was out of season), many women use suitcases, boxes under the bed or even black bin-liners. Clothing that is worn all the time often never makes it into the wardrobe; for ease of access, these items are kept on a chair in the bedroom or on a stair rail, to be grabbed on the way out of the house. Table 2.1 provides details about the wardrobes of the women in this study and how many items of clothing are contained within them. With the exception of Nom (who is only temporarily residing in Britain and has very few clothes), all women have spaces for both hanging and folding. Most women had a separate chest of drawers for folded clothing.

The majority of women had two or three wardrobes and chests of drawers; the largest number being Mumtaz's seven wardrobes and Rosie's seven. Both of these women have vast quantities of clothing (with Mumtaz having the most at 182 items). There is a correlation between greater wardrobe space and quantity of clothing, as all women I interviewed filled all available wardrobe space.

The Contents of the Wardrobe

The wardrobe's structure limits the possible ways in which clothes can be stored, but it does not necessarily dictate how women organize their wardrobes. Rather, drawing from Lefebvre (1991), 'space' is produced dialectically through normative ideas of how space should be used and the actual empirical use of space (Lefebvre, 1991, Shields, 1991). These normative models of how space should be used create a range of possibilities, which may or may not be actualized in practice (De Certeau, 1984). In the case of the wardrobe, it is structured to enable the dual practices of hanging and folding; this is mirrored in terms of women's practices, as women usually hang their clothing on the rails and place clothing in the drawers. However, the lack of time to organize the wardrobe often leads to clothing being stuffed rather than folded or items such as handbags and shoes colonizing the undesignated areas of the wardrobe, such as the space at the bottom of the hanging area. The wardrobe's structure and size also limits how many items of clothing women are able to keep within it. For most women I worked with, the amount of clothing they owned remained relatively stable; they filled all available wardrobe space, and newly acquired items of clothing ousted older ones, which were discarded or given away to make space. The numbers of items represented in Table 2.1 are based upon the initial wardrobe interview carried out with each woman and therefore represent a moment in the life-cycle of the wardrobe. Broadly speaking, those with more clothing tended to be older, reasonably well off and living in a permanent residence with more space for clothes.

Table 2.1 Participants' Spaces Designated for Clothing and their Total Number of Clothing Items

	Number of Ward-Robes (hanging)	*Number of Ward-Robes (folded)*	*Other Spaces for Clothes*	*Number of Items of Clothing*
Rosanna	2	2	0	135
Clare	1	2	0	64
Alice	1	1	2	67
Gemma	1	1	0	86
Akane	1	2	0	39
Helen	1 1/2	1	2	104
Emanuela	1	2	0	110
Nom	1	0	0	35
Anna	1	0	1	47
Louise	1	0	1	97
Lydia	1	1	0	155
Faye	1	2	0	73
Mumtaz	4	3	1	182
Patsy	2	1	0	176
Theresa	1	1	1	154
Sonya	1	2	0	109
Margaret	2	1	0	87
Joanna	1	1	1	83
Sarah	1	1	1	54
Marie	1	1	0	72
Sadie	1	0	2	81
Lisa	2	1	0	76
Sandra	1	1	1	110
Rosie	4	3	0	151
Jane	1	1	0	58
Pat	2	2	0	108
Vivienne	1	1	0	129

This general trend would seem to suggest that, rather than the wardrobes of younger women being overburdened with frivolous items of fashion, in fact the wardrobe is an accumulation of items over a long period of time. Women with more space are afforded the luxury of keeping such items within their wardrobes.

The general organizing principle of the wardrobe rests upon clothing that is hung up and clothing that is folded (often folding is less disciplined). The undesignated areas of the wardrobe, such as the bottom of the hanging area, invariably are filled with shoes. Such spatial practices emerge in the interstices of the dominant practices of the wardrobes, perhaps as a means of dealing with excess clothing or the practicalities of containing all clothing within one domain. The key determinants in positioning clothing as hung or folded that emerge are whether the clothes are considered special, the materiality of the item (type, fabric), season and domains. For example, Clare, a young woman who mostly wears jeans and a black top every day as she works from home or goes to university, hangs only four 'special' items, including a red velvet skirt and top, a feathered black dress, a two-tone satin red and purple dress and a raw silk bronzed skirt. Each item has been worn only once, placed on its own hanger in a clear plastic bag and is distinguished from the piles of clothing; by keeping each item separate, she is able to preserve the memory of the event. Like most women I worked with, Clare always hangs dresses and skirts (with the exception of perhaps casual summer ones). In part this is due to the materiality of the dresses; in Clare's case, she fears ruining or creasing the delicate fabrics by folding them. Although these dresses are unambiguously 'smarter' items, in many cases, the decisions over whether to fold or hang an item is based upon available space or the function of an item (such as a work top).

Clothes that are folded tend to be organized into more rigid categories than hanging clothes, with all women having a separate drawer for underwear, t-shirts (often further divided into long- and short-sleeved, pale and dark) and jeans and other casual trousers. As well as type, fabric and occasions, a fundamental ordering that emerged was organization into domains: home, work, holiday, functional (such as for sport) and going-out clothing. For some women, home wear has its own drawer; for others, because it is worn so frequently, it remains on a chair in the bedroom. Functional clothing is often kept in its own drawer, as is holiday wear (which coincides with seasonal wear, most women having summer and winter clothing). Organizing clothing into work wear is central to all of the women I worked with; clothing specified for work is usually not kept in a separate wardrobe or drawer, but work trousers and shirts are grouped together on the hanging rail, facilitating ease of access. How the wardrobe is ordered and organized enables the women to organize life realms through the clothing worn to different domains. Women are not just ordering shirts, but are also regulating their lives.

Similar to the ordering of work wear is the presence of a 'fun' order of the wardrobe; for example, Marie, who works in a second-hand book shop, has an entire 'fun' drawer full of 'interesting' tops in lighter colours with slogans or cartoon characters printed on them. Like other women who have these drawers, fun clothing falls in opposition to her dark-coloured, plain work clothing. The opposition between fun and work for many women is enabled through aesthetic distinctions; a small proportion of the women interviewed (four of them) consciously organized their entire wardrobe aesthetically. For example, Alice, a former fashion MA student, who has the most brightly coloured collection of clothing of anyone I interviewed, has ordered her clothing on the occasion of this interview into colour domains. The organization is incredible; her fifty-four hanging items are ordered thus (from left to right): nine denim items, four pink items, one peach item, one white and pink item, one navy blue, one blue and purple, one red, four green, one turquoise, white and yellow, one white and blue, three white, two grey, eleven black, one camel, two black and white, one camel, one pale brown, one beige, one cream, one camel, two yellow, one brown, one white, one blue and turquoise and one white. The colour domains are placed together so as to blend into each other in complementary hues. On another occasion, she reorganized her wardrobe in terms of prints and patterns in a similarly systematic way. In common with the other women who ordered their wardrobes aesthetically, the key ordering is based upon how the clothing appears; Alice wants her wardrobe to be a pleasing aesthetic totality. Such a conscious ordering has clear implications for how assemblages are made, because, on making selections, the wearer is presented with a colour spectrum.

When clothing is ordered in terms of type of clothing, an item is selected from a category, such as bottoms or smart tops. The outfit is conceptualized as an assemblage of types of clothing (such as a skirt, t-shirt and cardigan); the first decisions are made regarding what types of clothing will be selected, and the subsequent points for deliberation are colours and fabrics. In contrast, a wardrobe organized aesthetically lends itself to initial decisions being made regarding which colours will be worn; Alice decides what colours or prints go together, as the form and function of a garment is secondary (on occasion, she even wears skirts as tops in order to make the right colour combinations). This allows Alice to be creative in mixing colours and coming up with new looks. Lydia, who has an array of brightly coloured clothing but is less confident about her clothing choices, also orders her wardrobe into aesthetics. In Lydia's case, ordering her wardrobe aesthetically allows her to 'get it right'. She panics about putting the wrong colours together, and so organizing her wardrobe into colours mediates potential panics when dressing. What these contrasting examples show is that, even though how the wardrobe is organized clearly affects how women choose what to wear, this relationship is not reductive: how a woman organizes her clothing into colours or patterns does not dictate how she gets dressed. On occasion, a woman who organizes her wardrobe aesthetically may decide that she feels like wearing a skirt and blouse and will make her clothing choices according to types of clothing rather than colours.

Frequency of Wearing

When women are dressing in a hurry, one of the most important factors in deciding what to wear is ease of access. For the clothing that is folded, women are most likely to grab one of the top two items when they are late getting ready for work. Similarly, for clothing that is hanging on rails, the accessibility of items is crucial in affecting how often women wear items when there are several items on the same hanger. Some wardrobes have a sliding door or hidden recesses which are not easily accessible, as clothing that is rarely worn is pushed to the peripheries. This massively reduces the range of items women are actually choosing from. It was common during my ethnography for a shocked woman to encounter clothing she did not realize that she owned. Even for women who could see the whole range of their clothing, it often proved too overwhelming to select from the whole wardrobe every day. For example, Lydia has a large conventional-style wardrobe, with two doors that open in the centre; she only wears clothing on the left-hand side of the wardrobe. Characteristically, women have strategies for separating out their habitual clothing from clothing that they rarely wear to help cope with the sheer quantity of clothing they have. This helps women make quick decisions when dressing.

The percentages of clothing that women actually wore are represented in Table 2.2. The number of items worn is obtained from the initial wardrobe interview. The other percentages, relating to how often the clothing is worn, are based upon what women told me, their clothes diaries and my own observations of whether clothing was worn throughout the year. The *inactive clothing* incorporates unworn and formerly worn clothing; *potential clothing* incorporates clothing that is worn rarely or sometimes or clothing that is tried on, even if it never leaves the bedroom; *active clothing* includes work clothing and clothing worn often or habitually.

The broad pattern emerging from the data is that, on average, 12.20 per cent of clothing is inactive, 50.55 per cent of clothing has the potential to be worn and 37.25 per cent of clothing forms the active wardrobe, from which women select clothing all the time. The relationship between inactive, active and potential clothing raises issues over clothing that used to be worn all the time, inherited clothing, gifted clothing and clothing women wish they could wear. These issues will be discussed throughout the book. There are, however, evident discrepancies to the broad pattern above and worthy of mention here. Several of the women have significantly lower percentages of inactive clothing (Akane, in fact, has no clothes in this category). Such women are almost all younger (in their early twenties) and have not yet had time to accumulate vast quantities of clothing; moreover, as will be discussed throughout the book, younger women are more likely to discard clothing they no longer wear. At the opposite end of the spectrum are those women who have very high levels of inactive clothing (ten women have over 19 per cent of clothing that is inactive). These women tend to be older (in their mid-thirties to early sixties), and have acquired more 'former selves', memories through clothing and indeed have the space in which to store them.

Young women who had lots of inactive clothing usually had had a lifestyle change. For example, Louise has similar percentages of active and inactive clothing (39 and 34 per cent, respectively). She either wears her clothing all the time or never wears it, as she is unable to financially afford to buy new clothing she might not wear. In the instances of Vivienne and Gemma, their active wardrobe is smaller than their inactive wardrobe. Such a pattern emerges as both women are extremely habitual in their clothing, having a small number of items that they wear all the time rather than a range from which they draw. Similarly, there is a group

Table 2.2 Participants' Total Number of Clothing Items and their Percentages of Inactive, Potential and Active Items

	Number of Items of Clothing	*Per Cent Inactive*	*Per Cent Potential*	*Per Cent Active*
Rosanna	135	41.48	37.04	21.48
Clare	64	1.56	40.63	57.81
Alice	67	0	56.72	43.28
Gemma	86	26.74	52.34	20.92
Akane	39	0	58.97	41.03
Helen	104	21.15	55.77	23.08
Emanuela	110	4.54	69.09	26.37
Nom	35	2.86	51.43	45.71
Anna	47	6.38	46.81	46.81
Louise	97	34.02	26.8	39.18
Lydia	155	10.97	73.55	15.48
Faye	73	2.74	57.53	39.73
Mumtaz	182	21.43	51.65	26.92
Patsy	176	19.32	52.27	28.41
Theresa	154	24.03	46.1	29.87
Sonya	109	1.83	65.14	33.03
Margaret	87	2.3	50.57	47.13
Joanna	83	4.81	50.6	44.58
Sarah	54	11.11	53.7	35.19
Marie	72	4.17	30.56	65.27
Sadie	81	25.93	35.8	38.27
Lisa	76	2.63	35.53	61.84
Sandra	110	20.91	50	29.09
Rosie	151	10.6	47.68	41.72
Jane	58	6.9	56.89	36.21
Pat	108	0	53.7	46.3
Vivienne	129	20.93	58.14	20.93
Average	98.5	12.2	50.55	37.25

of women who have the highest percentages of habitual clothing, such as Clare, Marie and Lisa, all of whom do not have vast quantities of clothing, have clearly defined work domains and thus tend to wear all the clothing that they own. The key factors in considering why women wear the same items all the time and do not wear others are age, financial resources and the discrepancies between lifestyle and clothing.

Order and Disorder

This ordering into habitual clothing and inactive clothing is not one that is defined by the structure of the wardrobe. Here the process of spatialization (Lefebvre, 1991) incorporates the acts of wearing with practices of positioning clothing and with the existing structure of the wardrobe. The wardrobe's structure also has wider ramifications in terms of the normative discourses of order and control. As a spatial domain that promotes the rational organization of space, the wardrobe is designed for the ordering of clothing. The linking of ordered clothing to control is explicitly made in the discourses of companies that specialize in wardrobe organization. As Cwerner notes (2001), their aim is to enable people to control their clothing rather than the opposite: that clothing overwhelms the person. Such a normative notion of control is evidenced in the regular sort-outs that women felt compelled to do every few months, as the clothes start to escape from the confines prescribed by the wardrobe. An exemplary wardrobe in this sense of rational order is Theresa's, for whom all items in the wardrobe are clearly compartmentalized; clothing is ordered in terms of type, and within this scheme items are colour coordinated. She even has a separate section of the wardrobe for former clothing that she no longer wears but loves; even the memories are clearly organized and regimented. Even when items are worn, they find their place back in the same spatial location in the wardrobe. She also has a biannual switchover of her clothing according to seasons, as clothing is swapped from the bin-liners in her daughter's wardrobe to become current clothing in her wardrobe. Such rationalization of space is clearly evidenced in the rest of her home, and indeed in the rest of her life. Despite having two small children, there is no evidence of the customary children's toys littering the floor, as they are always packed away in designated boxes. The wardrobe reflects and is clearly part of her general sense of order in her life; yet, more than this, ordering her clothes helps her to 'get it right' when she selects outfits. Such ordering is evidenced to some degree in all other wardrobes—in particular, in the case of work clothing. Degrees of ordering clearly enable the process of getting dressed; this ordering of the wardrobe also facilitates the management of wider aspects of women's lives—such as dressing appropriately for work, for being a mother or for going to the pub with friends.

Not all women organize their wardrobes to such an extent. Rosanna exemplifies a defiance of this rationalization, as someone for whom 41.8 per cent of her clothing is inactive. Still in her mid-twenties, she has not had any major life shifts; instead, she is someone who has a rapid turnover of clothing, mostly acquired from car boot sales or second-hand shops. She buys vast amounts of cheap, brightly coloured, extravagant items, most of which she knows she will never wear. She is the only woman I interviewed who had a walk-in wardrobe, mentioned previously, and the presence of cheap and bright clothing is fundamental to her experience of dressing and of her wardrobe. Having a walk-in wardrobe, she is surrounded by exuberant, patterned, glittering items of clothing, even though the clothing she selects on a day-to-day basis forms a pile on the shelf at the back of the wardrobe: usually jeans and a vest top or jumper. She loves her wardrobe as a whole and the aesthetic experience of standing in it, yet her relationship to such clothing is rarely as potential clothing to be worn. Rather, it incorporates her fantasy of what dressing should be, even if her fantasy is only enacted when she tries on these items in the privacy of her home. This notion of fantasy also leads to the disorder of her wardrobe. Underneath the rails on the right-hand side and on the floor shelves, the space is stuffed full of tops; none are folded, but rather they wind about each other in spirals of colours and fabrics. This disordered state is not a mere accident, as, in fact, she clears out her clothing every three months; she actively cultivates this experience of being overwhelmed by her clothing. Whilst the rest of her flat continues the aesthetic of bright, exotic colours, and each room is painted a different, vibrant colour, the same level of disorder is not present; it is as if the separate room of the wardrobe is where such a fantasy is allowed presence. The disorder is ordered. In the opposite case of Theresa, in actualizing the rationalist philosophy of the ordering of wardrobes, she does so in order to give herself feelings of control over her clothing and, in turn, her life.

Conclusion

This research involved getting behind the scenes in order to understand both how and why women reject and select certain items of clothing. Although I have already made a case for studying women's clothing choices in the home, the actual practice of doing research was far from easy. Even if it is a pivotal moment in understanding why women wear what they wear; it is also a difficult aspect to research, given how private it is. A key concern for me was gaining access to this moment, and then hanging around enough to allow me to situate women's clothing choices within their lives. Given that fieldwork is an organic practice, the practice of ethnography was different dependent upon the woman. Some women kept daily clothes diaries for me as we discussed how they made choices; with those, I had a more in-depth involvement, and I sat in their bedrooms and watched them dress. My role as ethnographer was active in these cases, as I helped advise women what to wear, shared in their triumphs and commiserated in their disasters.

The starting point for this research was women's wardrobes, as how they are organized is crucial in terms of how women make clothing choices. There was an amazing commonality amongst the women I talked to in terms of how they ordered their clothing into function, style and domains (especially work, home and going out and fun clothing). Rarer was when women ordered their wardrobes aesthetically. This act of ordering their clothing meant that getting dressed was supposed to be easier, as women do not have to create an entire work wardrobe afresh every morning. Knowing which clothes are for going out and which are for wearing around the home helped prevent wardrobe panics. However, one form of ordering that was notable by its absence was that no women organized their wardrobes into outfits. The only exception was sometimes women had work outfits or outfits for special occasions (such as weddings). The implication of this is that, even for women with very ordered and organized wardrobes, they still want to feel that they are being creative when they get dressed. No women I worked with wanted to be reduced to always wearing pre-determined outfits as dressing is therefore always a creative act of assemblage. This creativity must always be seen in relationship to the ordering, as one of the main dynamics in dressing is between novel assemblages and pre-existing aesthetic order. Dressing is never an act of unhampered creativity, as evidenced by how few items women actually select from on a daily basis. Within the wardrobe many items are rarely—if ever worn—as they may be items that women used to wear but no longer have the lifestyle or the body to wear them. Rather than see this clothing as irrelevant to clothing choices, the next chapter will discuss the kept but unworn items as part of how women construct current identities through clothing.

–3–

But What Were You Wearing?
Clothes and Memories

The very fact that many women I interviewed had items they had owned for over twenty years hanging in their wardrobe along-side more recently acquired items raises the importance of considering the long-term relationship women have to their clothing. If an understanding of clothing and identity is reduced to the externally imposed temporality of the fashion system, then the relationships women form to their clothing may come to appear fickle and ephemeral. Instead, in this chapter the focus is upon the personalized temporality of the wardrobe, making it possible to arrive at an understanding of the identities women construct through their clothing as similarly constituted over time. This relationship will be considered in this chapter in terms of both how women use clothing as a means to remember former selves and how women may use who they were through clothing to construct who they are today.

As the previous section demonstrated, on average 12.2 per cent of women's wardrobes are inactive, which in certain instances rises to a remarkable 40 per cent. For some women, this is due to not sorting out the wardrobe regularly or high turnovers of styles, yet most of the women I interviewed regularly sorted through their clothing and have deliberately kept items that they do not wear anymore. The wardrobe sort-out is, therefore, an occasion on which women can also work through their biography. Inasmuch as choosing what to wear can be seen as an act of self-construction, so too, the act of sorting out former selves through clothing is also part of this process of engaging with self-identity. Giddens defines self-identity as 'the self as reflexively understood by the person in terms of her or his biography' (1991: 53). A continuity of biography is fundamental to the 'reflexive project of the self' (Giddens, 1991: 5). An individual can establish a sense of self through the reflexive awareness of his or her biography as a coherent trajectory, spanning from the past through to the future. Central to his argument is that self-identity is a project, and, as part of this project, biography, rather than just being a pre-existing given, is consciously engaged with, and indeed manipulated in order to establish a stable self-identity. Although Giddens is concerned primarily with verbal and written narrative biographies, to be discussed in this chapter is the possibility that the wardrobe may form part of this biographical project. This project involves sorting out the wardrobe and disposing of clothing as an act of both remembering and of the mirror process of forgetting (Forty, 1999).

One consideration will be the way in which clothing is used to both remember former versions of the self (Banim and Guy, 2001) and visualize potential future selves to which a person might aspire. In both cases, the wardrobe represents an external and material visualization as opposed to the internal and intangible nature of memory. Memories through clothing acquire a particular poignancy as they are evoked through the physical sensuality and tactility of clothing. In focusing upon the specific material ways in which clothing is able to hold former aspects of the self, it is apparent that clothing does not simply reflect an 'actual' event (Denzin, 1989, Stanley, 1992). Unlike a life story, which, if inadequate, can be retold using different words, the possibilities of manipulation in clothing are rather more limited: if clothing fails to capture the biography the person wishes to construct, the only available option is to throw the item away. If kept, the clothing confronts the person with things they may otherwise have wished to forget. Clothing is not just open to manipulation by the wearer, as the tear on an evening gown tells the tale not of chic sophistication, but of the bulging body beneath which defied its incarceration.

The implication of Giddens's theory here is that people define and order their past so as to legitimate and define a current identity as the culmination of a coherent, ordered biography. However, when we consider how women choose what to wear, on many occasions these former identities through clothing are not relegated to a terminated past. In wearing older items again, the past is reactivated, and the conventional biographical trajectory 'of development from the past to the anticipated future' (Giddens, 1991: 75) becomes problematic. As a documentation of a life from the cradle to the grave, both verbal and written biography follows particular conventions (Gullestad, 1996) of linear coherent temporality. Implicit within conventional narrative biographies is that the self is teleological, developing chronologically through previous acts in a manner that is 'progressive, accumulated' (Stanley, 1992: 12). However, when women reactivate former aspects of themselves, as they rewear items that have hung unworn in the wardrobe, such items can no longer merely be part of the past.

Personal Biography Through the Wardrobe: Ruptures and Former Selves

This chapter considers the ways in which the clothing in the wardrobe is used by women as a means to work through their biography; in the case of Theresa, the act of ordering the wardrobe into memories and former selves is part of her wider strategies of using the wardrobe as a means to order and organize her life. A quarter of the items of clothing in her wardrobe are no longer worn. Characteristic of other women with quantities of such clothing, Theresa has experienced a biographical and sartorial rupture. Such life shifts correspond either to a shift in relationship status (with the acquisition of a permanent partner resulting in the abandonment of 'on the pull' clothing) or to a change in working status. Theresa forms an example of the latter, as she and her husband have recently moved from central London, where she used to work in the corporate sector, to a rural suburb. Theresa is a white British woman and was born in the countryside surrounding London. Her wardrobe is one of the most striking in terms of the immense control she has over her clothing; her relationships, family, seasons, events and even her biography are clearly ordered. She continued working after she gave birth to the two children, yet, once the children's vocal capacities had developed from the wailings and screamings of babies to the persistent inquisitive musings of toddlers, Theresa was keen to relinquish her job and become a full-time mother. Her husband runs his own business, and as such they are in a secure financial position so that she does not need to work. Her primary occupation is now homemaker: looking after the children and engaging in various projects around their new house, such as decorating, feeding the animals and tending to the garden.

The clothing she keeps is not an accidental by-product of bad organization; as discussed in the previous chapter, Theresa's wardrobe is so regimented that even her memories are clearly ordered. The cessation of her working life became the occasion for a wardrobe sort-out, as many of her suits, dresses and shirts that were in good condition were given to her mother to sell on to a second-hand shop. Many she chose to keep. Hanging on the left side of her wardrobe are the remnants of her working life. The plastic suit bags which enclose them manifest her desire to preserve the suits, and the aspects of her self they embody. The items she has kept are those which she remembers made her 'feel really good when I wore them'. For example, she has a fitted, long, marl grey jacket which was her 'lucky jacket. I felt really confident in it'. Although she knows she will never wear it again, as it is too 'office-y', given the colour and the style, the mystical qualities she has attributed to it make her reluctant to part with it. In keeping the item, Theresa wishes to retain the memories and former aspects of her working self. One of the reasons such items of clothing are able to form a significant extension of who she used to be is that it was worn habitually; her entire working life was carried out in these clothes. All the clothing she wore was in a particular style: shift dresses and matching suit jackets, as they were worn over a period of 10 years, comprised a shape and look that became definitive of Theresa's working wardrobe. This clothing forms a stark stylistic contrast to her current aesthetic; because these items were worn only to work, they evoke vividly her former working life. As Hoskins (1998) points out, objects may be pivots for 'reflexivity and introspection, a tool of auto-biography, self-discovery, a way of knowing oneself through things' (Hoskins, 1998: 198).

Hoskins (1998) discusses how objects may be biographical in the example of the betel bag, amongst the Kodi of the Eastern Indonesian island of Sumba—a society which she notes lacks the tradition of telling life stories. As such, the past is accessed and understood through objects. The betel bag is carried around by adults all the time, and so the object is imbued with the owner's personality to the extent that, in some instances, a betel bag can be buried in lieu of a person. The notion of clothing forming an extension of the person is useful when considering these items women do not wish to throw away. Just as the betel bag is a constant companion to the Kodi, Theresa wore her work clothing every day and so this clothing is inseparable from her working self. When the self is extended through objects, the person is able to stand outside of, and reflect upon, themselves; and so, when Theresa is sorting out her wardrobe, she is considering her former working self through the suits and shift dresses. In keeping the items, she is able to retain these memories rather than rely on the intangible, unreliability of memory in the mind.

Her former clothing helps Theresa construct and legitimate her current position in life. Whilst not wishing to return to this lifestyle, she does not want to relinquish the knowledge that she used to be this person. Banim and Guy (2001), in discussing why women keep clothing they no longer wear, point to the connectivities between former items and current identities. One of the means by which this is achieved is through establishing continuity between the former and the contemporary, yet for Theresa such a continuity is achieved through contrast. This contrasting self is enabled through the disparity between her former and current clothing styles. In keeping this clothing, she is able to both acknowledge that she has the capacity to be such a different person and to legitimate her current status and lifestyle choice as a homemaker and mother. Even though she does not wear these former outfits, they are not relegated to her past entirely, as she uses them in the construction and justification of a current identity; like all forms of memory, they are seen from the perspective of the present.

In keeping her work clothing, Theresa's continuity of identity is established through contrast; in other cases, this emphasis upon a continuity of identity is even more important. Theresa still possesses a stretchy cotton and viscose dress she wore when she was pregnant, which, throughout the gestation period, expanded to incorporate her swelling stomach. Ordinarily with such fabric, the elastane fibres stretch over the body, retracting when the body is no longer encapsulated within and the clothing returns to its former shape. Given the extent of stretching and that Theresa wore it constantly throughout the nine-month period, the material is disfigured around the centre. She 'can't bear to throw it out', wanting to embrace and reminisce over this period: the transition to her current motherhood status. She has thrown out most of her other maternity dresses, which tended to be loose cotton. Central to this item is that it carries her personalized individual shape. The transitional and fluctuating stage of pregnancy is concretized and made permanent through the dress. Ordinarily the clothing that hangs in the wardrobe is characterized by its disembodiment, as it hangs lifeless on rails. Here the clothing, stretched and worn habitually, manages to presence this absence. She would not just be throwing out a dress, but rather she would be throwing out her own externalized pregnant body. Whilst this transitory period of pregnancy is not one she will return to, it is foundational to her current lifestyle as a mother, and so too is the dress which embodies this.

In addition to the pregnancy dress and many of the work clothes, there are many items in the wardrobe which cannot be worn again due to the physical state of the garment. Theresa still has a petrol blue silk shirt she bought almost twenty years ago. There are several rips in the fabric, and it is starting to fray in places through over wearing. It is soft and smooth to the touch; as Theresa talks about it, she strokes it fondly, telling me how it brings back so many memories—when she made her first cheeky foray to the pub at the age of sixteen and to the first eighteenth birthday party she went to. She remembers the excitement she felt at buying it as it was the first silk shirt she ever had and seemed very expensive at the time from Hobbes. It was her 'most dressy and exciting item', and even now she can recount how her hair spiked up when she wore it, how the soft fabric caressed her skin and how, in its volumi-nousness, when her body moved, so too the dress stroked her body in undulations of sensuous material. The feel of the soft silk on her hands enables Theresa to reimagine herself through the sensuality of the item, as she remembers what it felt like to wear the clothing.

The importance of such sensual aspects of wearing becomes apparent when cloth-ing is understood phenomenologically, from the perspective of the wearer, as an embodied experience (Entwistle, 2000). Clothing is imbued with meaning not only through how it appears, but also through how it feels, smells and sounds (Barnes and Eicher, 1993: 3). The wearer's perception and experience of the world arise out the bodily situatedness, as a clothed body. The touch of the clothing on the skin enables Theresa to be resituated as she is able to remember how it felt to wear the clothing. It is through this tactility that the wearer recaptures the potentialities of their former self as a particular synaesthetic experience of remembering is triggered (Kuechler, 1999: 54). Writing on wine collectors, Belk (1995) notes that on tasting each wine, people were able to remember exactly where they were when they first tasted it. With clothing this happens through touch and feel rather than through taste. Touching the silk shirt evoked the other sensations associated with wearing the item.

Theresa rarely wears the shirt now, mostly due to its state of disrepair; she wore it so often when she was younger that it is ripped and torn. The propensities of an object to age do not correspond with our desire to remember them (Forty and Kuechler, 1999); as the silk shirt is aging and falling apart, through its materiality, the shirt resists its full incorporation into Theresa's identity. She still loves the shirt and is able to keep it in her wardrobe but is not able to have the same relationship she once had to it; she fears it will fall apart completely if she wears it again. At the same time, the existence of the rips and tears serves to authenticate how much it was worn and loved. It is cherished for its age-value (Riegl, 1982) not because it embod-ies a particular period of her life or memories, but rather as it is worn continuously, through the material biography of the item, it is valued as it shows the generic pas-sage of time and wearing.

This silk shirt shows that women are often ambivalent about many items that are kept and the extent to which the past is truly terminated. Some of the items Theresa used to wear to work are recombined. In her summer wardrobe, she still has a linen long-sleeved jacket with a granddad-style collar. Being linen, the jacket hangs relatively

easily off the body, yet the jacket's structure is dictated by bulky shoulder pads, legacies of her working days in the 1980s. Despite being a delicate fabric, when worn
the effect is boxy, giving a square shape to the body. Theresa used to love wearing it
to the office because it is relatively loose and 'doesn't hug my body too tightly'; she
felt able to contrast it with tighter short skirts and a camisole underneath. The jacket
is not suitable for her current lifestyle, at home with the children; however, on one
occasion when I visit her, she is debating over whether to wear it to a forthcoming
parents evening. She despises the shoulder pads which locate the jacket in the 80s,
so she resolves to unpick the stitches and remove them.

Given that the jacket has no collar and the fabric is relatively informal, once the
pads are taken out and the shape is made more fluid, she feels it will be suitable to
her new lifestyle, worn with a pair of jeans. The formal rigidity of the office jacket is
relaxed to become assimilated into her role as a caring mother. Here an item initially
relegated to her past is reactivated to construct a new look: that of the effortlessly
smart, multi-tasking mother. Theresa has the appropriate skills of recombination to
not only make the item wearable again, but also to activate facets of her former
working self as part of being a mother. This reactivation, therefore, forms a challenge to Giddens's discussion of how biography links to self-identity (1991), as the
past is not terminated, but made present through clothing. Even though her working
life is over, as clothing is recombined with other items from different periods, the
biography through clothing is not terminated. Aspects of her working self may be
mobilized within a new outfit dependent upon how the outfit is assembled, as former
moments are juxtaposed with current or more recent items. The intersection of a
former item of clothing with current, worn clothing challenges notions of a linear
biography through clothing.

Frozen/dormant Clothing

Theresa's linen jacket is a work item that can be worn again because it can be altered
to fit her current identity. Many other women cannot rewear items of clothing because they do not fit their current life stage. Mumtaz, a British-Asian woman in her
forties who is also Theresa's sister in law, is a case in point. She currently lives in her
parents' house in North East London with her husband, two children and her parents.
She has lived in Uganda, Kenya, India—where she married her first husband—and
London—where she met her current husband Adam. She then moved to Paris with
Adam's job to set up a family and has now finally settled back in London. She works
part-time in the family business; she and her husband are extremely well off, and she
does not need to work. She relishes the closeness with her family, having lived out
of Britain for years. Her wardrobes are fascinating as she has the largest amount of
clothes of anyone I interviewed and has seven wardrobes. However, despite being
financially well off, she does not spend a great deal of money on clothing, preferring

instead to buy clothes from lower-end high street shops. Within her vast selection of folded clothing are numerous short stretchy Lycra skirts; a particular favourite of hers being a dulled down chocolate brown leopard-print skirt. She used to wear the skirts resting on her hips and teamed them with loose hanging tops, so an inch or so of the tight skirt peeped out from under the flowing masses of her tops. This way of dressing was Mumtaz's definitive style when she lived in Paris. However, despite being in her late forties, now that she lives with her parents she feels unable to wear such short skirts. Her mother dresses in saris every day and would disapprove of such clothing as both inappropriate and revealing too much of her legs. Mumtaz still loves these skirts, and, although she no longer wears them, she cannot abandon the possibility that she may wear them again. It is likely she and Adam soon will buy their own home in London, so, away from the watchful eyes of her parents, she will be able to wear them again without being disrespectful. The clothes lie dormant, hopeful in the possibility of being reawakened. She does not plan to make alterations to them to make them befit her current status, but rather hopes to return to wearing them in the state in which they are now.

Both the items of clothing and the former aspect of herself that they embody remain temporally frozen, their potential reactivation projected into an imagined future. Of Mumtaz's seven wardrobe spaces, six are for what she calls her Western clothing, and one is for her Indian clothing. The latter contains mounds of silks and satins in sky blue, verdant greens, silvers, whites, pinks and vibrant reds which are delicately adorned with embroidered patterns. When she lived in Paris and in India, she used to have a wardrobe for her saris, and each one was hung up individually; now they are folded in piles in an inaccessible wardrobe, and she rarely wears them. When she lived in India with her first husband, she wore saris most days; she has acquired the requisite skills to stand and move in such items. However, now she wears these items only if she goes to the temple (she's Sikh) or attends an Indian function or a wedding, when she will be merely required to stand around looking, as she states, 'decorative'. She prefers to wear *shalwar kamiz,* now finding saris impractical and uncomfortable, as she is no longer used to wearing them, the feat of retaining the shape and dignity when wearing them being a conscious perpetual effort.

Keeping these items of clothing is very important to Mumtaz because they help her retain a fundamental part of her identity. She also keeps the saris because she hopes her daughter will one day wear them. As her daughter has been bought up in Paris and London, although she has been raised a Sikh and has been taught Urdu, Mumtaz is keen to inculcate this facet of identity in her daughter. Clothing is central to how children are socialized into gender-appropriate roles (Barnes and Eicher, 1993); for children, gender-specific expectations are instilled in them through the wearing of clothing bought by the parents. The patterns of socialization are particularly dependent upon intersecting factors such as ethnicity, class position and family relationships. In this instance, the sari is an externalized form of Mumtaz's Indian gendered identity and, as such, is a particular means through which this can be passed on to the next generation. As a long drape of material, saris can fit any size or shape of woman, and will fit Mumtaz's daughter in the same way they fit her. In the case of Theresa's maternity dress, the fact that the item takes on her body shape is central in personalizing the item; yet for Mumtaz it is the very opposite feature that would allow her daughter to take on the sari as an aspect of her own identity. As Hall (2005: 94) has argued, we are all 'ethnically located', yet this does not mean that we always choose, or are forced, to make this an explicit aspect of our identities. On this occasion, Mumtaz is explicitly attempting to pass on an awareness of her 'ethnic location' through the traditional item of clothing. In turn, if her daughter chooses to wear the items, she too will be actively taking on this aspect of her identity. At the moment, these saris are in storage, as a 'past', but as this past is used in the construction of an imagined future, the saris are 'bridging across a lost present to a desired future' (Kuchler, 1999: 60). The present identity of the saris is frozen or 'lost', yet even as the saris lie unworn in the wardrobe, there is still a connection between the past aspect of Mumtaz's identity and her aspirations towards the future. This one garment externalizes both the actual and aspired-to identities of Mumtaz and her daughter; characteristic of items of clothing passed down to daughters or friends, items of clothing do not just externalize an individual identity. As Stanley notes of verbal biographies, they are often constructed as an isolated individual life story, with other figures being relegated to the secondary position of shadows (Stanley, 1992). In contrast, when items of clothing are passed down from mother to daughter, multiple histories are woven into the cloth, and so the biographies of several women can coexist in the clothing.

Complex Continuities and Contemporary Histories

The majority of Mumtaz's saris are rarely worn, but she keeps them in the wardrobe in the hope that both she and her daughter will wear them in the future; within the piles of saris, there is one particular sari that Mumtaz still wears whenever she has occasion to, and in wearing it she establishes a continuity in her identity. She has had this particular sari for fifteen years; she bought the fabric, Chantilly lace—a material she thought was particularly beautiful—from Paris. To have it cut into the right size piece, she took it to a tailor in India where she always takes her clothes to be adjusted or made when she visits twice a year. Because Chantilly lace is see-through, under the connecting fibres, she had a white under-layer sewn in. This sari combines Mumtaz's love of beautiful fabrics and her notion of being fashionable through the beautiful fabric bought in Paris. Moreover, as the fabric was made into a sari, it draws in her Indian identity. The item is as global as she is, as the various different threads of her life are woven together in the one garment. Different moments from her various pasts all come together within this one sari to form a contemporary identity, and this sari serves to connect the various periods of her life.

Mumtaz has worn this sari on various formal occasions over the last fifteen years. When clothing is worn through life stages, it allows for a continuity with the past. Vivienne (who is discussed in more detail in the next chapter) is a political campaigner who is practically retired now; she is in her fifties and has many items which she has worn throughout changes in her life. She was born in Britain, her mother was an Austrian Jewish woman, and her father was Czech. Having family in both these countries and because her two husbands (from whom she is now divorced) were from Iran and Palestine, she has connections all over the world. She has also traveled throughout the world, doing research for the campaigns she has worked on. She has a dress from Pakistan in her wardrobe which is long, loose, cotton and heavily embroidered. The basic colours are large blocks of bright colours placed in vivid juxtaposition: burgundy, green, royal blue, arterial red. It was bought for her sister's wedding some years before and was worn several times in the interim, including to her own second wedding (she has been married three times but now lives alone). She was pregnant when she got married the second time; as the dress is loose, it was able to be worn as a pregnancy dress. The adaptability and multi-functionality of the dress incorporated various events and progressive changes in Vivienne's life. The various temporal threads of Vivienne's life are woven together as the clothing allows her to maintain constancy in her self in the face of other shifts in her life.

In both Mumtaz's and Vivienne's cases, still wearing these items allows a connection to the past, a bringing together of multiple histories, as they establish a coherence and continuity in their identity through clothing. In other instances, women are able to create a connection to the past through reintroducing former items of clothing into new outfits. It is through women's clothing choices, and the subsequent act of wearing an older item with a newer one, that women are able to draw from their pasts. If choosing what to wear is the back-stage to the public presentation of the self, then the act of wearing clothing can be seen as a kind of performance of the self. This performance is achieved through women's 'habitus' (Bourdieu, 1977), the internalized social scripts which are enacted through bodily demeanour and behaviour. In moments of creating a new outfit, this performance becomes more deliberate and self-conscious, as women may be unsure how to walk in the outfit or how they are expected to behave in a particular outfit. Wearing a new outfit is often an occasion for women to try on an identity as they wonder whether this is 'me'; when women are wearing an outfit made up of new and old items, they will be wondering whether this is 'still' me.

The ways in which choosing what to wear can involve the past being made present through performance resonates with Kuchler's (1999) discussion of Malanggan, a ritual performance in New Ireland which constitutes the finishing of work for the dead. Whilst her discussion of how the past is reanimated in this ritual is culturally and contextually specific, it is useful by way of an analogy here. She explains that, in this ritual performance, elaborate architectural structures are first constructed as a locus for the display of effigies, ritual performances and activities and later are destroyed, liberating the soul of the dead. Importantly, she argues that this is not an act of remembering the past, but rather that the past is momentarily reanimated through performance in the act of iconoclasm. Here ritual efficacy comes not from remembrance but from this momentary reanimation. This distinction between reanimation and remembrance is important in considering what happens when women decide to rewear an item of clothing from their past and combine it with a more recently acquired item. When Theresa decided to wear a former work jacket again after making alterations, she was not trying to reenact or to remember her former working self. Instead, the former item and the current habitually worn jeans involve a juxtaposition of the past and present within one item. In the act of wearing both simultaneously, Theresa is able to conjoin her former and current selves, as through the act of assemblage it is possible for the past to coexist with the present in the transient moment of wearing the outfit. For both Mumtaz's sari and Theresa's reworn and altered jacket, various pasts coalesce into a present.

Knowing Who You are: When to Throw Out and When to Keep Clothes

All three women discussed—Mumtaz, Theresa and Vivienne—have deliberately kept in their wardrobes items of clothing they no longer wear. To be discussed here is the difference between items women store but do not wear and the items women have thrown away but are able to vibrantly recount through stories. For all of the women I worked with I conducted life-history interviews, and, notably, everyone was able to recount past clothing disasters and successes. A good example of this is Rosie, a married management consultant in her thirties who lives in a house in Hampstead with her new husband; she has not kept many of the items she used to wear, yet she was able to vividly recall her self through her remembrances of her clothing. Her earlier years were characterized by a progression of defined clothing styles: Goth, hippy, 'on the pull'. Her early teens coincided with her Goth clothing. She no longer possesses any of these clothes but clearly remembers the hours taken to get ready after school, applying layers of black eyeliner and the clothing as unanimous in its blackness. The school she attended was an all-girls school, where no make-up or jewellery was permitted. Pat, her mother, recounts one particular occasion when Boy George (Rosie's idol at the time) was visiting the nearby shopping centre. In a frantic rush after school to arrive in time for Rosie to catch a glimpse of her hero, there was no time to apply the elaborate make-up or even to change her clothing. Although slightly dismayed that Boy George did not see her in her Gothic get-up which she habitually wore, she was unconcerned as none of her friends would know this. However, the moment of securing his autograph was captured by a local photographer, and a picture of a bespectacled Rosie, in her full school uniform appeared in the newspaper the next day. Rosie was mortified. Rosie's wardrobe at the time incorporated two aesthetic domains: her school uniform which she wore begrudgingly and her Gothic clothing which embraced her entire lifestyle and selfhood, signifying which clubs she went to and what music she listened to. The clothing did not match the situation she found herself in, with humiliating consequences. Characteristic of sub-cultures is the complete adherence to a look (Hodkinson, 2002); the transition to a new sub-culture does not involve a gradual phasing out, but rather a complete repudiation of the previous look. In her 'hippy' years, the clothing fell in complete distinction to the unflinching harsh blackness of her former clothing, and, as such, the Goth clothing was thrown out.

Despite having thrown out such clothing from her earlier years, there came a point at which Rosie started to hold on to items. Therefore, an important aspect of contrast between clothing that is kept and that which is discarded lies in the issues of age and experimentation. Resounding through all of the examples is a sense that the women become themselves at some point in their biography. As such, items from this point onwards have the potential to be recombined (items kept from before this point tend to be mementoes, as a separated past). Whilst Rosie did have many years of experimentations, she is now a high earner and is more settled, having just gotten married and having bought a house. The clothing she now favours is expensive and carries a designer label; particularly impressive is her range of shoes, which are all housed in their own wardrobe, stored in the boxes for safe keeping. Although there are still shifts in her clothing styles, they are more gradual. She has an array of 'fun' glittering, brightly coloured shoes and tops; a particular favourite is a vest top from Monsoon. The vest is patterned with bold red and fuchsia prints in a psychedelic vortex of superimposed flowers and butterflies which swirl into and over each other, dizzying and disorienting the viewer. The drama of the top is reminiscent of her former clubbing days, yet now she combines it with white trousers for a more understated look.

The last ten years of her life, as she has moved from a single girl going clubbing to a married home owner, has not seen any dramatic shifts in the clothing she wears, but rather a gradual evolution of styles. Hemlines are lower, tops are adorned with less glitter, and translucent clothing is replaced by opaque. She still purchases new items that are exuberant, yet teams them with her more staid designer pieces. She recently purchased a new denim mini-skirt, which she has worn with a black fitted shirt and brown knee-high boots rather than with a see-through or cropped top, as she may previously have done. Adaptations in her clothing enable her to negotiate a transition in her lifestyle, a shifting continuity, as she still wears clothes she feels fit her aesthetic preferences yet are more suited to a settled, married woman. In her youth, she participated in a series of defined fashions, whereas more recently her sartorial continuity is enabled through adopting clothing of the past and reintegrating in into her more sensible clothing.

Rosie is able to recombine such items as they coincide with the fact that she now has a clear sense of her self and, as such, has the confidence to attempt to express and externalize her self through clothing. The instances where clothing is kept relate clearly to notions of success. When women throw out clothing, often it is when they are trying to discard a part of themselves. The process of forgetting as well as remembering is a conscious act (Forty, 1999). The decision to keep clothing is analogous to the decision over whether to place a photograph in an album. Photographs that are deemed as insignificant or that were taken on an unhappy occasion are usually culled (Belk, 1995, Chalfen, 1987, Sontag, 1979). As Bourdieu points out (1990), on being placed in an album, the 'good moment' is transformed into a 'good memory' (1990: 27). Within the wardrobe, the outfits which embody bad memories or were a failure are thrown away; in contrast, keeping clothing that is no longer worn involves a woman identifying with who she used to be and therefore that she has the capacity to be this person. Women keep these items as a memory, or a reminder, even if they no longer have the lifestyle to wear them. Equally, such items cannot be recombined if the period of their wear was before the woman 'becomes' her self, as many biographies through clothing have a pivotal point. However, this does not signify that after this point uncertainties, failures and ambivalences are no longer present, as will be evidenced in the next chapter.

Clothing as Constitutive of the Biographical Self

Examples of women deliberately keeping items they do not wear proliferated within my fieldwork. In many cases, women were using their clothing and wardrobes as a means of working out their personal biographies, as clothing is able to embody and evoke memories so emotively, and through the tactility of clothing women are able to resituate and reimagine themselves. These items of clothing do not just reflect or passively represent a 'real' life which precedes and is independent of externalizations and representations. Instead what emerges from this research is that clothing is fundamental to and constitutive of both the woman and her biography. Clothing is employed as a means to enact a change in a person. Therefore it does not just reflect a working life or being a mother but constitutes the person in that role. Emanuela was born in the North of England, yet has two Italian parents; she is in her forties and lives in Nottingham with her husband and eleven-year-old daughter. She just completed an MA in textiles, and she has previously been a teacher. Three years ago, she received a diagnosis of breast cancer, for which a partial mastectomy would be necessary. Understandably devastated by the news, she managed to muster the strength and emotional control to emerge from the operation with a stable outlook. However, the radiotherapy that followed was more distressing. Emanuela entered a period of depression, the radiotherapy draining her of any vitality; she spent most of her days listlessly moping around her house, watching daytime TV, with no impetus or drive for activity. A friend of Emanuela's who had been diagnosed with terminal cancer twenty-five years ago, advised her of a diet she had followed that helped her to get through this period. In tandem with the radiotherapy, Emanuela went on this extremely strict macrobiotic diet: no meat, coffee, tea, fats, sugars, herbs or spices. This strict diet gave her surprising stores of vitality. The other effect of the new healthy regime was that Emanuela lost a great deal of weight. This period of time was characterized by ambiguity: having just been diagnosed with cancer, having major surgery and suffering bouts of depression as a result of the radiotherapy, at the same time, she was brimming with new vitality and had attained a new svelte physique—it was a period of optimistic pessimism.

A facet of her previous listlessness had been characterized by not taking proper care of her appearance, staying home most days watching daytime TV and not even managing to keep the house in an orderly fashion. She felt she could not be bothered to engage in the usual rituals of getting ready. Her daughter used to comment despondently when Emanuela did go out that she had not brushed her hair again. Understandably, her family was concerned, and on one of her trips home, her father took her clothes shopping in an attempt to instill some of her previous vivacity. Despite usually relishing such an opportunity, she was unable to muster any enthusiasm and ended up trying clothes only to placate her father. One item her father coerced her to try on was a greenish grey trouser suit. Contrary to her expectations, she loved the shape of it; the trousers are fitted and slightly flared at the bottom. The jacket is the part she likes the most—it is single-breasted, and the buttons are at waist level, so when they are fastened, an hour glass silhouette is achieved. Her lacklustre trying on of the item was confounded by the flattering shape on her body. She saw her new body outlined to perfection in the changing room mirrors. The new item enabled this vision rather than making her feel drained by colourless, sloppy clothing.

She loves the combination of the suit being both smart and comfortable. It is still her favourite outfit. When she first tried it on, it transformed her, as she was forced to develop a self-conscious awareness of the image she saw before her. When she tries it on on the occasion of her first interview with me, it has the same effect. Once her dad saw her in it and saw the optimism it had invigorated, he bought it for her, and a massive shopping spree ensued. In retrospect, Emanuela realizes what a change this made to her life. Wearing the suit made 'me feel good about myself for the first time in a long time'; this shopping spree marked a transition in her wardrobe. From this moment, she decided that she was going to start making an effort with her appearance every day, wearing her favourite clothes all the time, not only on special occasions. She mobilized the capacity of certain items to transform her through wearing them every day. This enacted a change in Emanuela's life: gone were the listless days of hanging around at home; she found a new lust for life. The shift in clothing along with body and health changes meant that Emanuela looked better than she had in years. Previously she had suffered from anaemia and insomnia, with her medical misfortune culminating in the breast cancer. With her new diet, she only needed five hours of sleep a night and was incredibly slim and buzzing with life. Her clothing routines and regimes forced her into new rituals. A combination of seeing a more positive image in the mirror and of forcing herself to undergo the various daily beauty routines meant that she could be bothered to go out and to tidy the house.

As her father's purchases enabled her to enter the socialized life of clothing, she returned to her full existence as a social being. It is clothing here that activated a biographical shift for her, rather than being a secondary effect of a 'real' or prior change. By undergoing daily rituals of beautification, she was making herself participate in life again and perform ordinary daily routines. Forcing herself to go through these processes daily was, in alliance with her new diet, the catalyst for her renewed vitality. In tandem with buying these new, smarter items, she started buying colourful clothing again, as someone pointed out to her that she tended to wear darker clothing. For a long time, she had not really reflected on her wardrobe, but rather through a continuous period of working at the Buddhist centre and being a mother, she ended up in something of a sartorial rut. Clothing here is agentic, as she buys brighter clothing, anticipating that it will lift her mood and enable her to participate in life again. Here clothing is a catalyst for a shift in her self and biography. The shifts in her clothing choices precede any actual biographical shifts and can therefore be seen to be foundational in reconstituting herself biographically.

The ambivalence and uncertainty about her body, health and appearance were channelled into a positive transition in her clothing; Emanuela was able to move from being depressed and listless to enthusiastic and vital. The clothing enabled her to go out, to participate in the social world. The sartorial shifts that this period engendered are ones that Emanuela still tries to consciously cultivate. There are times when she feels herself slipping into old patterns of wearing scruffier clothing or not being bothered day in and day out. Yet she makes a conscious effort to buy colourful clothing or smarter clothing because she knows it makes her feel better. Now in her wardrobe there is less of a division between day wear and night wear. The smarter clothing that she loves she wears all the time. Emanuela is constantly battling against her former self and former wardrobe as she utilizes the transformatory potential of clothing.

Conclusion

The ways in which clothing manages to enact a transformation in Emanuela form a clear challenge to the notion that clothing merely 'reflects' a pre-existing life. The notion of 'retail therapy' is widely recognized and indeed practiced in contemporary Britain, as shopping is a means of mood enhancement or as an instigator for a 'new me', usually subsequent to a relationship break-down. Indeed I found the practice to be quite widespread amongst my informants; however, this process takes on a primary significance in Emanuela's case. The clothing forces Emanuela to consider her newly acquired body shape and her reflected image as it propels her into the next life stage. The daily rituals that are involved in appearance management have to be engaged in: hair brushing and hair styling, skin regimes and make-up, selection of suitable outfits and accessories. Emanuela becomes part of these daily rituals and activities which inhere within the socialized life of clothing. The clothing is not only important as a moment of transformation, but carries on being important every day; she becomes vitalized, socialized and activated by these processes and becomes able to go out more and reenter her social life.

Implicit in this example is that, through managing her clothing, Emanuela is in fact taking control of her life; she is aware of clothing's capacity to transform and uses it to keep herself from relapsing into her former self. This raises three key points about how current clothing choices need to be understood in the context of women's long-term relationship to their clothing. First, in keeping items of clothing in the wardrobe that are no longer worn, women are managing and ordering their biographies from the perspective of a current identity. This notion of the manipulation of biography through organizing the clothing in the wardrobe resonates with Giddens's discussion (1991) of the self as a reflexive project. Through ordering and sorting out their wardrobes, women can construct their biographies in accordance with their current life point. However, when this self-narrative is engaged with through the wardrobe rather than just through verbal biographies, it is clear that having clothing that women no longer wear gives them the sense of having a past. Memories exist in a tangible form, and so women can remind themselves that they used to be that person as they feel the fabric on their skin again; in particularly vivid and sensual ways, they are able to reimagine themselves.

The second point links to the ways in which clothing does not reflect a pre-existing life, but in fact enacts transformations in the biographically constituted self. As items of clothing have been worn over a period of time by a particular person, the garment's history is woven into the item of clothing. As such, these materialized pasts are embedded in the clothing and become one of the ways in which women can use clothing to transform themselves. The agency and materiality of clothing comes from its texture, style, shape and colours and also from the histories of its usage. Inasmuch as a woman might choose a top because it will make her feel more sexy, she may also choose a jacket from her former working life because, in reminding her she used to be this person, it makes her feel more confident. Women can draw upon former aspects of themselves as they are materialized and externalized in items of clothing.

Women wear former items of clothing with newer items to create an identity through clothing that is appropriate to a current occasion. This raises the third point to emerge from this chapter, which is the ways in which a biography through clothing differs from conventional narrative forms. None of the women I worked with ordered her wardrobe chronologically; ordinarily, as the last chapter made clear, clothing is ordered in terms of function or aesthetic qualities. So, when women select clothing to wear, they are not looking at their wardrobe as a chronology. Rather, from the array of clothing displayed before them, the older items form part of the continuum of the wardrobe, as the various past moments punctuate the arrays of clothing. And so, whilst women may still keep certain items as memories or former aspects of the self, they may also, on certain occasions of dressing, conjoin various pasts in order to make a new identity through clothing. On such occasions, even if clothing gives women a sense of having a past and a biography, it can never simply be relegated to the past if it is worn in the present.

–4–

Looking Good, Feeling Right
The Aesthetics of Getting Dressed

This chapter focuses upon one of the main concerns women have when trying on an outfit: whether the separate items go together. All women I interviewed had a clear sense of what items can be combined together in an outfit and an even more emphatic sense of what cannot be worn together. This often deeply entrenched sense of what goes with what is cultivated over a woman's life time. In Bourdieu's terms, taste emerges as a result of a particular 'habitus' (1977), as particular dispositions, competences and taste preferences are the sediments of women's upbringing, arising out of social and cultural positioning (Devine, Savage, Scott and Crompton, 2005). These tastes and dispositions are activated, or perpetuated, in particular social conditions or, in Bourdieu's term, 'fields'. When these tastes are considered in terms of women's clothing choices, it is evident that they are also embodied, as a woman's sense of what she likes arises from how clothing feels on her body. This applies as much to the tactile relationship of clothing to a woman's skin as to how she sees her own body image. Women's sense of what goes together involves not only questions of colour and style, but also whether the outfit 'goes' on her own body. Even if the ways in which women view their own bodies is influenced by the beauty ideals that are perpetuated through media images, such images do not remain at the level of an abstracted ideal as they are considered in the intimate encounter between women and their reflected images in the mirror.

Women's sense of what goes therefore brings together wider social expectations and beauty ideals with their own personal preferences; in this chapter, the wardrobe is discussed as a personal aesthetic—that is, a woman's individual sense of what can be worn together based upon colour, texture, style, cut and pattern. What goes together is taken in terms of what feels right, as the question 'does this go?' elides women's sense of themselves with how an outfit looks. The links between 'how I look' and 'how I feel' suggests that women's sense of themselves through clothing is inseparable from the aesthetics of clothing. The consideration of colours, fabrics and styles is a material means through which women negotiate their clothing identities, as aspects of a woman's self-identity are externalized in the items of clothing in the wardrobe. The wardrobe can be seen as an example of Gell's (1998) understanding of individual style (as opposed to generic artistic styles) as 'personhood in aesthetic form' (1998: 157). In this chapter, the personal aesthetic I interrogate is the wardrobe from which women engage with their identities daily. As material culture, clothing is not seen to simply reflect given aspects of the self but is a material means through which women engage in an act of self-construction. Applying Gell's theory (1998), women choose an outfit as a medium through which their intentions are externalized into a form by which they can affect how other people interpret their appearance. A woman may wish to look powerful for a job interview and so chooses a shirt and jacket that will allow her to be perceived as such. The shirt and jacket do not just reflect her identity, but through the structured collar and the shape of the shoulders, she is able to convince others that she is businesslike.

However, the emphasis that would follow a reading of Gell would be on clothing as a medium through which women can successfully impact upon others. My ethnographic material shows this is far too straightforward and uni-directional. Putting on clothing is a form by which one exposes one's self to the outside world. The clothing becomes a conduit which allows other people's intentions to penetrate deeply into the intentions of the wearer. This often actually prevents the wearer of clothing from becoming the kind of self they would otherwise have wished to construct, let alone influencing anyone else. As will be discussed throughout the case studies, the result is very different from our usual assumption, as championed by post-modern accounts, that this would become simply a study of the self expressing itself freely through clothing.

Combinations of the Self

Through considering the material microscopics of particular women's personal aesthetics, the focus is upon how clothing mediates this relationship between the individual woman and the outside world. As such, it is the medium through which women consider their social roles and normative ideals of how they should look. As clothing is worn next to the body, such external factors cannot remain abstract, but rather enter the realm of the intimate as a private dilemma for the individual. In looking at how women relate to the external world through clothing, a consideration of getting dressed makes clear that this relationship is particular to each occasion. Even for women who are ordinarily extremely confident in their ability to get it right, on occasion this everyday confidence can still be disrupted. The individual event as an occasion for women to question their usually entrenched sense of what goes is demonstrated by the case of Rosie, a married management consultant in her early thirties who was invited for the first time to dinner at The Ivy restaurant (a renowned haunt in London of the fashionable and famous) with four of her female friends. Greatly excited by the prospect of attending such an exclusive location, the issue of what to wear was one of grave consideration. In selecting her outfit, she wanted to look as if she belonged at such a venue, as adequate for the occasion in the context of such famous and fashionable people. Throughout her life, Rosie has participated in a series of clearly defined subcultures—Goth, hippy, student, camp club culture, single girl on the pull—persistently dressing to fit in with various established groups. Such a desire to conform to the place and people that constitute The Ivy can be seen to form part of Rosie's sartorial trajectory of adhering to categories of clothing. On this occasion, her anxiety to fit in is exacerbated by the novelty of the occasion. As a highly paid professional with no financial dependants and a house in Hampstead, her concern does not centre on her financial position. She certainly possesses an abundance of designer clothes that would appear to befit the occasion. Ordinarily she relishes an occasion to show off her clothes and is renowned amongst her friends for her fantastic style.

However, she remains unsure of what to wear and spends hours futilely trying on various items from her seven wardrobes. In order for the unprecedented occasion of going to The Ivy to live up to its anticipated expectations, Rosie feels she needs to wear something new and dynamic. Overwhelmed by the mass of clothing in a myriad of colours, patterns and styles, she is unable to differentiate between them, and her usual capacity for aesthetic combination is lost. In this moment of panic, she falls back on her favourite black leather knee-length Maxmara skirt as a lifeline of security in the ever-expanding vortex of clothing that engulfs her room, piling up on the bed and floor. The fit of the skirt is perfect, clinging to the hips, gradually triangulating out, ceasing just below the knees. Rosie is extremely slim and ordinarily does not worry about whether an outfit makes her look fat. She perceives her problem area as her stomach, not being as taut as she would wish. This 'problem' is not sufficient for it to be a constant source of concern to her; however, on occasions when she has no idea what to wear, this confidence is shaken as she questions not only her capacity to put together the right outfit, but also the flatness of her stomach. This particular leather skirt is, therefore, perfect for her on such occasions, because the strong leather fabric holds the stomach in, giving Rosie the illusion of having a flat stomach. Despite being leather, the skirt's refined shape and style and its blackness give it an understated effect when worn with her usual black cotton cap-sleeved top. Viewing her wardrobe through the lens of the unprecedented invitation, the vitality of her favourite outfit is drained. The sombre blackness fails to give voice to the ambiguous facets of her personality needed for the occasion: trendy, youthful, stylish yet also successful. Resolving to still wear the skirt, the search begins for a suitably funky yet fashionable top, as the increasing mounds of failed tops obscure her bedcovers.

The sheer mass of clothing leads her to panic, as she doubts whether a suitable top will ever be located. Finally, she resorts to another tried and trusted item and opts to wear the skirt with her favourite one-shoulder khaki fitted top, which is dusted with silver glitter. The combination of khaki and glitter is unexpected: a casual combat look coexisting with the feminine and sexy. Khaki is ordinarily used by the army to present a uniform dullness in which no individual stands out, but here the glitter—which catches the light as the contours of Rosie's body move in the light—enables the eye to ambiguously be drawn to her. In her panic, Rosie ended up resorting to two items that she knows how to wear, that she knows are 'her' and that fit her usual aesthetic: the top from the funky order of clothing thus enabling her exuberance and the skirt personifying chic stylishness, being made of luxuriant leather bought from an expensive boutique. To complete the outfit, she wears knee-high leather boots and a three-quarter-length leather coat. Because both are the same fabric and colour as the skirt, the combination seems like a safe one—the shiny blackness should all blend and merge—leaving the top to stand out.

By her own admission, she felt that the outfit hadn't worked. The leather skirt, jacket and boots, which Rosie thought would go together, instead of placing promi-nence on the funky top, dominated the outfit and undermined the subtle sexiness of the skirt. She said she felt like a member of Liberty X (a raunchy popular music band renowned for a self-conscious creation of an overtly sexualized style through the wearing of all-over leather). Rosie felt aware of her age in the outfit—being in her early thirties and having now adapted her ordinary aesthetic to her mature, more settled position in life, it was 'a bit glitzy and a bit too much like a young, clubbing girl for me'. The outfit harks back to her days as a younger woman 'on the pull'—inappropriate for The Ivy, where there is a sense of having 'arrived'. The crucial element in Rosie's discomfort here lies not in the items themselves, but in how the items were combined. She failed to anticipate the heavy dominance of the shiny blackness, which swamped the outfit, eliminated all pretence of subtlety and extricated different facets of her personality. Instead of looking chic, stylish and so-phisticated, she felt overdressed and uncomfortable; the smooth, structured contours of her skirt concretized into a perpetual physical awareness of the heaviness of the leather oppressing her. As part of her 'distributed personhood' (Gell, 1998), the outfit should have externalized her intentionality in order to impact upon those present into seeing her as a chic, fashionable individual. However, here the agency of the clothing becomes apparent; Rosie failed to anticipate that the leather in the boots, the skirt and the jacket would articulate together in such a way as to impede her own intentions and create unwanted effects.

Rosie's sense that she had got it wrong also relates to the particularities of place. By opting for those garments that had become most unequivocally expressions of herself, ironically Rosie ended up neither looking nor feeling like herself. Because, by definition, a safe self could not create what needed to be an unprecedented self, where fit had to include place as well as person. An aspect of the self here is therein anticipatory—seeing herself as who she could be at The Ivy—fashionable, chic, successful—refracted back onto her wardrobe. On this occasion, Rosie's anticipation is mediated through the images she has seen in numerous magazines of various glam-orous celebrities photographed emerging from The Ivy. Because she has never been to the Ivy before, the ways in which she imagines herself there involves positioning herself alongside these images. Much has been written about how the media perpetu-ates an idealized body image through the constant repetition of seemingly identi-cal bodies in magazines and on television. The female body becomes the 'object of idealisation' (Thesander, 1997: 71), something women are measured against and expected to aspire towards. This ideal is in part created through the various media of the fashion industry, images which emerge out of, and reinforce, wider societal norms of gender, femininity and sexuality (Gunter and Wykes, 2005). What is apparent on this occasion is that whilst, on an everyday basis, Rosie does not see herself as inadequate in relation to a normative model of beauty, on this unprecedented occasion she finds herself questioning everything. This may not be caused by images of fashionable bodies, but, as one of the main sources of knowledge of the restaurant, it certainly exacerbates her anxieties over getting it right.

Rosie's example is one of aesthetic disjuncture; however, equally common amongst my informants were joyous moments when an outfit 'is me', when the combinations made constitute an aesthetic fit with the wearer. Mumtaz is a married mother of two in her mid-forties; she has lived extensively in France, India, and Uganda. Her husband was made partner in a prestigious law firm in London four years ago, which was the impetus for their move from Paris to London, where they now live with Mumtaz's parents and their own two children. Last year she was invited back to a wedding in France of one of her husband's former colleagues. The decision over what to wear incorporates the normative expectations of what is acceptable wedding attire. In addition, she will encounter old friends after an absence of several years. Mumtaz confides that, when living in Paris, the significant investment women made in their appearance led to her own constant rigorous maintenance programme. Even a trip to pick up her children from school turned into an event wherein clothing had to be closely considered. Having been out of this cycle for a significant period, Mumtaz feels the imagined expectations of the others particularly keenly.

As someone who loves clothing and fashion, Mumtaz, rather than panicking, relishes the opportunity to create an outfit afresh. Rather than purchasing anything new, she searches through her many wardrobes, three of which contain Western clothing and one that contains Indian clothing. The final outfit she decides upon consists of a white linen short summer dress with thin spaghetti straps worn over her 'ethnic' trousers—fitted black cotton trousers with colourful embroidery encircling her ankles (the trousers are, in fact, from New Look, a standard UK chain with no particular Asian connection). To finish the outfit, she draped around her shoulders one of her *chunis* (the scarf part of one of her many shalwar kamiz). The particular *chuni* is jade green with round embroidered sections which shimmer in the light (she calls it her 'spotty scarf'). The stark effect of the dress and trousers is invigorated by the playful shimmering of the *chuni* and the embroidery that surrounds and defines her ankles. Mumtaz has drawn on her existing wardrobe, yet has made a unique combination: wearing a dress over trousers and mixing her Indian and Western clothing.

On this occasion, the outfit was a considerable success; Mumtaz spent the afternoon basking in the admiring glances and comments of her friends. Not only did she manage to conform to the social mores, but she managed to look chic, stylish and most importantly individual—she looked and felt 'like herself'. What Mumtaz combined here is not just colours and fabrics; she also combined aspects of her self: former parts of her biography—her life in India, her global existence—and brought together the diverse items within one outfit. The surface of her body here is the site for the construction and presentation of her self, constituted biographically and relationally. Strathern (1979), writing on self-decoration in Mount Hagen in Melanesia, demonstrates that, for the people of that region, appearance is regarded as anything but superficial. Focusing explicitly upon body decorations employed by men on formal ritual occasions, Strathern points out that such elaborate make-up is not a form of disguise, but rather a way to display the self—'bringing things outside' (Strathern, 1979: 249). Although the context considered in my ethnography is vastly different, an analogous process can be seen to be happening. The different facets of Mumtaz's self—her past, her ethnicity, her global travels—are objectified in the clothing hanging in her wardrobe. In the act of dressing, she places her self around her body, bringing attributes of her personality and aspects of her self into the surface of her outfit. She is able to make visible things which on other occasions may remain private and concealed.

In this moment of selection, Mumtaz draws together disparate threads from her four separate wardrobes. Rather than expressing recidivist tendencies like Rosie going for 'safe', Mumtaz makes a novel combination. Such eclectic assemblage is something Mumtaz does frequently, befitting the multiple facets of her self. Furthermore, eclecticism is a defining feature of fashion, the fortuitous consequence of Mumtaz's diverse combinations leads to her outfits appearing fashionable and original. The self is here backwards looking—through considerations of her previous experiences of dressing in France and through her past sartorial biography. Yet simultaneously Mumtaz's imaginary projection of herself in the eyes of others at the wedding successfully refracts back on her wardrobe to lead to the unprecedented assemblage. Like Rosie on the actual occasion of wearing the clothes—in this case the wedding—wearing her self round her body, she is exposed to the judgements of others; the adulation she receives reinforces her sartorial confidence, validating her decision.

Vivienne's Wardrobe

Whilst Rosie's and Mumtaz's clothing is fundamental to their self-conceptions, Vivienne, a political campaigner in her fifties, appears to be the opposite. Politically aware and motivated, she insists that her appearance—clothing and otherwise—is not fundamental to her beliefs or values. The real important self is inner, intangible and invisible. She professes to have no interest in fashion, despises shopping and just 'throws on whatever' every day from her one and only wardrobe. She relates with relish instances wherein her work colleagues roll their eyes in despair at the sight of her in ripped jeans and fraying old sweaters. It has become so important to demonstrate that clothing does not matter to her, she now actively cultivates the unkempt look of the 'unlooked'. Her idea of not wanting to be judged by her appearance means that she has to consciously cultivate a 'natural' un-thought look. Vivienne wears such clothing with the intention of convincing others that she does not care about her appearance, but the outcome is ironically that, like everyone I interviewed, she does care what others think of her appearance.

Her sole wardrobe contains her skirts, shirts and dresses. Piled at the top are various jumpers and fleeces, with many of her pairs of shoes rammed at the bottom. Her only other receptacle for clothing is a chest of drawers that contains her underwear, Pilates clothing, winter jumpers and t-shirt tops. Now retired, she partakes only in the odd political campaign which concords with her beliefs. Even during her full-time working days, as there was no dress code, Vivienne does not have separate work and casual clothing. The clothing she wears is continuous across the different domains of her life: whether she is going in to work, having dinner with a friend, seeing one of her daughters or spending time at home. The styles, fabrics and colours tend to cohere around particular configurations defined by her own aesthetic. The main points of disjuncture from this are clothing worn to weddings and clothing for travelling—where the external influences of social, cultural and religious expectations come into play. However, even in these cases, in order for her to feel 'comfortable', Vivienne's dominant aesthetic widens to incorporate such events. The notion of comfort incorporates both a physical sensation of comfort and, in a more nuanced sense, the notion of aesthetic fit: the wearing of clothes which are 'you'. This link between a sense of self and the appearance resonates with Holliday's (2001) discussion of comfort as a link between 'inner' and 'outer'. This arises out of her research into lesbian and gay identities through clothing and people's own perceptions of how they construct their appearance and as it is seen by others. Her informants, using video diaries, use the word *comfort* to articulate an 'authentic' relationship to clothing and, in particular instances, as a rejection of mainstream femininity. This has resonance for Vivienne's example, as, although she is heterosexual, her use of the word *comfort* can be taken as part of her anti-fashion stance and indeed the femininity that this condones.

Vivienne articulates comfort as linked to practicality and eschews any notion that she has a defined aesthetic whereby how she looks links to how she feels. However, what emerges from an analysis of her wardrobe is that this comfort is also crucially aesthetic, material and embodied. Ordinarily, Vivienne wears casual combat trousers and perhaps a sweater during the day in the winter time; she asserts that the loose, navy blue cotton trousers are 'comfortable and practical'. Large cargo pockets protrude on both sides; such bulky evident pockets, allied with the multiple toggles and zips that cover the trousers, create an aesthetic of functionality. Not only are the trousers practical—being of a hardy fabric, loose with large pockets—they are also designed to look functional. Vivienne was given them by her niece, who used them during her gap year. Although initially she only wore them in the garden, she now wears them all the time, much to the dismay of her daughters and niece, who complains 'they don't do anything for you!' These trousers allow Vivienne to wear practical sensible clothing, yet also importantly to create an image of herself as being purely practical, with no interest in the combinations of her clothing. The image of the trousers to others therefore does matter; the anticipated effect of the trousers is to make others think she has made no effort; the incredulity of her niece makes apparent the efficacy of the trousers as an objectification of this intention.

Vivienne's clothing falls primarily into three colour domains: dull colours (black, navy and grey), earthy colours (stone, olive green, browns) and warm colours (red, burgundy, yellows). Although such colour palettes do not solely correspond to certain events or domains, Vivienne does express a tendency to favour the brighter, lighter colours in the summer months. Rather than being an isolated preference, the dominance of darker, duller clothing throughout Britain in the winter months is overwhelming. In tandem with the practicalities pertaining to the weather (darker colours absorb heat and therefore are inappropriate in the summer, and lighter colours tend to get ruined in rain and bad weather) is an overwhelming sense of social appropriateness. Such a normative expectation is manifest in the colours available in retail outlets; many women I interviewed divided their wardrobes into winter and summer clothing, with a biannual switchover of clothes in May and September. Vivienne is part of a broader trend wherein the clothing practices and shifts in colours, fabrics and wearing of open-toed shoes in effect creates the seasons (given that the division between summer and winter is characterized more by unpredictability than by binary weather polarities). Here there is a semiotic 'fit' to the outer environment; similar to Rosie's case—where clothing is selected to be appropriate to the occasion and the people she will be meeting—here the 'sunny clothes' are worn to greet the anticipated sun. Comfort here involves the fit to external rather than internal factors.

The ways in which Vivienne wears colours are quite particular: in strong, contrasting blocks. Such contrasts are made either through combination of items or within one item of clothing. A striking example of the latter is a long, flowing cotton dress from Pakistan that she possesses. The predominant colour of the top half is burgundy with defined green, burgundy and blue rectangles printed on. The bottom half is a striking arterial red colour and terminates at the ankles with strong bands of burgundy and navy. Rather than being colours which merge into each other, the blocks of colour stand in stark juxtaposition, challenging the viewer. Although she no longer wears this dress (given the political connotations of wearing it), she loves the colours, patterns and style of it. Seemingly in contrast to the uncompromising boldness of the colours, the fabric is soft, worn cotton that falls in loose flowing waves around the body. This stylistic paradox is central to Vivienne's aesthetic.

Another facet of this aesthetic paradox is that, whilst the colours exist in strong blocks, Vivienne's penchant for habitually wearing the same items of clothing for periods often in excess of twenty years leads to a softening of the material and fading of the colours. For example, Vivienne possesses a loose, long-sleeved cotton top in a faded shade of orange with large yellow sun prints on it. This top was given to her when she was sixteen by her boyfriend; it was purchased in Kenya. During summer, when the weather turns slightly cooler, she always wears this top because 'it is the colour of sunshine. It cheers me up so much to wear it'. On wearing the jumper, her mood is lifted by the brighter colours, and the coolness of the weather is balanced by the sunny print. Having worn the top frequently every summer for the last thirty-five years, the fabric has softened, and the colours have faded through exposure to light and persistent washing. The orange colour has become diluted. Vivienne has had similar sartorial preferences all her life—a practice which is confirmed by the presence of numerous tops she has had for over thirty years. The seeming contradiction of the harsh blocks of bold colours on the soft, faded worn fabric is symptomatic of her wardrobe. Furthermore, such continuity of styles is evidenced in the sartorial coherence of her wardrobe.

Assembling Aesthetics

As Rosie's example makes apparent, how combinations are made is crucial in realizing a particular aesthetic. Despite Vivienne claiming she has no concern with what colours go together, there are certain combinations that are always made. She possesses three red shirts, and each one is only ever worn with black trousers or a skirt. All of Vivienne's skirts are floor length, with a slit up the back to mid-thigh. When she walks, the trailing leg is almost entirely exposed. This facilitates ease of movement, yet simultaneously Vivienne confesses she likes exhibiting her legs. Her daughters Sandra and Tamsin regularly buy her skirts with a slit, insisting this is her best bodily feature. Whilst being appropriate for a woman of her years and status, the outfit is practical in not impeding her bodily movements, yet at the same time is sexualized. As regards the colours, not only is the contrasting effect of red and black quite striking—furthermore the combinational potential of the shirts is severely limited. Although the red shirt and black skirt were not bought as an outfit, they only find communion with each other. Vivienne feels that neither item goes with anything else. McCracken (1988) points to the need to understand the complementarity of goods; Vivienne's sense of what goes with what is based upon her particular sense of order. The internal categorization of the wardrobe along such lines is common to all wardrobes investigated in my fieldwork. Vivienne's example shows that this sense of what goes together can be extremely constraining. The colours—black and red—and the styles—a loose shirt and a skirt—articulate with each other in such a way that she feels she cannot intervene. What she feels to be the logic of the clothing means that she will only combine these items with each other.

In this instance, it is both the colours and the styles of the items that are restrictive; more generally throughout Vivienne's wardrobe the stylistic combination of a loose, relatively unstructured shirt with a long skirt is a common one. She has an array of silk shirts: one purple shirt that hangs alone on a hanger and four that all hang together in the following colours: camel, olive green, pale brown and a darker brown. They were acquired explicitly for travelling, in keeping with local cultural and religious sensibilities, predominantly within the Middle East, where she was carrying out some research. In Iran, given the extreme heat, she wore flimsy cotton summer dresses beneath the obligatory long coat which concealed the body. In Egypt, she borrowed a couple of pairs of raw silk trousers from a friend, which she wore with her silk shirts: clothing that was comfortable yet would not draw attention to her. Here the fit is functional, as the clothing had to coincide with Muslim sensibilities.

These shirts are also now her standard wear for when she is compelled to dress more formally. Although Vivienne's clothes are relatively continuous across domains, slight modifications are made for formal wear. A particular combination she favours is a long grey skirt with a greenish shirt and a fitted grey woollen waistcoat. The thickness of the waistcoat's material and its rigid seaming serves to structure and formalize the waistcoat—designating its appropriateness for smarter occasions. Yet, because it is covered with small green and red floral embroidery, this softens the effect. Vivienne admits that she loves to wear an olive green shirt with this waistcoat in part due to the coordination between the green embroidery and the selected shirt. This outfit recapitulates the ambiguity at the heart of Vivienne's aesthetic hinted at earlier: the fluidity of the draping shirt and skirt coupled with the rigid structure of the waistcoat, which is softened by intricate floral embroidery.

This outfit is both appropriate to formal occasions and simultaneously allows Vivienne to feel comfortable; the comfort is enabled by the ease of movement and by being a particular look which Vivienne habitually wears. This issue of comfort is crucial to understanding Vivienne's wardrobe. She owns a range of poncho-style tops, all purchased about fifteen years ago from a South American shop in London. The authenticity of the items, being made in South America from llama wool, is important to Vivienne in her self-conceptualization as a global, politically astute person. As she was born in Britain, her mother was an Austrian and Jewish, her father was Czech, her first husband was Iranian and her second husband Palestinian, her sense of being global arises not only out of her traveling, but also out of her ethnic location, as she defies clear categorization and conceives of herself as global. Only one of them is an actual poncho (wherein the head goes though a neck slit at the top, and the material falls like a cape over the shoulders, leaving the arms free). Two of the others follow the principle of a pashmina (a large strip of material which is flung around the shoulders like a shawl). However, the commonality lies in the fabric and patterning and in the effect and function of wearing them. She tends to wear all of them in autumn and winter; being made from llama wool, they are rough to the touch and are worn over her usual clothes for an extra layer of warmth. Being impractical in the rain (merely getting sodden and waterlogged), she favours them on dry winter days and often doubles them up and uses them as rugs in the park.

One particular poncho is crucially tied to Vivienne's notions of comfort. The poncho is in earthy browns, with bold stone and terracotta stripes. On the front part of the body, the stripes run vertically, yet as the material slopes over the shoulders, so too do the stripes, resulting in them curving with the arms, as they become diagonal and gradually horizontal as they reach her lower arms. As the neck is a wide v-neck, in conjunction with the softening of the shoulders through gently curving stripes, the effect is to make the neck area expansive, and the overall look is unstructured. The shape of the body is softened, rounding off the shoulders, physically engendering a sense of casualness. When worn, particularly on winter evenings at home when there is a chill in the air, the masses of woollen fabric enswathe and enclose her body but still allow the free movement of her arms. The coziness of the poncho is further facilitated as she is able to hug her own body with her liberated arms whilst still being subsumed by a layer of fabric. Similarly, the other poncho-style tops permit such a sense of comfort and of being surrounded in cozy warm layers of fabric. The pashmina-style items are thrown around the shoulders, thus enveloping the body when worn. This sense of the voluminousness of fabric and looseness is prevalent in much of Vivienne's clothing. As already mentioned, the silk shirts she wears are wide and baggy, as are the other shirts she wears informally. Her primary concern is to remain unfettered and unrestrained by the clothing she wears; the clothing she selects enables movement, allowing this feeling of comfort as the clothing embraces her body.

The ponchos materially enable comfort and coziness, particularly in the home (where Vivienne often wears them). The comfort engendered is not merely an obvious physical sense (in particular given that the material is harsh), but rather as something which coincides with her ordinary aesthetic. The ponchos are wrapped round the body; as 'ethnic' clothing, authentically obtained, in the autumnal colours she favours, the ponchos therein 'fit' her self conceptualization. The ways in which Vivienne's clothing externalizes her political stance and ecological moralities exemplifies clothing's capacity to carry 'fundamental values' (O'Connor, 2005: 41). Vivienne's relationship to her clothing in some ways mirrors the explicit use of clothing by Gandhi as a materialization of his pacifist, pro-Indian, anti-imperialist politics (Bean, 1989). Inasmuch as Gandhi's choice of clothing was a means to demonstrate his political stance, for Vivienne, woven within her ponchos is her sense of global political awareness.

The looseness of the fabric is crucial; even in her more formal items, already discussed, rigid shapes are not those Vivienne favours. The relationship between structured formality as required by an evening/smart event and soft fluidity is encapsulated in her skirt, silk shirt, and waistcoat combination already discussed. Here, through appropriate combination, Vivienne is able to feel appropriately smart and aware of the formality of the occasion through the rigidity of the waistcoat. Yet she is simultaneously allowed her usual comfort through the flowing shirt in her usual blocks of colour. The fact that it is silk, a sensation apparent as it sensuously caresses the skin, also defines it as appropriate for a smart or special occasion. Sexuality is heightened through the slit in the skirt which suggestively reveals her legs when she walks. Because the skirt's slit allows both the practicalities of movement and, through taking a healthy stride, a glimpse of the leg, it is elevated beyond the level of mere function. Both factors are equally important to Vivienne. Within this look, it is not merely that each item allows distinct facets, rather it is within the surface of individual items (the shape of the waistcoat yet covered with delicate ornament) that this happens. Comfort involves a combination of not only particular colours and fabrics, but also within the surface of each item is a complex interplay: the complexities of the items ambiguously contradict and enhance each other. Part of what is being combined is aspects of her self and biography, cultivated through this aesthetic. Such an outfit shows the complexities of the surface through clothing—not only are different items layered upon each other to differential effect, but furthermore the nuances and subtle antagonisms of function and sexuality interact and interchange with each other within the feature of a single item of clothing. Also players in this interchange are aspects of Vivienne's biography, of her personality. As in Strathern's (1979) discussion where attributes of the person are brought to the surface, here with the movement of Vivienne's leg to a different angle, such attributes may be activated, then temporarily submerged, only to resurface again.

One of the most interesting features about Vivienne's clothing is the means through which she acquired it. The vast majority of her wardrobe has been passed up to her by her two daughters—items they no longer wear or want yet which are not yet completely threadbare, often things which are already second-hand. Many of her items are faded through perennial washing and wearing. Like the orange top discussed earlier, along with many items procured from charity shops, the biography of many items in her wardrobe is already extended over a long period of time, testing the durability of fabrics to their limit. Until clothing has physically disintegrated, Vivienne perseveres in wearing it. In wearing her clothing, Vivienne is bringing her familial relationships, political orientations and ecological moralities all within the act of dressing. Combinations of clothing involve a moment of totalization: of incorporating the diverse threads of her life within her clothing. Given that Vivienne's aesthetic is relatively coherent and continuous, the aesthetic totality that constitutes her wardrobe is able to bring together multiple facets of her self—as constituted biographically, relationally, politically and ethically. Like Mumtaz, what she combines is not just colours and fabrics, but fragments of her self.

Such an aesthetic totality only crystallizes over time, as part of her 'habitus' (Bourdieu, 1977); yet this concretization of taste is also crucially material, as the clothing softens through wearing, so too the clothing becomes integral to being a part of her. In wearing the same clothes over a period of time, the fabric starts to relax. The persistent washing and wearing of a sweater drains the colour and softens both the appearance and the texture. Through perpetually wearing the same items of clothing, it is as if they age with the wearer, becoming like a second skin. When wearing them, there is no awareness of constraint or of a seam that rubs or chafes; rather, the items soften in the places where the body is most harsh on the clothing—the elbows of a jumper or the knees of trousers. The relationship between the clothing and the person becomes symbiotic; the hardness of the body softens the fabric. Having occupied such a relationship to clothing all her life, Vivienne loves to not have to feel conscious in the clothing she is wearing. When the clothing is already worn and aged, the boundary that separates the clothing and the person starts to disintegrate and the clothing is able to 'become' the wearer. Bayly (1986) has pointed to the links between biography and clothing, wherein the porosity of cloth and as something worn by individuals next to the body enables a fusion between person and clothing. Through clothing's capacity to age, yet being similarly durable, this symbiotic relationship between person and clothing is created—where the wearer feels comfortable in her clothing. What Vivienne makes apparent is that she is equally able to do this when someone else has worn the clothing in for her.

Isolated Nodules of Clothing

Given that she no longer works full-time, does not need the money and only works if it is a campaign she is particularly passionate about, Vivienne is able to wear such clothing all the time; however, as has already been suggested regarding her more formal wear, she widens her ordinary aesthetic to accommodate such necessities. Vivienne's wardrobe does contain certain isolated outfits compelled by particular social occasions. Despite despising wearing rigid formal clothing, on the occasion of her brother's wedding, her anticipated potential discomfort is subsumed to familial relationships. The purchased outfit consists of a cream top and burnt umber skirt, both made of cotton which shimmers slightly in the light. The top is short-sleeved and hangs loosely; at the bottom, where it is at its fullest, the top is layered with asymmetrical jaggered fabrics. The natural undulations of a loose top are enhanced by the extra layer of material at the bottom. The skirt is in exactly the same style and falls to near the floor. When wearing such an item, the body of the wearer recedes in prominence, and the overlapping waves of fabric dominate and become the focus of attention. Moreover, the body is still able to move freely underneath, albeit with the material swishing and catching against the legs with every step. Vivienne has worn this outfit to two weddings and would probably wear it to another, as she felt sufficiently comfortable in it, although she professes she would not wear it to any other occasion as she would feel too 'self-conscious' in it, 'over the top'. Although such a domain forms a distinct nodule of her wardrobe, it is apparent that it still corresponds to her particular personal aesthetic in its colours and style. Whilst she ordinarily favours clothing which is like a second skin, here the fit to the external event and the expectations of those attending means she is able to feel comfortable wearing it.

Such relatively formalized wear is able to be incorporated within Vivienne's overall personal aesthetic; whilst only wearable for particular occasions, she still feels comfortable in them. Vivienne's wardrobe constitutes an aesthetic totality in the convergence not only on particular colour combinations, but in her incorporating into her clothing her family and her global political orientations. As a result of this clearly defined aesthetic totality, on occasion Vivienne turns down invitations to formal events if she is not able to wear her everyday clothes. She turned down an invitation to a very prestigious awards ceremony last year, solely on the basis that she did not want to get dressed up. She hated the thought that she would be forced to walk in a 'mincing way', wearing shoes she would be unable to take a full stride in; 'I just wouldn't be able to be!' On this occasion, Vivienne vividly imagines the discomfort she would feel at the event and is able to opt not to attend. The way in which she moves and stands is fundamental to her 'being' and is enabled and facilitated by the clothing she wears. Despite professing to throw 'whatever' clothing on, her decision not to attend an important event is based upon clothing and the discomfort the wearing of formal clothing would entail for her.

Wearing loose clothing which has softened to her body over long periods of wearing, Vivienne is able to feel comfortable. Yet the potential discomfort caused by going to this event also relates to her 'being seen'; she would be forced to engage with her reflection in a different way. In Rosie's case, the place she was dressing for was The Ivy, a place which is renowned for being a haunt of the rich, fashionable and famous. As such, images of people coming out of The Ivy are often found in fashion and celebrity magazines. Whilst Rosie is not comparing herself directly to a particular image of someone, in dressing she is forced to imagine herself in the context of such people. Gunter and Wykes (2005: 32) have pointed to the links between how media images construct ideal femininities and how women conceptualize themselves. Their research points to a correlation between the mass promotion of narrowly defined beauty ideals and an increase in women's dissatisfaction with their body shape. They suggest that dissatisfaction arises when women measure their own bodies against the increasingly unrealistic ideals that are presented. In Rosie's case, she is forced to see her clothed body in relation to these images on this particular occasion. The influence of ideals of beauty and idealized bodies is felt all the more keenly. In not going to such places, Vivienne is able to evade measuring herself by these ideals and allows herself to just 'be'.

Conclusion

The fact that Vivienne turns down prestigious invitations based upon her refusal to wear certain clothes makes it clear that clothing is just as significant for her as it is for the explicitly clothes-conscious Rosie or Mumtaz. For all three women, their wardrobes have been analyzed as forms of extended personhood, wherein clothing becomes a means through which disparate facets of their selfhood are objectified (Gell, 1998). Gell's theory points to the ways in which a person's intentionality may be distributed through objects; in this example, it shows the immense potential of clothing to influence the minds of others. Such actualized potential is seen in Vivienne's cultivated image of lack of cultivation, resulting in the despondent groans of her daughters. However, what becomes apparent through closer analysis of all three cases is that 'how I look or feel' turns out to be anything but merely a personal and free expression of the self. One of the supposed characteristics of post-modernity is that 'everyone can be anybody' (cited in Featherstone, 1991), which translates sartorially into the wealth of often contradictory styles and identities to experiment with. What the examples here make clear is that there are numerous constraints which prevent this free exertion of agency through clothing.

The first constraint comes at the moment of assemblage: the individual has to commit to a particular outfit, combinations which in turn are unequivocally associated with that person. On any particular occasion, one cannot be all the possibilities or looks that are present in the wardrobe. Although a degree of ambiguity can be incorporated within one outfit, the multiple identities offered by fragmented and ephemeral fashions cannot all be present within one assemblage. Rosie's many wardrobes are overburdened with post-modern possibilities, offers of identities or selves Rosie may try on. This abundance of choice offers not greater freedom, but leads to her inability to choose and indeed in the end making what seemed like a 'safe' choice, but was in fact unsuited to the occasion. What is constraining here for Rosie is the fact that in the moment of dressing she has to perform an act of aesthetic totalization to create her self. In Vivienne's case, the opposite is true; her wardrobe is already a totalized aesthetic, as it incorporates not only particular colour domains and soft, flowing fabrics, but incorporates all aspects of her existence—an aesthetic comfort materially cultivated through a lifetime of wearing. However, such a complete aesthetic coherence can be just as constraining as Rosie's multiple possibilities. So enclosed are her aesthetic parameters that she is unable to attend events where she cannot wear these clothes.

The second major area of constraint is that of the clothing itself, in terms of both its material propensities and also its own internal logic of combinations. In positing the agentic capacities of objects, Gell (1998) critiques the assumption that autonomous human agents have intentions which are imposed upon passive objects. Instead, agency emerges in the context of a web of objects and people—and 'agents thus "are" and do not merely "use" artefacts' (1998: 21). Gell refers to objects as secondary agents; they are not therefore seen to have independent intentions of their own, but rather are the material embodiment of this intentionality—part of the matrix of its generation and actualization. Implicit within this argument that objects are part of the externalized mind which may impact upon the mind of others is the potential for failure. As the objects carry people's intentionality—yet in Gell's argument are not passive—then through the materiality itself objects may thwart our intentions. For Rosie, the black leather skirt which was meant to make her feel sophisticated in the end sits heavily upon her, as she cannot ignore its physical sweaty presence. The clothing does not act as a medium for her intentions but produces quite the opposite effect, as the combined black leather items comes to have their own efficacy and dominate the outfit. On other occasions when clothing produces an effect other than that which a woman may have intended, this can make the clothing an unexpected success. For Vivienne, as she has worn her clothing habitually over extended periods of time, the clothing now draws out facets of her self and biography through its own logics independent of the wearer. The slit in the long skirt allows the surfacing of Vivienne's sexuality yet also of her practicality and desire for mobility. The fluctuating processes of surfacing and re-surfacing of facets of the self are actualized within complex aesthetic dialogues which interweave the agency of the wearer and the logics that arise from the materiality of the clothing.

The third aspect of constraint comes from the way the clothing interiorizes the anticipated judgments of others. Discussed earlier was the possibility that clothing may be a means by which women are able to externalize their intentions in order to impact the will of others. In terms of Gell's (1998: 96–153) theory, clothing opens up the person to wider layers of externalized, potentially distributed, mind. But this opening up has made them vulnerable to penetration by the anticipated gaze of others. Clothing may be regarded as a conduit which, in opening up the potential impact upon the minds of others, also allows the fierce judgments of others to strike deep within. In order to select the outfit that will make Rosie feel fashionable and chic, she has to envision the clientele that attend and how she might appear to them. This act of imagining is not so much about the friends she is going with but about who else might be there—imaginings which are mediated through ideals of fashionability. The impact of these beauty and body ideals is therefore always particular to place and occasion; on going to The Ivy, Rosie cannot help but see herself in light of the images she has seen in the media of this particular location and the celebrities and models who frequent it. The result is that Rosie's usual capacity for combination and selection of outfits is lost. Despite having seven wardrobes, Rosie's selection not only failed to express her, but, from her perspective, quite betrayed her, turning her into what she imagined others saw as aspects of herself she would never have wanted revealed at that time. In understanding such moments of anxiety, we need to examine how clothing as a medium that relates surface to depth is as much the fibres that conduct the judgments of others to the inside as the intentions of the self to the outside.

–5–

Looking in the Mirror
Seeing and Being Seen

The act of dressing starts with women standing in front of the wardrobe considering the items of clothing that hang in front of them. Sometimes women have already been mulling over which items to wear before they face their clothing; yet equally likely are times when women stand gazing at their personal collection with no idea of what to wear. Items of clothing may be taken out of the wardrobe and deliberated over on their hangers or held against the body as women consider which items are suitable. In Miller's sense (1987), the creation of identity involves considering the self in an external form. When getting dressed, women are considering their identity through the material form of clothing, to see whether individual items are 'me'. When women are still not sure what to wear, the deciding moment often comes when they stand in front of the mirror and their reflected bodies. Looking in the mirror involves the reciprocal relations of seeing and being seen (Melchior-Bonnett, 2002: 5). In this moment the idealized person women imagine they can be is faced with the actuality of what they have managed to construct from their wardrobes.

This moment in front of the mirror involves women imagining themselves as other people see them. In Mead's terms, when the self sees itself as an object as others would, it is the 'I' that perceives the 'me' (1982: 102). Women look at themselves in the mirror as the 'I' who imagines how others will see the 'me', as measured through wider body ideals or normative ideas of what is appropriate to the social occasion. On successful occasions, there is an aesthetic fit, as discussed in the last chapter, when the self women hope to project or enact through clothing matches the image they see before them in the mirror. This 'fit' happens when women look in the mirror and, when the outfit is worn to go out, the woman receives the appropriate admiring comments and glances of others. Equally possible are moments of failure, as women are not only trying to find an outfit that is 'me', but also one which must also 'fit' place, occasion and the expectations of other people. Women have to consider whether the items go together and whether the outfit is right for the occasion. Importantly, this also involves consideration of the body, often as it measures up against wider body ideals that are perpetuated through magazine, film and television images (Hollander, 1993).

Looking in the mirror is therefore a marriage of the intimate and the generic, as women consider their own dressed bodies in light of wider social ideals and expectations. The generic gaze is specific to individual women as it is racialized (Hall, 1997, Mercer and Julien, 1994), gendered and framed through women's sexual orientations. The theory of the male gaze assumes the heterosexual desire of a man for a woman (Berger, 1972, Mulvey, 1975). The notion that women exist as objects of the male gaze is well documented, linked to the power relations inscribed within looking (Bonner, Goodman, Allen, Janes, and King, 1992). However, it is the contention of this chapter that 'the gaze' is neither homogeneous, pre-existing, nor constant. If dressing is understood as a process, it becomes apparent that the gaze emerges, and is constructed, dependent upon women, location and occasion. This chapter uses examples of women getting dressed, both to go out and as part of their daily routine, to consider how women choose what to wear dependent upon the specific occasions of wearing, the normative expectations of acceptable wear and the self women are trying to construct. Focusing upon the role of the mirror in dressing, I consider examples of occasions when the gaze of others is actively sought and examples where it intrudes unwanted as women are forced to consider themselves as 'seen'.

Constructing Natural Appearances

All the women I worked with wanted to appear as if they had not made an effort. Even Vivienne, who was discussed in chapter 4, a woman whose approach to her appearance was clearly idiosyncratic, is an example of this trend whereby women adopt a rhetoric of authenticity, stating they don't want to look 'made-up', 'fake' or 'not like me'. Despite having this attitude, every one of these women was engaged in the act of constructing her appearance, whether it was by having her hair cut in a particular style, shaving her legs or maintaining a tan. In some instances, women just styled their hair and applied face cream; at the other extreme, 'not one part of a woman's body is left untouched' (Dworkin, 1974, 113–4). Whilst none of the women I interviewed had had cosmetic surgery, there were several women who underwent extensive daily, weekly and monthly rituals of bleaching, tweezing, moisturizing and styling. The ways in which women construct themselves as 'natural' beauties will be discussed here in the example of Sadie, aged nineteen, as she gets ready for a date with Warren, a man with whom she is currently in a casual relationship. She lives with friends in North London and works in a high street retail outlet; prior to this, she did a foundation degree in art but was disillusioned by the emphasis on conceptual art. The legacy of her days as an artist hangs upon her bedroom walls in the form of a painting of a shell in cream and peach hues achieved by a gradual layering of tones. The major manifestation of her creativity now is in her daily processes of self-aestheticization. For many women I interviewed, going on a date is as much about the rituals of getting ready as the actual date; for Sadie, the leisurely process of getting ready takes over three hours. Even on an ordinary morning before work, she would rather be late than not carry out her usual one and a half hours of getting ready (which includes a shower). For Sadie, it is the process of getting ready, as much as the final look created, that is central to the self she constructs daily.

In her flat, there are two mirrors in her bedroom, one of which is full length; two more full-length mirrors are in the hallway outside her bedroom, and a small square mirror is in the bathroom. Walking through her small flat from her bedroom to the bathroom or kitchen, one is constantly faced with one's own image; there are few places in the flat where the reflected self is not present. Getting ready starts with a shower; having washed her hair, she twists her long, curly and unruly hair into a hair clip. Having worked full-time all summer and unable to afford a holiday, she is dismayed by the pallor of her legs, and applying self-tanner is the next part of her routine. After moisturizing her freshly shaved legs, her fake tan is applied; it is a pale brown colour that darkens over the next few hours. Its application rapidly becomes a two-woman job; with my help, we rub the lotion into the back of her heels so there are no blotches or marks which betray the fakeness of the tan. She then embarks on styling her hair, which, if left alone, would spill in long, undulating waves. However, today she wants to make her waving hair appear as if it falls into natural spiral curls. The last time she went out with Warren, she wore it straight, so to test his preference for her hair type, she opts to wear it curly. She stands in front of the full-length mirror in her room and rubs in the 'curl definition' mousse; then, upturning her head, with her hair cascading down in front of her, she runs her fingers through her hair, scrunching it into curls. She is careful not to let her damp hair flick onto her legs, possibly leading to disastrous streaks, which would tell the tale not of olive skin ripened in the sun, but of a quick fix from a bottle. The onerous process of drying and styling her hair begins with the fringe. She dries the main body of her hair in individual sections. The dryer is held up at all times; it is quite large and heavy and requires considerable effort for the twenty-minute period of drying her hair. Resolving to conquer her wayward locks, she intensifies her efforts and bends over almost double so that her hair hangs upside down. Likewise, she turns her hair diffuser upside down and compresses her hair within it. When her hair is finally dry, she is so exhausted she has to sit down briefly after the strain. Whilst she is sitting down, she applies her deodorant.

Because the effort to make her hair look naturally curly is so immense, she opts to finish the process later, and, as a diversion, she tries on her outfit. A few days previously, she acquired some new clothes: a cream cord mini-skirt and a salmon-pink sleeveless vest top, which Warren has yet to see. They are suitably casual so as to look as if she has not made too much effort. Facing the mirror in her room, she tries on the outfit with her pink flip flops and turns to the side to see the profile view of the skirt. The short skirt causes particular anxiety, as she rarely exposes her legs; whilst she does not think that she has bad legs, she does not see them as a particular asset. Warren has only ever seen her in tight jeans, and he often compliments her on her bottom, as the jeans accentuate it. Sadie, like the majority of other women I interviewed, is not in a state of constant body dissatisfaction. It is typically on the occasions of trying on a new outfit, when women have put on weight or when they are dressing for a particular event that this ordinary relationship is disrupted. The material from my ethnography therefore challenges many of the assumptions of public debate and the constant polls taken in women's magazines over women's perceptions of their body image. This is not to question the excellent analyses of the media representations of women's bodies, which point to the ways in which the repetitive and reiterated body images serve to 'normalise' (Bordo, 2003: 25) what a body should look like. What is problematic is if this is assumed to be a model 'against which the self continually measures, judges, "disciplines" and "corrects itself"' (Bordo, 2003: 25). Even if on occasion these issues come to the fore, none of the women I worked with were in this state continually.

Although Sadie is not in a state of inadequacy constantly, when she does question her body image, the focus is always on a specific body part. Almost all the women I worked with perceived a particular 'problem area', and, when they were trying on new clothes, this was invariably the issue that concerned them. Sadie does not see her legs as a problem daily, but she does briefly worry as she tries on the mini-skirt, which exposes a part of her body that has not yet drawn comment from Warren. As such, her anxiety focuses upon her legs as she peers over her shoulder and tries to catch the image of her rear view in the mirror behind her. The view is unsatisfactory; as I am seated on her floor, she bends right over me so I can see up the skirt: 'can you see my arse?'—worrying her g-string will be visible. The inadequacies of the mirror are resolved by the presence of a second person. My opinion becomes another reflection, to enable a totalizing version of her clothed body. She then puts on her 'ugly but functional' strapless bra, which, whilst it may not be attractive in itself, from the outside, gives her body a balanced shape—a shape she checks by looking at her reflection sideways in the mirror. She turns around in front of the mirror to examine herself from every angle. She is not considering her whole reflection to consider 'is this me?' but rather is seeing her body in fragments.

In order to dress her skin, Sadie moves from viewing herself through her body parts to a microscopic view of the pores of her skin as she tries to cultivate a naturally looking radiant, blemish-free complexion. In order to get a close enough look at her skin, she presses her body against the full-length mirror in her bedroom with a tissue to squeeze her spots and comments, 'it's amazing how you have to go through something so hideous to look so beautiful'. In the same position, she then embarks upon tweezing her eyebrows. She pulls the eyebrow up into an arch with one hand and plucks out the hairs with her other hand. This daily ritual has become crucial, as her eyebrows are naturally bushy; 'it just shows nature isn't always right!' Her aim is to create the impression of a natural arched shape which frames her eyes. These micro-rituals of the skin are ultimately directed towards influencing how others will grasp the overall effect of her face. She stands back from the mirror every so often to consider how they look in the context of her face. By engaging in such processes, with the eye focused upon the pores or errant eyebrows, she has in mind the overall 'natural' radiance of her skin. She has carried out these procedures for so many years that they are part of her daily routine, and so there are no moments of doubt or reflection.

Her face is now cleansed and moisturized in preparation for make-up; in keeping with the aesthetic of natural beauty to which she aspires, the tones she has opted for are neutral ones. Starting with her eyes, she paints a peachy colour over the upper eyelid to 'make my eyes look more awake'. In even swirls, she delicately brushes on a white shadow from beneath her eyebrow down to meet the peach shades, so they blend together seamlessly, aiming to make her eyes look vitalized. She applies an orange eye-shadow in a curved line which follows the lower side of the bone which forms the eye socket; the line is thinner on the inside of the eye and gradually widens towards the outside. It is then blended in as a boundary between the two other colours. When her eyes are open, the orange shade is the most visible beneath the lightening effect of the white, making the eyes appear wider and longer. All selected colours are from the same palette, being similar tones and blended subtly. Her eyelids are the canvas on which she layers and blends the colours. Even as she cultivates the illusion of a completely natural look, beautification involves extensive aesthetic procedures and a constant battle against unruly eyebrows and hair. The creation of 'nature' becomes who she is, her self as a work of art. From the pores in her skin and the ringlets of hair outwards, making up her body is also an act of 'constituting that self' (Peiss, 1996: 323).

Despite going for a natural look, she opts to further accentuate her eyes by applying mascara. She brushes her upper lashes with more than twenty rhythmical strokes, applying more on the outer eyelashes. To do this, she tilts her head backwards and opens her eyes wide. After a brief respite, she puts on a second coat of mascara; 'I like lashes to be nice and big to match my hair'. She then stands back a few steps to gain perspective and looks at her eyes from a distance and in the context of her whole face. The final stage in make-up is her foundation, which she blends onto her chin, nose area, cheeks and under her eyes. She applies cheek gloss along the cheekbone and blends it gently; aiming for a dewy, glowing complexion, she stands back and tilts her head to see how her cheeks catch the light. For Sadie, once she has showered, the process of getting ready starts with her hair and continues with the pores of her skin and its texture, scent and make-up. In doing her hair, eyebrows and her pores, she is creating the canvas upon which she prepares her make-up.

She now returns to her hair to sort out her fringe. In the hallway, she assembles the ironing board in front of the full-length mirror and plugs in the iron, turning on the fairy lights which frame the mirror in the hallway and twinkle around her reflected image. Her hair straighteners have broken, and, unable to afford any new ones, the perilous ritual of ironing her hair is now part of her daily regimen. She applies hair-straightening serum, loving the exquisite smell that is unleashed every time she moves her head. She then gets on her knees in front of the ironing board and brushes her hair onto it. Placing a piece of plain paper on top of her hair, she irons over both the paper and her hair. 'This is where I burn myself!' she exclaims.

She used to iron not only her fringe but all of her hair every day; marks where the iron has scalded her blemish her hands and face—battle wounds in her incessant struggle with her untameable waves of hair. She then stands up and brushes the fringe. The process is repeated three times until finally she stands up and takes a step back to look in the mirror, and then she decides to trim her fringe. She goes back to her bedroom and stands a few metres back from the mirror in that room, ruffling her hair. Most of the activities she carries out in front of the mirror happen in micro-fragments of attending to the hairs of her fringe or the shape of her eyebrows. Yet this happens in conjunction with occasionally stepping back to consider her whole reflection. Through this process of distancing, she is able to consider her hair in the context of her overall look. Now dressed and made up, she puts on her silver jewelry: a heart necklace, two butterfly necklaces and her giant hoop earrings. She then puts perfume on her wrists and sprays it in front of her and walks into it so that the scent clings to her as she moves through the mist. The perfume is enhanced by the delicate, feminine fragrances of her scented body glitter; it is applied with a velvet pillow that caresses the skin and is brushed all over her arms and legs. She checks her reflection one last time in her mirror and is satisfied with what she sees. The elaborate process of getting ready is finally finished, and she is ready to go out.

What is striking in this example is the amount of time and effort that go into looking as if she has not spent much time on her appearance. As Warren has never seen her without her make-up, what becomes important is not a pre-existing 'natural' face, but rather the 'nature' that she cultivates. This is as true for the woman who has very limited make-up routines as it is for someone who spends hours apply-ing make-up. In no instances does the body or the face merely exist in a natural or authentic state; the cultivated appearance becomes the real and the natural. These acts of dressing the face and body are also acts of self-construction, which relates to Goffman's discussion of the self (1974), which he argues is 'performed' through cultural expectations and learned repertoires of behaviour. He sees everyday life as a performance in which the self is enacted (1971a). Part of this enactment is the clothing worn, but also the daily rituals of preparing the appearance can be seen as part of this performance. In Sadie's case, the rituals she carries out daily are part of these learned patterns of behaviour, such that getting ready is not an occasion for questioning her self and her appearance. These rituals are both central to creating the appearance she sees as 'herself', but also the very act of carrying out the rituals is part of how she sees herself.

A crucial part of this performance of the self involves living up to the individual's conception of him- or herself, an 'idealised' (Goffman, 1971a: 34) self one believes one can be. This is applicable as much to appearance as it is to behaviour. Sadie, as she dresses, has in her mind the final appearance which is who she 'really' is. When she carries out the various stages of getting ready, she does so with this idealized image in mind. Following Goffman, this ideal is the self that an individual imagines that they can be and aspire to be, which is mirrored in Kaiser's discussion of the 'ideal', which she discusses explicitly in the context of women's image they have of themselves in their mind (2003). Kaiser's position is important here as a challenge to the ways in which the 'ideal' is often discussed or written about, as it gets reduced to discussions about the beauty ideal that is perpetuated through fashion magazines. It is certainly true that the repetition of almost identical images in various media (not restricted to fashion) produce a model of what the body should look like, a model against which women are alleged to measure their own flawed bodies (Bordo, 2003). This ideal is presented as both out of reach yet simultaneously attainable. Since the early twentieth century, the development of the mass cosmetics industry has redefined beauty as something all women can achieve (Peiss, 1996: 323) through the use of cosmetics. This same possibility for changing the appearance is also an expectation which has become even more marked since the 1980s as bodies can be altered and controlled (Thesander, 1997: 14). The body can be altered through going to the gym or having plastic surgery. Extreme manifestations of this are in television programmes such as '10 years younger' in the UK and 'The Swan' in the US, as ordinary women undergo extensive cosmetic surgery in order to remake their bodies to match normative beauty ideals. Television makeover programmes both present a beauty ideal and also show and condone a means through which this ideal can be altered with new clothes, make-up and cosmetic surgery. Women's bodies therefore become a 'legitimate site of reconstruction' (Gunter and Wykes, 2005: 48).

In light of this, the implication is that women carry out daily beauty rituals in order to attain this ideal. However, what my ethnography shows is that women's relationship to their 'ideal' self and body is far more complex. Women I have interviewed do not constantly see themselves as inadequate in relation to this media-presented ideal; in fact, women are considering themselves in relation to their own aspirational version of themselves, which may or may not be influenced by images in the media. This ideal is in turn mediated by women's experiences, upbringing and multiple other factors to the point that, for the women I worked with, one cannot see any direct relationship between these images and how they saw themselves. How women see their own bodies is dependent upon what their 'project' (de Beauvoir, 1997) was; the person they hope they can be is dependent upon the occasion they are dressing for. On the occasion of her date with Warren, Sadie's aspired-to look is effortlessly beautiful, casually sexy. On previous occasions, she has been successful in constructing this particular idealized self, which is confirmed when her reflection in the mirror has coincided with the aspired-to image she has in her mind. She is therefore confident of the procedures she must carry out to be successful and attain an aesthetic fit, and so these rituals of getting ready are ones she has not necessarily felt pressured into doing by articles she has read or programmes she has seen, but ones she has learnt through practice. These rituals not only allow her to attain the appearance she feels is 'her', but, moreover, they are a source of immense pleasure. She loves the scents of the make-up and the touches of the make-up brushes and pads, as she listens to her music and dances in her bedroom whilst she gets ready.

Recruiting the Gaze

On the occasion described above, Sadie was getting ready for a date with a specific man, which raises the issue of whose eyes she was dressing through. The various possibilities range from how she thought Warren wanted her to look, what other men have previously liked, what her friends have suggested and what she imagines constitutes 'natural' beauty. These complex and overlapping issues are often simplified in popular discourse in terms of whether women dress for men or whether they dress for other women. What this fails to account for is the multiple opinions women have to balance and the differences between dressing for an individual man and dressing for men in general. These issues clearly resonate with the academic discussions of the male gaze—that is, the power relations inscribed within the gendered act of looking. Mulvey's discussion of Hollywood films (1975), which she argues are produced from a male viewpoint, raises the problematic question: if women exist only as the object of the male gaze, how can women position themselves as viewers? These issues form the focus of this section, as I address how women's encounters in front of the mirror are both the 'self's dialogue with itself' (Melchior-Bonnett, 2002: 145) and simultaneously the 'confirmation of the gaze of others' (2002: 145).

To access these multiple coexisting gazes, I will continue with the same case study. Sadie has always been explicitly positioned as the object of the male gaze. She has lived in London for a year now; when she lived in Manchester, she had multiple jobs (mostly retail jobs) and also worked in a beauty salon and as a hostess in a bar. The latter job she acquired when she was just eighteen, in a bar which was also a renowned celebrity haunt. A couple of men worked as cocktail waiters behind the bar; otherwise the staff were attractive, slim young women, all dressed in black. Irrespective of the qualifications of the female employees, they were rarely situated behind the bar, the manager stating that he wanted them 'out where everyone can see you'. On popping in one afternoon to meet the manager, Sadie's 'interview' consisted of a few cursory questions about what jobs she had done previously; all the while, she tells me, she felt his physical assessment of her as he looked her up and down. Despite never having worked in a bar and having no experience of mixing cocktails, she was employed right away, with the manager's leaving remark, 'you know how good we expect you to look don't you?'

Sadie's usual outfit was fitted black trousers and a wrap-over black top, low enough to reveal the red lace on her bra as it peeped out of the top. She was soon promoted to being a hostess, which entailed chatting to the businessmen and other rich male customers whilst they consumed their drinks. Such a job positioned Sadie as the object of the male gaze: placed standing by the bar to lure rich men in, to be looked at and lusted over, being compelled to flirt with men she admits in a normal situation she would not wish to know—but, as it was her job, she had no choice. This resonates with Mulvey's discussion (1975) of the impact of the male gaze; she argues that, if the gaze is encoded as male, then this would imply that women can only be viewers of themselves in a surrogate male position—in effect objectifying themselves. In his discussion of the painting *Las Meninas,* by Velasquez, Foucault (1970) concludes that, to make sense of the painting and complete its meaning, viewers have to subject themselves to the discursive meanings of the painting. Such a position, where the subject is only able to create meaning from within the regime of truth, could be extended to considerations of 'the gaze' to imply that women are only able to valorize their appearance through a male gaze which objectifies them.

In Sadie's case, the male gaze is specific to a particular bar; yet this cannot be seen in isolation, as the expectations male customers have of female attractiveness is, in turn, mediated and produced through wider representations. Given the ubiquitous and endless (Levy, 2005: 30) repetition of the same images of body and beauty ideals, the notion of what is attractive in a young woman is reduced and narrowed. This can be applied as much to the expectations of men as to the ways in which young women construct their own appearances as a 'male construct of what sexual desire is supposed to look like' (Kelly Holland, cited in Paul, 2005: 111). In the bar where Sadie worked, there was a conformity in terms of the women who were considered attractive, slim, relatively tall, usually having long hair and always dressed in an appropriate manner. The ways in which Sadie constructed her appearance were not in a direct measure against these wider media images, but these impacted upon how she was able to dress in a manner which was sexualized yet in a relatively conventional, classic manner. She realized whether she had got it right through customers' reactions and responses to her.

In fact, not only since then but prior to working in that bar, Sadie has always solicited the gaze of others in such a way, finding that having male admirers is a validation of her attractiveness. Sadie has clearly internalized a way of being and making herself attractive is as 'the object of the gaze of another, which is a major source of her bodily self-reference' (Young, 2005: 39). She has therefore been positioned explicitly as the object of the gaze and consensually now enters into it. There is, however, a clear point of ambivalence. She wants men to find her attractive, to be the object of their gaze, yet she is similarly forced into it, often by older unattractive men. In dressing for that job, she had to consider this objectified male gaze, to 'continually survey herself' (Edholm, 1992: 155) through this imagined gaze. At the time, this was part of her job, yet even now she still admits to wanting men to find her attractive, feeling despondent if she doesn't have a troupe of admirers. This 'gaze' is internalized; at times she feels oppressed by it, and at other times it is a source of self-confidence. When it is a source of confidence, it is clearly empowering; as Hall (1997) has pointed out, potentially objectifying gazes may be disrupted, citing the example of 'Black is Beautiful', where previously denigrated black beauty becomes a domain of empowerment, as the terms of valorization are reversed. Sadie is not attempting to challenge the sources of this gaze, but she does use it as a source of self-esteem and a way of gaining advantage, as her appearance helps her to jump the queue at prestigious nightclubs and acquires her many male admirers.

Given how central this gaze is in how she sees herself, classifying it as the 'male gaze' is insufficient. When Sadie was getting ready for her date, she admitted that, even if she was going out with another man, or even a friend, she would still carry out the same processes of getting ready. It is not just his eyes she sees herself through, but it is also how she sees herself, and so the application of Mead's theory to getting dressed—how the 'I' sees the 'me' through the experiences of interacting with others and remembered reactions—only offers a partial explanation. In this instance, Sadie's gaze and self-regard has become autonomous as she is cultivating a relationship to herself. Given that she is in her bedroom for hours every time before she goes out, her own gaze becomes crucial as she pampers her body and skin. The gaze she has internalized in this instance has become her own, as it is separated from the men who used to gaze at her. It is almost as if the man is an excuse to get ready in this fashion, as she concedes on the occasion of another date, 'it's nice to have an excuse to spend ages getting ready'. Sadie therefore, on occasion, dresses for herself; she enjoys the ways in which she is able to make herself look and also the actual rituals involved in doing so. On a night in, she will often experiment with new make-up and try on her clothing, either alone or with friends. The presence of others mediates the gaze, as they all discuss with each other which outfits work and what looks good.

Even if Sadie is, on occasion, considering what Warren will think or what men in general will think about her appearance, the very fact that so often she gets ready with her girlfriends questions any straightforward understanding of the male gaze. The male gaze can be seen as part of what Butler discusses as the 'heterosexual matrix' (1990), which normalizes heterosexuality, as a woman is seen as the object for the straight man to look at. The male gaze is clearly challenged if one considers how 'queer subjects both desire the objects of their gaze ... and want to be their desired object' (Holliday, 2001: 229). In Holliday's research, how lesbian women look at other women involves how they see their idealized image of themselves. When the desiring subject and the desired are the same gender, then the power relation between the spectator and the object is problematized. What Sadie's case makes clear is that heterosexual women do not just dress for the male gaze. Even when Sadie dresses for a man, it is mediated through her friends and what she likes. More often than not, for Sadie—as for many other women—the man fails to make the right comments, and so the presence of female friends is a necessary part of constructing the self through the eyes of others. On a night in with her girlfriends, Sadie often wears some of her beautiful silk or satin underwear—items which, on occasion, she has worn for a man. However, more often than not, the man fails to appreciate it and is more interested in removing the underwear than the intricacies of the lacework. Her friends can be relied on to admire the underwear, and Sadie is able to construct herself as sexy and beautiful in the presence of her straight female friends.

Many overlapping gazes come into play in the act of choosing what to wear, mirroring King's (1992) point that there are multiple ways of looking. As Foucault points out in the discussion of *Las Meninas,* within the painting there are multiple gazes and layers of representation: 'the gaze, the palette and brush, the canvas innocent of signs ... the painting, the reflection, the real man' (1970: 11). So, too, in the act of dressing, there are many different points at which different gazes and layers of representation emerge. Applying Mead's theory of the relational self (1982) to dressing, a crucial aspect of considering an outfit is seeing yourself as others see you. In this case, being objectified through the imagined opinions of others is not necessarily disempowering or 'objectifying' in the negative sense Mulvey and subsequent writers imply. The nature of the gaze is dependent upon the context of looking: in the bedroom, in a shop window and the occasion for which women are dressing. On occasions when women see their own bodies, the remembrance of a boyfriend's comments, or a friend's admiration, can be more important than the distorted images in magazines. And so it is important not to just reduce how women see their own bodies in relation to the airbrushed, silicone-enhanced images of magazines, against which women supposedly see themselves as deficient. For Sadie, as for all the women I interviewed, the gaze is always multiple, shifting and contested. The gaze might be through a woman's own eyes, the remembered opinions of other people or even a generic male gaze.

The Intrusion of the Gaze: Anticipating the Party

Whilst Sadie invites the gaze, there are occasions when it is oppressive and unwanted. This is felt as an intrusion for women like Louise, a young English-born former student living with her boyfriend in Nottingham, who dresses not to be noticed or 'seen'; she only performs a cursory glance in the mirror on a daily basis before going out to check that labels are not poking out. She has no cultivated relationship to the reflected self. Each morning, Louise has a shower and brushes and briefly styles her hair in front of the mirror before she goes to either university (where she is doing a part-time MA) or to her part-time job. She examines her skin for blemishes; if any are encountered, she attempts a swift cover-up with make-up concealer. Her clothing is selected next; on opening her wardrobe, the first thing she does is go to the pile of ten pairs of jeans at the bottom, and, as she is rarely seen in anything else, she selects a pair. She then peruses the tops hanging in the wardrobe and, on most occasions, ends up wearing one of her many black long-sleeved ones. On leaving her flat, she checks her appearance in the mirror briefly.

Like most women I interviewed, Louise's daily act of dressing is a clear routine, consisting of selections which she does not reflect on extensively but are made in a similar manner most days. Her aim on looking in the mirror is to verify that there is nothing out of the ordinary in her appearance. She actively seeks to avoid being noticed or being the focus of attention. The gaze of herself is therefore not important; she wants to appear socially acceptable, to measure her appearance in relation to social norms, yet in doing so not to attract the unwanted attention of others. However, this is not to suggest that Louise's appearance is in any way 'natural'—she still selects particular clothes to make her 'not seen', has her hair cut and tries to get a tan in the summer. For Louise as much as for Sadie, her appearance is part of how she 'enacts' (Goffman, 1974) her self every day. On one level, Louise and Sadie appear to be extremely different; however, both women get ready in a routinized fashion almost every day.

The ordinary relationship Louise has to her clothing can be easily disrupted by a particular occasion. On one of my visits to see Louise in Nottingham, it is her friend's birthday barbeque in a week's time and will be the first time she has seen many of her friends since graduating the previous year. As she attempts to select an outfit, she stands before her wardrobe, flicks through the clothes and is faced with an overwhelming dominance of blacks, blues and greys. Her friends always comment that she wears the same sorts of clothing, and she is dying to buy something new. However, she is still doing her Masters' degree, with no real source of income, and so cannot afford it. Her paucity of new, exciting clothing is exacerbated by her friends' relative affluence. The girl whose birthday it is works for a top fashion designer, another works at an exclusive high street shop and many of the others have a similar penchant for designer clothing—along with the requisite money to fund such a preference. 'It's so unfair', she wails, wishing she could afford to buy something new. The clothes she does have, appear to her as alien objects, unrecognizable. She can no longer remember what it is that she used to wear. She panics as even her trusty black top and trousers appear boring to her now, dreary and uninteresting. In that moment, it becomes inconceivable that these items of clothing could ever have been so reliable; the imagination of what her friends might be wearing drains the vitality out of her wardrobe, and she yearns for something new. Haunted by images of Calvin Klein dresses and ensembles from Paul Smith, her clothing becomes an inadequate alien entity; the clothing is fine when it is out of focus, but when the spotlight is on it, it appears inadequate and undeserving of attention. She imagines the fashionable, expensive clothing that her friends will be attired in, relegating her own clothing to drab anonymity.

She cannot believe it is only a week until the party. A few days later, she is galvanized into action when one of her friends texts her to inform Louise she's wearing a mini-skirt and pleads with her to likewise wear one. Although apprehensive, as she has not worn a skirt for a while, she has no other real ideas and so roots around in her wardrobe, trying on various skirts. She reluctantly decides on an outfit: a black mini-skirt and relatively new black vest top. She tries to imagine herself at the party; yet the reflection that faces her is not one she can envision receiving admiration. She is not only alienated from the clothing in the wardrobe, but from the clothing as it looks on her body. On this occasion, she is forced to look properly at her reflection in the mirror, and her insecurities about the flatness of her bottom come to the fore. Deep down she knows she is not going to wear her selected ensemble. Not only does she not have the confidence to wear a short skirt, she also knows that the only item of clothing that gives her a sufficiently curvy posterior is the right pair of jeans. The next day she is having a despondent wander around Nottingham city centre on the way to college and spots a girl on the street wearing some cropped denim jeans. In a contemporary fashion, they are fitted, three-quarter length and gathered slightly at the bottom. She had seen them in Top Shop, as Louise already had some full-length jeans that looked similar. She couldn't get the jeans out of her mind: being jeans, they were suitably 'safe' for her to wear, yet were also quite fashionable and represented a slight disjuncture from her usual style. There was no alternative: on the Saturday of the barbeque, she went into Top Shop in the morning and bought them. She couldn't afford them and so had to open up a store card using her parents' address.

Louise's dilemma in front of the wardrobe is a common one: being faced with a special occasion and a collection of clothing that appears alien, from which it is impossible to recognize the outfits that she so loves, always wears and looks good in. With this specific event, the way she looks at her wardrobe is changed; her gaze is refracted through the imagined gaze of her friends. The wardrobe is only alien and inadequate for this moment. The collection of clothing is faced at a distance and is no longer just un-thought-about habitual clothing that enables her to blend in. Bartky (1982: 66) has argued that, when women compare their own defective bodies to the media ideals, they see their own bodies in a relationship of 'distance'. Here Louise sees not her own body as 'other', but her clothing. She sees it mediated through the perfect wardrobes she imagines her friends to have, and she can no longer relate to it. Most of the time her wardrobe appears sufficient and positive in terms of her identification through her clothes, but it is this event that has re-configured her wardrobe as alien so she cannot even recall her normal relationship. The implication of this example is that wardrobes settle into routine, relatively unconscious selections which become comfortable, until they are disrupted by an event which matters and which casts a woman in a relatively inferior light. The degree to which this happens differs among women. For Louise, the failure of her wardrobe is only momentary as she imagines her clothes as they would appear in front of her friends. As Louise pictures herself at the party, she also thinks about the person she wishes she could be. Louise wants to be seen as confident, attractive and stylish, and this means choosing an outfit that will allow her to be this. As Goffman has argued, in the social situation, in order to make this idealized version of the self a reality, the person has to believe that they have the attributes they 'appear to possess' (1971a: 28). However, Louise sees herself in the outfit and imagines how she would look to others; under this imagined gaze, she is unable to believe that she is the fashionable, trendy person she wishes to project. All of this happens before the actual event—'back-stage' rather than 'front-stage'—(Goffman, 1971b) and she has to buy something new out of fear of shaming herself. The imagined projections and fears of her own inadequacies make her vulnerable.

Intrusion of the Gaze: The Opinions of Others

Louise's everyday relationship to her clothing is an attempt to make her mostly invisible, yet the anticipated occasion of the party positions her and her clothing under the spotlight—leading to a vulnerability in her clothed self. In Sadie's case, having been positioned as the object of a gaze, the internalized gaze comes to be autonomous, and her own admiration acquires a self-sufficiency. However, the opinions of other people can still shatter her confidence when she changes her routine beauty procedures. In the last few months, as part of a broader shift towards a healthier lifestyle, Sadie has joined a gym and goes every day after work for at least two hours a night. Inasmuch as the processes of making up her face were acts of making up the self (Peiss, 1996), so too her new body project is as much a new attempt at self-construction, as the body and self are inextricably interlinked (Bordo, 2003, Turner, 1984). Eschewing carbohydrates as highly calorific and detrimental to weight loss, she is trying to follow a diet of protein, vegetables and salad. Although she still spends time and effort on her appearance, the focus now is more on the 'body beautiful' than on make-up or styled hair. Moments in front of the mirror are spent now examining the relative firmness of her abdominal muscles and pertness of her bottom, rather than studying her face and hair. Moreover, as she goes to the gym straight after work, application of make-up is impractical given its propensity to run off the face with the rivulets of sweat, the result of vigorous sessions on the running machine.

Sadie has been astounded by the number of comments she has been receiving from people at work, as they approach her to ask what's happened or what's wrong. When she replied she was fine, the standard response was, 'you just don't look like yourself'. Such was the level of comments about how awful and peculiar she looked that, during her break, rather than having a customary chat and drink with her friends, the time was spent in the toilet frantically applying make-up: mascara to return her eyes to their habitual prominence and under-eye foundation to conceal dark circles and bags. Having not really noticed how her own face looked different prior to work, she was struck that, as her work colleagues have never seen her without make-up, the 'natural' look that she spends so many hours cultivating daily is believed by her friends to be her 'actual' look. She finds herself trapped in a cycle where make-up is essential in order to continue looking like herself. Here the make-up, jewellry and clothes are not an external artifice but rather are the actuality of her appearance. As a result of her laborious daily self-constructions, the irony is that when she wears no make-up she cannot really be herself.

The external perception of her friends forces her into re-engaging with her ordinary practices of self-cultivation in order to look like herself. This also relates to her own engagement with her reflected self. On a recent day off from work, planning to spend the day shopping and then meeting her friend to go to the gym, she selected some newly acquired sports wear to put on: tracksuit bottoms, trainers and a fitted sports zipper top. Because she was planning to go the gym, she chose not to wear make-up nor style her hair. A cursory glance in one of her many mirrors before leaving the flat led her to exclaim in horror, 'oh my god, I look so different, I'm just not me!' This reaction starkly contrasts to her previous cultivations, where the process of 'objectification' (Miller, 1987) was complete; when she looked in the mirror, there was an aesthetic fit, as her attempt to transform herself through clothing and make-up was successful in creating 'me'. On the occasion described here, had the look been successful, the potential self—a sporty, healthy, attractive person—would have become actual when the clothing was worn on her body. A crucial part of the process of 'objectification' (Miller, 1987) involves the idealized image women have of themselves. Therefore, women consider themselves in the external form of clothing and also in the internal image in their heads of how they wish to look. This is successful when the mirror image of the woman in the clothing is the same as this idealized image. However, this objectification is a failure when there is a discrepancy between the self a woman thought she was projecting and the reflection that faces her. The discrepancy between the 'perceived self and the ideal self' (Gunter and Wykes, 2005: 4) leads to a dissatisfaction with her body image. In fact, Sadie confesses now that every time she looks at her face in the mirror she cannot help but stare at her reflection, trying to reconcile what she sees facing her with the self she has been cultivating all her life. When I quiz her on whether this could merely be a new era in her life, she says that she will go back to wearing full make-up again. This outing into town wearing her exercise clothes is the first time such clothing has not been confined to the gym. On the way there, she glances at her reflection in the bus windows and cannot believe how 'awful' she looks, setting her on a paranoid constant search for her appearance in every fleeting reflected image, trying to grasp the person she saw as herself.

Sadie's physical sense of disjuncture arises not only when she visually encounters herself in the mirror, but is also present in how she feels in her body. Ordinarily wearing lots of heavy silver jewelry, its absence makes her feel light and self-aware. Although she feels physically comfortable in the loose cotton fabrics, she simultaneously feels an aesthetic discomfort as she constantly senses the absence of weight on her ears or the feel of gloss on her lips. She has returned to the rituals of make-up and hair styling when she goes to work and even when going to the gym afterwards. She is keen to live up to her friends' expectations that the cultivated image is her 'true' appearance. The image of being a sporty, healthy person with a toned body is one she desires, yet equally the aesthetic this engendered was one which was in disjuncture with her sense of self. She is caught off guard when she sees her new sporty reflection, as she no longer sees it as her real reflection. Over time, she got into the habit of spending hours every day cultivating her image and a relationship to her self. When she emerges into the world and the actual gaze of other people, she is filled with utter confidence, projecting onto others her own admiring gaze. Sadie's paradox is that the self she has created is so robust through this constant and entrenched daily process of getting ready in the same manner each day that she is unable to change it without making her self vulnerable. In Sadie's case, like the other women I interviewed, what makes even the most confident woman vulnerable is often the opinions of others. Even for a woman who feels supremely confident after seeing the admiration in the eyes of friends at a party, she cannot control the leering comments she encounters on her walk home alone. The gaze can therefore be objectifying or empowering dependent upon specific situations and social contexts of looking.

The 'Authenticity' of Mirrors

For both Sadie and Louise, their routinized relationship to getting dressed means that ordinarily their selves through clothing are relatively robust. For neither of them is clothing a major source of anxiety every day. However, on the occasion of a specific event for Louise, or when there is a change in the routine and an uninvited comment for Sadie, this ordinary relationship is disrupted. The unwanted gaze intrudes. This is something which happened on some occasion to every woman I worked with, and many women had adopted strategies to avoid this unwanted intrusion of the gaze. For many women, this involves a routinized act of getting dressed which helps them avoid the daily dilemma of choosing what to wear and a crisis of self-image. Interestingly, it is incredible how many women try to avoid these daily crises not only through what clothing they choose to wear, but also how they deal with mirrors, either through avoiding them or only looking in specific ones. I found that women's attitudes towards mirrors were ambivalent: mirrors were seen to tell an objective truth about appearance, yet at the same time women recognized that their reflection in mirrors differed dependent upon the location and type of mirror. Mirrors are thought to give a complete and comprehensive geography of the body, enabling the viewing of all sides, and, in doing so, are purported to be able to tell women how they 'really' look. Yet, at the same time, women know that the image offered in a mirror differs dependent upon lighting or the size and style of the mirror. Margaret, a Welsh-born primary school teacher now living with her Irish husband in North London, doesn't possess a full-length mirror. In her previous flat, she used to have one and constantly used to change her outfits, as she saw herself in her totality and felt that her upper and lower body were not in proportion. Now she has a half-length mirror in her hallway; every morning she examines her upper body in it; she then stands on a chair and peers down to see her lower body. She admits that now she rarely changes her outfit.

The totalizing geography of the body is not possible in Margaret's mirror, and she happily escapes the tyranny of the mirror, as she knows there are no full-length mirrors in her place of work. Margaret becomes complicit in her own deception; although she knows the shape of her body and the problems she used to have, as she will not have to encounter her total body reflection, she does not have to care. When faced with her image before, she felt she had no option when presented with this 'reality' but to change her clothes. It is as if, when she faces her reflection in the mirror, she is forced to see her own image in line with the many images she sees in magazines or on the television telling her how she should look. When looking in the mirror, her reflected image becomes 'real', she sees her self as she appears, yet is simultaneously positioned as both the subject and object of that vision. She is uncomfortable with the 'seen' being 'me'. Margaret employs the half-mirror as a way of protecting herself and making that self robust. Many of the women I spoke with neither looked in mirrors nor made an effort with their appearance, and as such they too do not allow themselves to become vulnerable to the gaze or the tyranny of their own reflected appearance.

Conclusion

The facts that some women avoid seeing their reflection in a mirror and other women will spend hours in front of mirrors makes clear how central mirrors are in helping women decide what to wear. They become so important because this is the moment when women encounter the self they want to construct through clothing. Having selected items of clothing from the wardrobe, standing in front of the mirror is the moment when women decide whether the outfit has worked. The process is successful when there is an aesthetic fit, when the idealized image women have in their heads matches what they perceive to be reflected before them. Two key points emerge from this chapter. First, this moment in front of the mirror is not just a visual relationship, as the mirror moment impacts upon how comfortable women feel in their clothing. 'Comfort' is not a natural feeling engendered by the softness of a fabric; instead, what emerges from this chapter is that in fact comfort emerges in a dialectic between how clothing looks and how it feels. When Sadie looked at her un-made-up face, she was unable to recognize the reflection as her self, and she felt uncomfortable in the soft, loose clothing. Because the reflection she sees does not correspond to how she has imagined herself, she becomes aware of the clothing she is wearing as external. Comfort also relates to what it is that women usually do; for both Sadie and Louise, their routinized relationship to their bodies, clothing and image means that every day they enact and perform themselves through clothing successfully. For both women, it is the unwanted opinions of others or the new event that disrupts the success of this routine.

Second, the ways in which women view themselves in the mirror are extremely complex and multi-layered and cannot be reduced to the male gaze or the impact of media images. One of the ideas this chapter has aimed to highlight is the many layers of viewing that are present within the reciprocal relations of 'seeing' and 'being seen'. Women see themselves through the fantasy image in their own minds, fuelled by past successes, good photographs or admiring glances and comments. They consider their reflected dressed body in terms of what they aspire to look like, which may in turn be refracted through wider media images of body ideals. However, what emerges from watching women getting dressed is how, when the 'I' sees the 'me' (Mead, 1982), it is specific to the social occasion women are dressing for. Despite many of the women I talked to mentioning a 'real me', in fact through clothing—even if there are many continuities across different domains of their lives and the clothing they wear—this is always occasion specific, as women imagine themselves through the eyes of men they are going out with or friends they wish to impress. This gaze is made even more specific as the normative expectation of acceptable wear is specific to ethnicity, class, generation and occupation. Given the particularity of this act of seeing, it is hardly surprising that the women I watched dressing often expressed shock when they saw how they looked in the mirror, as how they imagined themselves did not match up to how they saw their reflection.

–6–

Mothers, Daughters, Friends
Dressing in Relationships

Throughout my fieldwork, I was struck by the quantity of clothing women possess that has been gifted to them by their mothers or partners or has been borrowed temporarily from sisters or friends. These items women have not chosen for themselves show that women's clothing choices are anything but a free expression of individual choice. Women may keep these items in the wardrobe as mementoes of a particular person and are considered too precious to wear. A close friend's penchant for ethnic clothing may not match a woman's own sense of style, and so the item may be rejected on the grounds of taste. However, it is often this very dissimilarity that leads women to wear gifted or borrowed items, as it allows them to experiment with new looks and expand upon who they could be through the taste and style of a friend or relative. Choosing what to wear therefore also involves expanding the self through a woman's significant relationships to others, as dressing involves not only personal preferences but is also the consideration of a mother's love and the closeness of friends. Through the clothing in the wardrobe, women negotiate their sense of self, their individuality and their autonomy, yet also their continued dependence and connection to family members and loved ones. The argument in this chapter is that women's identities through clothing are intrinsically bound up with these connections to others.

Traditional anthropological discussions of kinship focus upon obligations and mutual dependence at the expense of any discussion of self-construction. This implies that kinship and relationships exist in opposition to the self, which is free from ties and obligations. Conversely, in the case of British kinship, Strathern (1992) has argued that kinship both produces and depends upon the individuality and autonomy of persons. Individuality here is not seen in opposition to social relations but as part of the same cultural matrix. Connections and ties between people are not solely a result of enforced obligations prescribed by role or the constraints of kinship but, as Macfarlane (1987) has argued, also arise out of choices made. In a British context, Strathern (1992) has argued that there is a complementarity between kinship and individualism. In the case of the pivotal parent-child relationship, whilst the parent may act out of normative expectations of parenting and providing for children—and, as such, come to 'stand' for the relationship—the development of the child is signified by its growing autonomy and individual identity.

Strathern introduces the complex ways in which connectivities and dependence may exist in a culture where there is a core value of individualism. The implication of Strathern's argument for an understanding of clothing is that, when women choose what to wear, they are not free to simply express themselves. Throughout my fieldwork, I was struck by otherwise autonomous and independent women passing clothing back to mothers to dispose of, still shopping with their mothers and relying on their husband's opinions. These same women are clear and explicit about their autonomy and individual self-sufficiency, but in a way echo Strathern in recognizing that their individualism is the product of these relationships. An example of this is the sought-for respect of mothers and husbands that gives women confidence in their subsequent relationships to others. In as much as this can appear contradictory or even clumsy as an observation when verbalized, it is often the more subtle material practice which demonstrates this complementarity between relationships and individualism. When a person is considered through the multiple constituent parts of his or her relationships (of which clothing is one), the myriad clothing practices allow the possibility of simultaneous dependence and autonomy. Macfarlane (1987) emphasizes 'choice' in British kinship, as individuals redefine and construct relationships as a negotiated process. Because clothing is non-verbal, it lends itself to becoming a means through which people can acknowledge the aspects of a relationship that they do not want to or cannot explicitly acknowledge. The independent woman may be dependent; the friend may express her jealousy or admiration of another. As a subtle material practice, such contradictions are possible as they are not made explicit, and as such clothing does not necessarily cohere with the rest of the relationship.

Mothers, Husbands, Sisters, In-laws: Managing Multiple Relationships

My fieldwork makes clear that the most important relationship that is negotiated through clothing is that between mothers and daughters, from the household provisioning of children, the socialization into certain clothing preferences and a continued, yet redefined involvement in adulthood. As the women I worked with were all over the age of eighteen (although I carried out informal conversations with women's children), the mother-daughter relationship is discussed primarily in terms of how women negotiate this relationship into adulthood. As many of these women were also mothers—with children ranging from two years old to daughters in their mid-thirties—I will discuss how clothing is used by women as they negotiate their self-understanding as simultaneously mothers, daughters and often as wives. One such example is Theresa, a mother of two small children who lives with her husband and still has a close relationship to her mother. In the third chapter, Theresa was discussed in terms of how she uses her wardrobe to order her sartorial biography and memories; to be considered here is how she uses the wardrobe in a similar manner to manage to multiple relationships in her life. Theresa is largely responsible for buying clothing for and feeding her two children. These roles are not particular to Theresa, but were something I found throughout my ethnography—that women are the primary purchasers of children's clothing (Clarke, 2000, Corrigan, 1995, Miller, 1997), as part of the more general patterns of domestic consumption (DeVault, 1991, Jackson and Moores, 1995, Vickery, 1998). In all cases I looked at, this was a relationship of both economic dependence and simultaneously a means through which both taste preferences and gender-appropriate codes of behaviour (Holland and Adkins, 1996, Mann, 1996) are instilled. One of the primary mediums for this gender-specific socialization is through clothing, which is crucial in establishing gender identity (Barnes and Eicher, 1993).

The ways in which clothing is used to inculcate taste and normative dress codes is well documented for babies and small children. The assumption is often that, when the child becomes an adult, this involves a rejection of the mother's preferences, or at least a divergence to new, more fashionable styles. However, this assumption is problematic when seen in the case of Theresa's wardrobe, as hanging alongside items she has bought for herself are many items gifted from her mother, her mother-in-law and her sister—all of which she wears. Many of the items from her mother have been handed down as items which her mother used to wear. The dominant style of clothing is loose-fitting tunic-style jumpers or cardigans made from luxurious natural fabrics such as cashmere or silk. Made of good quality fabric and having been well cared for, they have maintained their shape and softness. Theresa has clear remembrances of her mother wearing these items when she was younger. The good state of repair of the garments means that Theresa is able to wear these tops. A particularly cherished one is a charcoal grey open knit tunic jumper in soft wool, which she wears as the chill sets in on a summer's evening, slipping it on as a chic yet easy piece. As this jumper was worn next to her mother's body, in the very act of wearing it, Theresa is brought into physical contact with the item she so strongly associates with her mother. As discussed in the chapter on biography, it is through the sensual experiences of wearing clothing that Theresa was able to recapture the former potentialities of herself. Here, in a similar manner, through the soft wool touching her skin, Theresa is situating herself—at least in one small measure—in the position of her mother.

Theresa's wearing of her mother's old clothing can be seen as a continuation of the ways in which the taste preferences of the child develops, which arises out of wearing items of clothing bought for them. Through borrowing and wearing these items that belonged to her mother, she has developed a preference for wearing cashmere and velvet tops in a loose style: items which she now buys new for herself. There is, therefore, a convergence between Theresa's and her mother's aesthetics. Even if they have this relationship now, it has not just continued unproblematically. Theresa, like all women I worked with, had a period of experimentation with styles in her teenage years, as she asserted her clothing autonomy. It was perhaps less marked for her than it was for other women I interviewed. In developing from girls to women, this period meant negotiating often-conflicting social norms and relationships: friendship groups, family, partners and a new occupation. The development of women's autonomy in their teenage years is often made manifest in the rejection of the mother buying clothing for them and the assertion of their own preferences. As women start exercising their own choices, the clothing relationship between mothers and daughters can become one of contestation (Corrigan, 1995). Miller (1997) has argued that, with reference to middle-class mothers in North London, infants are initially conceptualized as an extension of the mother. There were examples in my own fieldwork of mothers who select clothing for their daughters that manifested how they wished they had dressed at that age. What Miller's work highlights is how the mother's understanding of her connectedness to her child becomes problematic as the child grows up and starts exercising his or her own choices regarding clothing, negating this initial narcissism.

My ethnography shows that this assertion of radical autonomy by young women is not absolute. As Theresa's case shows, as women mature, often their preferences start to converge with that of their mothers as a signifier of a redefined relationship with their family and their past. This revision of the relationship also signifies a shift in women's self-image. Kaiser (2003) has argued that, as girls grow into women, through multiple social interactions, this self-image that was cultivated through familial relationships is either perpetuated or redefined by the clothing choices women make. Even if most women move away from their cultivated tastes through their families, returning to them often accords with a shift in their own status to being a mother themselves or becoming more settled in their lives. This often involves re-investing in a tradition and religion that they were socialized into (discussed more in chapter 8).

However, this style convergence is only partial for Theresa and for other women I worked with. Women still assert their autonomy through their clothing choices. There is a large section of Theresa's wardrobe which is dissimilar to her mother's, all items which she buys for herself. They include expensive 'treats' bought to perk herself up, items from when she was still working in London and practical items, such as a fleece for keeping her warm around the house. In the main, she buys herself 'fun, fashion' items—such as stretch jeans with embroidery or glitter on them or gypsy style tops—from relatively cheap high street outlets. The contrast between the types of clothing in her wardrobe shows her ambivalence: she purchases for herself fun and fashionable items, yet at the same time she allows herself to be dependent, to be mothered. Theresa adopts more than one strategy through clothing; in choosing items from the shops based upon choices and preferences she knows do not coincide with her husband's or mother's, she is creating a space through clothing that is entirely individual. She allows a continued connection to her mother by wearing her hand-me-downs, and yet also exercises her individuality in other areas. The relationship to her mother is reinforced by the fact that her mother aids Theresa in her wardrobe sort-outs. She helps her choose which items to dispose of and takes the better quality clothes, such as old work suits, to sell in a second-hand shop in her home town. She does the same for Patsy, Theresa's sister; she gives to and takes away from Theresa's and Patsy's wardrobes. Even though all three women are financially independent and buy most of their own clothing, Patsy and Theresa return clothing to their mother to dispose of. When the daughters have stains or marks on their clothes, they give them to their mother to sort out because 'she can work magic with stains' (Theresa). Theresa is very practical in such matters, and, if she stains an item, she will re-dye it and carry on wearing it.

Patsy is not quite so pragmatic, and her propensity to stain clothing is an evident source of anguish at times. Patsy is meant to be buying her first house, yet every time I look at her clothes there is another purchase that I am forbidden from telling Theresa about: 'I'm so naughty!' Although Patsy does appear to enjoy playing the role of the younger, disobedient sister, she was particularly concerned on one occasion when I visited her about a new camel coloured suede skirt she had bought from Morgan. Having bought it on a Saturday, she wore it out that same evening to go out for dinner to celebrate a friend's birthday, teamed with a new white ruffled shirt, also from Morgan. A few glasses of wine later, during one of Patsy's anecdotes, an over-exuberant sweep of the arm also flings an oil-drenched piece of avocado on her fork onto the bottom of the skirt. An attempt to rub it on the spot merely spreads the oil. The next day she tried applying her 'trusty' Dry Clean spray. The end result is a large white patch at the bottom of the skirt. Patsy is crestfallen. It was her favourite (although she did buy another 'sneaky' skirt to 'cheer myself up'). She now has had the cunning plan of dyeing it plum red so 'no-one need ever know!' Patsy is a mature, responsible adult, but, in the context of her family and her clothing rituals, she still occupies the position of a naughty girl. She has a high investment in fashion and clothing, and she buys clothing according to her own personal preferences; it is in the rituals surrounding clothing that there is a continuity, as her mother is still defined as the provisioner. Her passion for shopping is well known, and in this arena in relation to her mother she is allowed a degree of irresponsibility as this is how she exists and performs in relation to her sister and mother.

The continuities in Theresa's relationship to her sister and mother coexist with the newer relationships to her husband, children and mother-in-law (who also buys clothing for Theresa). The new relationships in her life are incorporated through new clothing practices, seen in the practice of dressing for dinner. Theresa's mother-in-law Alison was someone who never worked outside the home and spent each day at home looking after her two children and preparing dinner for her husband on his return home from work. Each evening she engaged in the ritual of dressing for dinner, changing out of the clothing she wore during the day into a new outfit, even though ordinarily she and her husband only ate dinner at home. Theresa's life follows a similar pattern of staying at home in the day looking after the house and the children. She does not have to concern herself with clothes that her husband will like and wears clothing she sees as fun yet comfortable and practical. She has a penchant for 1970s-style hipster trousers and flared jeans with glitter embellishments and gypsy-style tops, which Simon her husband dislikes, preferring a more 'classic' look. He hates hipsters because they 'cut up a woman's shape'. She dresses for dinner every evening when he returns; as the children watch DVDs from 6:00 to 7:30 p.m., Theresa has her evening shower. She selects an outfit to wear from the wardrobe, often thinking in terms of what Simon might like.

The children are then read a bedtime story and put to bed. Theresa finishes making the supper, opens a bottle of wine, and her husband arrives home at about 8:00. Theresa, through this practice, is assimilating herself into the practices of her husband's family; continuing the tradition of her mother-in-law, yet also dressing in clothing she imagines Simon would like to see. This is also important in the context of food, as her mother-in-law Alison is renowned for being a fantastic cook; Theresa knows this not only from Simon's constant comments, but also from having sampled Alison's culinary creativity. Theresa spends a great deal of time cooking and regularly phones Alison for advice and recipes. She is always delighted when Simon compliments her on her cooking. Through food preparation and clothing rituals, she aspires to live up to Simon's expectations of his mother. In trying to be a good mother and wife, she aspires to live up to the models of her mother and her mother-in-law, and clothing is one of the means through which she is able to do this. Through clothing, Theresa is able to bring together her dual membership of two families, her existence as a daughter and as a desirable wife and mother. Theresa is able to manage her existence in multiple, often overlapping, relationships; at the same time, she manages her autonomy and individual preferences through her separate collection of fun clothing.

The Burden of a Mother's Love

Theresa's example of managing shifting and continued relationships through clothing exemplifies Macfarlane's (1987) point about the element of choice in how relationships of dependence and autonomy are negotiated. The case to be discussed here, Joanna, is where the love and aspects of relationships present in clothing may become a burden, as women feel that they are not able to, or do not want to, exercise their choices through clothing. The continued handing down or the buying of clothing by a mother initially inhibits Joanna's ability to incorporate new relationships into her life. Joanna was born and brought up in Korea and five years ago married an English man and moved to London. She is notable by her desire to be a 'good wife' and expresses very little desire for autonomy in her clothing choices. This is in part a product of the cultural context of her upbringing. This is not to suggest that her passivity and lack of desire for autonomy is something which characterizes all Korean women (Kibria, 2002). Rather, the particular ways in which she emphasizes the importance in her life of being a 'good wife' and the centrality of family is a product of how she was brought up and socialized in a South Korean context. The vestiges of Confucianism and traditional Korean values has led to the development of what Cho has termed a 'mass society' (1995), with few communal or voluntary organizations, leading to the centrality of the extended family. Joanna's mother only started working once the children were at school, and then only part-time; she devoted most of her time to her family—in particular, encouraging her children's educational progress. Typical of many middle class South Korean women, the family was her occupation (Cho, 1998). Even in this context, Joanna is extreme in wanting to be constituted entirely through her familial relationships.

Joanna met Mark through her church, and straight after the marriage she moved to London to be a Christian missionary. Although her English was practically fluent, she had never visited Britain before. Whilst Theresa was able to negotiate the shift to being a wife through many continuous, if subtly shifting, clothing practices, for Joanna, the rupture—both cultural and in terms of relationship status—was so marked that this was not possible. When Joanna lived in Korea, her mother bought and selected all of her clothing for her and for her brother, father and sister (who asserted her own tastes at the age of thirteen). As a child, teenager, and even a university student, her mother selected jeans and either checked shirts or casual brightly coloured aertex-style tops, short-sleeved t-shirts with a little collar and buttons. When she finished her degree and started her MA, her mother decided that it was time for Joanna to start dressing in a more mature fashion and bought a range of navy and grey skirt suits for her, despite the fact that other students were still wearing jeans. Joanna still wore the suits, having accepted that her mother bought and selected her clothing. As a product of never making her own choices, a strong degree of passivity is inculcated in Joanna. In part this is due to her upbringing, through which she has developed certain traits and values. In South Korea, the cultural heritage of Confucianism and associated ideologies position women in particular ways (Bedeski, 1994), as they are expected to be 'mild and faithful' and follow their husbands (Cho, 1998: 28). Whilst cultural shifts have led to a diminishing emphasis upon this for younger women in the last twenty years, these values are still present in particular in Joanna's mother's generation and, as such, have affected Joanna's upbringing. Keen to please her mother, and thinking that aesthetic decisions do not concern her, Joanna allows her mother to make selections for her. She therefore has failed to develop ordinary skills and competences in assembling and selecting clothing.

Joanna did have a brief period when she attempted to buy clothes for herself while she was at university, living in halls of residence with other girls. Liberated from her familial home, she attempted to consolidate this freedom through asserting some of her own aesthetic control. Despite having the desire and will to choose her own clothes, she was unable to. Never having faced the clothing in shops before, she was overwhelmed by the options. Without her mother's guidance, Joanna was unsure in which direction to turn. Floundering in the immense variety of styles, shapes, colours and textures that surrounded her, she ended up buying an array of party dresses.

Ultimately, she had no need for such dresses, and, because they were so different from her usual understated aesthetic, she was far too self-conscious to wear them. Not only does Joanna therefore lack the experience and skills of shopping and assemblage, her aesthetic as developed through her mother's clearly defined style has a rigid in-built conservatism. After this brief failed foray into sartorial decisions, she happily relinquished aesthetic control back to her mother.

The occasion of her marriage and subsequent move to Britain was an occasion of immense rupture, in terms of lifestyle, culture and indeed clothing practices. When Mark came to Korea for the wedding, her mother's aesthetic dictatorship first started to crumble, as he purchased a couple of items for his bride: a pale blue long-sleeved jacket and matching shift dress and a plain black skirt suit. Joanna's mother dislikes the pale blue suit in particular, yet both are now staple items for Joanna. Such a transition from maternal aesthetic to that of her husband's became accentuated when they moved to London. Getting married involved a shift in her priorities and a redefinition of herself primarily in terms of her husband; for every item of clothing we go through in her wardrobe, she tells me whether Mark likes it. She always agrees with him; as she is someone who is completely pliant and has no clearly defined opinion on such things, her aesthetic judgments are always derivative. The clothing she wears and thinks is most appropriate depends on her relationship with a particular person.

However, wearing clothing that her husband wants to see her in is extremely problematic as he does not buy clothing for her in the same manner in which her mother did. When Joanna first arrived in Britain, she unquestioningly carried on wearing the same clothing as before; as her clothing has always been selected and provided for her, clothing rarely occupies a major position in her thoughts. The first time she met her father-in-law, Roger, she wore a dress she had bought with her mother just before getting married. The dress is navy coloured, knee length, with short sleeves and a distinctive white sailor-style collar. A couple of months after she had been in England, she was going to another important dinner and unthinkingly picked out this same dress. Prior to going out, Mark delicately informed her that the outfit resembled a school uniform. Joanna started to panic; not only did she want to please her husband, but also she became aware that there might be a distinct English aesthetic, rendering all her Korean clothing inappropriate. Whilst many of her friends are Korean, in the context of her husband's colleagues, she feels self-conscious and out of place. The clothes she had been previously able to wear without reflection suddenly became visible as Korean clothing, as her mother's particular taste. Unable to wear anything from her former life and worried about letting her husband down, she settled on a black suit that Mark had bought for her. Such a moment is one of transition for Joanna, as she realizes that she must cultivate her own aesthetic; she can no longer rely on clothing decisions to be made for her. The ways in which she was socialized into clothing preferences is very different from other, British-born, women I worked with, where the mother-daughter relationship is primarily characterized by both dependence, but also importantly, the mother is still expected to be responsible for 'nurturing a specific type of self within the daughter ... mothering the self' (Lawler, 2000: 1). For Joanna, a dependence was inculcated into her, not only in terms of taste, but also in terms of the actual act of shopping for clothing. This is challenged in this instance as her husband Mark expects her to be able to do this for herself.

Mark has little interest in what she wears per se, yet it becomes incredibly important to her to dress in a way she imagines he would like. Clothing becomes important to her as it is an aspect of their relationship which does not live up to or cohere with the totality. For Joanna, being a good wife is foundational to who she is. She wants all aspects of her relationship to fit in with this, having no desire for an autonomous identity through clothing. She is unlike Theresa, who manages the potentially contradictory aspects of her self and her relationships through different material forms, verbally and through food and clothing. As Mark rarely expresses an opinion on what she wears, she is forced to choose clothing that she imagines he would like. She knows that he has extremely defined opinions about aesthetic preferences and is extremely minimalist, as is apparent in their interior décor. When they moved into their flat on a council estate in North London, the first step they took was to paint every flat surface white. On the walls are a few photographs of family members, but they remain relatively sparse. A great deal of the furniture is from Ikea, being both affordable and fitting in with the minimalist look. Such minimalism translates into his own clothing, as he likes to wear 'neutral, classic clothing'.

Joanna's mother still sends clothing to her, which exacerbates Joanna's clothing dilemmas because the items fall within Joanna's old aesthetic: bright aertex tops and patterned, stripy shirts. Joanna decides to articulate Mark's comments on the parcels to her mother—that the clothing is too garish and bright. Joanna is jubilant when, after two years of sending clothing unwanted by Joanna and Mark, the next parcel contains a selection of plain, round-necked blue and grey t-shirts for both of them to wear. The resolution of Joanna's problem is her mother selecting items based upon what Mark has stated. Here Joanna is able to circumvent making any choices over clothing, as her mother interprets and imagines what Mark likes. She therefore is able to negate the autonomy that Mark bestowed on her and be both dependent upon her husband and mother in different ways.

Now that the problem of what to wear is partially resolved, there still remains the issue of what to do with the many things that Joanna's mother has sent in monthly parcels over the last few years. Although recognizing the love and kindness behind such packages, they are greeted with a slight feeling of dread as they are opened to reveal clothing, foodstuffs, saucepans, and other items such as cushions and duvets. The unwanted items amass and find a home in their storage room. It is filled with mounds of saucepans, unwanted kitchen equipment and, most evidently, oceans of clothing which engulf the space. The lids of large crates on one side of the room cannot be fastened because the jumpers and shirts stuffed within defy their incarceration and spill out over the top. The room is filled with piles of bin-liners, each one restraining the mass of clothing which threatens to overwhelm the room. Such clothing is not evidence of a shameful, hidden propensity to materialism, but rather the problematic gifts and provisions that Joanna's mother keeps sending.

These items are a source of dispute between Mark and Joanna, as Mark wanted to give away the unused and unworn items. Joanna agrees with him in the case of saucepans and duvets, which are seen mainly in functional terms. Some of the household items are kept 'just in case', and some are given away. However, the clothing is a different matter. Although not a forthright or argumentative person, Joanna stood her ground and stated that 'these are not just clothes, they're my mother's love. It's her heart. I can't throw them away'. It is the clothing, and not the other items, that Joanna cannot throw away. When she sees the colours, the patterns and the fabrics of the clothing, she sees the style she wore for the first twenty-five years of her life. The checked shirts embody and constitute a crucial aspect of Joanna's relationship to her mother. It is through this clothing style that her mother has socialized her, provided for her and loved her as she grew up. In contrast, saucepans have never been bought for her before, and so Joanna is able to see them in purely functional terms. The clothing is a materialization of her mother's love, and this is precisely why it matters and in the end why these clothes become such a burden.

The ways in which gifted objects are inseparable from the giver are well documented anthropologically (Godelier, 1999, Mauss, 1992, Osteen, 2002) and evidenced here in the items sent to her by Joanna's mother. Joanna cannot see the items in terms of their functionality, as she cannot separate the items from her mother's love. Clothing is not a separate expression of her mother's love in their relationship, but a particular material manifestation of that love, constituted through years of providing for her daughter through clothing. Joanna's decision to keep this clothing is important as she wishes to hold on to the love the items externalize, but it is also important that she chooses not to wear them. Theresa is happy to wear the items her mother used to wear as a way of accepting this aspect of her relationship to her mother and establishing a continuity between them, despite the fact that in the rest of her life she is no longer dependent upon her mother. However, Joanna cannot wear the items as this would be a form of acceptance of her mother's role as aesthetic judge in her life—a relationship she now wants with her husband. In keeping the items yet not wearing them, she is redefining the relationship. She is still the recipient of her mother's love, and her mother is still able to provide for her. But, because these aspects are separated out from the role of aesthetic arbiter, Joanna is able to accept aspects of the relationship yet reject others.

The Relational Self

What Joanna's case highlights is how central women's connections to others are to their self-definition; for all women I worked with, their self-identity is defined through their relationships to the significant others in their lives: as a mother, as a friend, as a partner or as a daughter. The most central relationship in terms of self-identity is usually the parent-child relationship, considered in this book through the mother-daughter relationship. This is true for women not only when their children as still growing up, but as my ethnography shows, even as they grow to adulthood. Numerous women I interviewed, who were financially independent, either let their mothers buy clothing for them or more commonly took their unwanted clothing to their mother to dispose of. The mother is no longer a provider but, through disposing of items of clothing, is still able to be a caring mother (Jackson and Moores, 1995, Miller, 1997) without threatening the daughter's independence. Therefore, the acts of maternal care and domestic responsibility and the ways in which 'mothering' occurs (Clarke, 2000: 88) can be seen through my ethnography to be extended and continued into adult relationships.

Another major transition in the ways in which women define themselves in relation to others is through living with a partner or husband. This transition is particularly marked given that, unlike Joanna, most women I interviewed had had a period of independence prior to moving in with their partner, living alone or with friends. For example, Helen is twenty-two and lived at home in a small town in Scotland until she was eighteen; she then moved to Nottingham to live with friends whilst she completed her degree. On graduating, she got married and now lives in Nottingham with her husband. Her husband is in full-time employment, and she is still a student, doing an MA in fashion design. Her prize possession in her wardrobe is a pair of brown three-quarter-length cord trousers, which she purchased from the Karen Millen sale after Christmas. She bought them at a time when she had been through a phase of buying lots of clothes: jeans, boots and cardigans. She could not bear the thought of telling her husband that she had made yet another clothes purchase as their finances are limited. Moving in with a partner involves a renegotiation of her previous carefree independence and autonomy; these negotiations often centre upon finances. Even though Helen used her own money to buy the trousers, her experience evidences the fact that very rarely do women spend guiltlessly (Wilson, 1995). Although she knew he would not be angry, her feelings of guilt led her to hide them from him for a few months. During this time, she wore them only when she knew he would be leaving for work before her and she would be able to change furtively before he returned home. After a few months, she was hankering to wear them with her reddish brown boots to an evening event they were both going to. She slipped them on, hoping he would not notice. He commented that they were nice trousers and asked if they were new, and Helen replied, 'I've had these for ages!' Once she had had them for months and the fact they were no longer new made her feel less guilty about them. During the three-month period of concealment, she made fewer clothes purchases, thus justifying the trousers. As a relatively new bride, only married for six months when she bought the trousers, a new form of provisioning and budgeting had to be negotiated. Even though Helen only makes clothing purchases for herself and is self-financing, as she is married, she feels accountable to someone else. She has been forced to rethink her identity, as the ways in which women construct themselves as a wife links to their capacity to budget (Delphy, 1995). Her clothing practices show an ambiguity of being both independent yet simultaneously constructed through her relationship to her husband.

Processes of Exchange: Short Term and Long Term

The focus of this chapter so far has been the negotiations between women and their mothers, sisters and partners. As such, the practices involved are the long-term provisioning and gifting of clothing. However, I also encountered in my fieldwork the rather different practices of swapping and borrowing of clothing amongst friendship groups. This is common amongst young women, and the example chosen is that of four young women—Sandra, Jane, Lisa and Lizzie—all twenty or twenty-one years old and living in a shared house. They are all second-year university students and in a relatively impoverished position; as they are all keen on clothing and fashion, they find that borrowing each other's clothing is a way to expand their own wardrobes. They form an interesting example of the ways in which women with limited financial resources are still able to be creative and innovative in their clothing choices. As they met at university and have only known each other for a couple of years, none of the items are jointly owned. However, an extremely high level of sharing and borrowing of clothes goes on. When one of them makes a new clothing purchase, they show it off to the other housemates, a process which usually involves all of the women trying it on for future reference.

One of the key reasons for sharing is that, as is typical of many young women, their changing tastes are incompatible with their financial resources. Because they live together and socialize together, they are constantly exposed to each other's clothing choices. Before a night out, the women all look through their own wardrobes and, if an outfit is found lacking, they search through the house. For example, on a recent night out with Lizzie, Jane was adamant she was going to wear her red knee-high suede boots. As a self-confessed shoe addict, she wanted the boots to be the focus of the outfit. She therefore decided that a short skirt would best show off the boots and opted to wear Lizzie's short pleated black mini-skirt, a skirt she regularly borrows. In order for the boots to become even more of a focal point, Jane thought a black top would be most appropriate. Many tops are scattered about in various locations, so Jane set about trawling through the house trying them on until she found a suitable one, again one of Lizzie's, yet currently located in Lisa's wardrobe. The potential clothes from which the outfit would be selected were not just her limited wardrobe, but all the clothes in the house become potential outfits to try on.

Clothes are in a continual state of flow; when an item is borrowed, it does not reside for long in one wardrobe. The dominant items being borrowed are tops and skirts (all the women are practically the same size on top); trousers prove more problematic. They do not tend to borrow items such as jumpers or tops to be worn in the day, but rather the sharing of clothing is linked to social occasions in the evening. They often go out together as a group to the pub or to a party, as they have friends in common. Going out, and the sharing of clothing, is in part how their shared life together is constituted, with the rituals of getting ready beforehand being part of this. The fact that it is mostly going-out clothing that is shared signifies that, unlike in Theresa's case of wearing the items her mother wore, these women are not trying to 'take on' aspects of the other women. For Theresa, the fact that her mother wore these items day in and day out is important as the clothing embodies aspects of her mother, and the act of wearing the items becomes the shared bond between mother and daughter. Yet in the shared house, no item is ever borrowed for long. It is in the processes of exchange of clothing in the house where value and friendship are created, 'rather than value being located in specific items of clothing and their wearing' (Gregson and Beale, 2004). What matters here is that these acts of borrowing are swiftly moving and ephemeral. This happens in conjunction with the four of them going out together, whereas many other aspects of their lives are entirely separate: they do different courses and have boyfriends and separate family lives and friendship groups.

Even though the passage of clothing creates an aspect of their friendship, this borrowing of clothing is also important in terms of how each woman is able to expand upon the possibilities of her self. All the women state that they share their clothing and all are technically free to borrow each other's, yet, in practice, this sharing relationship is not equal. Despite all other aspects of their friendship seeming to be equal, at the level of clothing, Lizzie clearly occupies the most central position. Although both Jane and Lisa acknowledge that Lizzie has some 'really cool' clothes, on no other level is she designated as being 'cooler' in terms of music tastes or her personality. In effect, Lizzie is the fashion pioneer, introducing new styles into the group. Ever since Lizzie bought the black pleated short skirt that Jane borrowed a few months ago, there has been a gradual trend towards all of the women starting to wear short skirts. Prior to this purchase, none of the women regularly wore short skirts. At some point, all of the women have tried on the skirt, and both Jane and Lisa have borrowed it to go out. Lisa, on a recent shopping spree in Top Shop at Oxford Circus, bought a denim mini-skirt with wide pleats going all the way around it. The skirt forms departure from her normal style of clothing, but she was so taken with Lizzie's skirt that she started borrowing it all the time. She admits she used to have a real phobia about wearing short skirts and baring her legs, but now thinks 'it's so much fun wearing short skirts!'

The primary reason for Lizzie's status as fashion leader seems to be a combination of having the most clothes and the fact that she tends to buy items which break out of the norm. Her clothes seem more interesting and exciting, enticing the others to try them on. The colours of the clothes in Jane's wardrobe tend to be, as is typical of most British women's wardrobes that I encountered, dominated by neutral colours such as black and grey and the fabric denim. Jane has been borrowing many of Lizzie's red tops recently, really loving the colour, but admits she probably wouldn't buy anything in that colour in case she didn't wear it. The clothes she buys tend to be safer, but she utilizes the bolder choices of her friends to enable her to be more adventurous.

At a verbalized level, or indeed in any other area of their relationship, there is no sense in which 'status' is an issue, yet it becomes apparent through looking at these processes of borrowing that Lizzie becomes the fashion leader. Rather than status being important as a homogeneous, unthinking emulation (Veblen, 1899), here it is both non-verbalized and in fact crucial to how each woman is able to construct her self. This status is created through the exchange processes. In the case of the cycles of clothing exchange in the household, as it is Lizzie's items that are most borrowed and in demand, her items come to seem more desirable and accrue status (Osteen, 2002). However, whilst the items may be shared, the distinction between possession and ownership is important here. Weiner defines inalienable goods as something which is 'imbued with the intrinsic and ineffable identities of their owners' (1992: 6). Although these items are shared and worn, each woman only possesses the item temporarily so the original owner is always recognized. As clothing carries such an intimate connection to identity, the item remains linked to the original wearer. This connection is enhanced as on no occasion of borrowing the item do the women ever borrow it for indefinite periods, whereby it would become linked to the new wearer. The swift passage of the item of clothing is essential. Were it to remain with one woman, her identity may become woven in the cloth. Its ephemeral passage throughout the house enables status to accrue to the owner of clothing through the other women possessing it temporarily. As such, when the other women wear her clothing, Lizzie is expanding the possibilities of her self (Osteen, 2002). When her skirt is worn by all of the other women, this allows the creation and reinforcement of herself as a fashion leader, as 'cool'. For the other women, the wearing of Lizzie's items allows them to be more exuberant or to experiment with being cool and fashionable. Through wearing Lizzie's items, they are exploring the aspects of themselves that do not exist in their own wardrobes or clothing, but which they see as potential personality facets.

Whilst the relationships between the housemates is manifest in clothing through constant borrowing and short-term exchanges, the women also have more long-term swaps with family members and old school friends. The items that are loaned long term create and reinforce a relationship of trust. When loaning an item to an old school friend, there is no need for an equivalent item to be swapped; this echoes Weiner's argument that long-term alliances are not created through reciprocity but through delayed return. Weiner uses the specific example of kula exchange cycles—a system of inter- and intra-tribal trade in the Trobriand Islands (Campbell, 1983, Malinowski, 1922). The trade of shells in the form of bracelets and necklaces is one of immense prestige and a means through which men's subjectivities, relationships and statuses are constituted. The acquisition of a particularly prestigious shell is a source of status for men, yet simultaneously the shell carries within it the obligation to pass it on. Of particular relevance here is how, through exchanges, alliances are formed. If someone has in his temporary possession a valuable kula shell, several parties will be interested in receiving the shell and will compete to become an exchange partner. In vying to receive the shell, each interested party will give a smaller shell as a kind of down payment. However, if the shell is reciprocated immediately with an equivalent shell, this signifies that any attempt to establish a partnership has been rejected. Alliances are created through delays and many small gifts before the giving of the desired shell. Weiner (1992) makes the point that reciprocity, as assumed by traditional exchange theory in anthropology, and equivalence do not create long-term alliances. This point is held out in other discussions of exchange, such as Sahlins's (1972) investigation of the opposition between immediate and generalized reciprocity and that pertaining to the short-term self-cancelling exchanges of bride-wealth and the long-term alliances created through dowry (Bell, 1998). When considered in the case of clothing, it becomes apparent that long-term lending, and the non-equivalent delayed return of items, is the basis upon which alliances and trust may be created. This is useful in understanding the differences between the flow of clothing in the women's house and the more long-term swaps they have with other friends.

For example, Lisa has many such long-term exchanges with her friends from home and her sister. The swaps with her friends from home are more long term; clothes might be returned months, maybe even a year, after the initial borrowing, as these friendships have developed over a longer period. The basis of trust is one which does not necessitate immediate return. Within a similar paradigm are Lisa's swaps with her sister. Lisa sees this as more risky than swapping with her friends as they have a more volatile relationship. Her sister is a couple of years younger than Lisa and slightly slimmer, so Lisa is open to charges of making clothes stretch as well as spilling things on them. Lisa borrowed her sister's dark green silk bias-cut top to go to a friend's birthday party the day before Christmas Eve. During the revelry, Lisa managed to besmirch the top with a small watermark. As often typifies family rows, the arguing was immense and communal, involving their mother and grandmother. Although there is still swapping of clothes, Lisa fears borrowing anything from her sister; on their return, her sister scours items for stains or rips, attempting to reveal Lisa's carelessness.

The contrast between Lisa's sister and her friends from home is interesting, in that both involve relationships that have developed over a long period of time, and therefore one would expect a similar pattern of clothing exchange. However, what becomes apparent is that the relationship with her sister is taken as 'given', rather than something they have to create or at which they have to work. They have shared parents, a shared home and a shared history. In contrast, whilst her friends have a similar shared past, clothing becomes a means through which this longevity and trust can be continued and created. As in Weiner's discussion (1992), what is important here is precisely that the items are not equivalent. If an item were to be given back immediately, or indeed were Lisa to demand an item back from one of her friends, this in effect would be a rejection of the strength of the friendship. As they now live in different cities because Lisa has moved away to university, the presence of clothing in the other person's wardrobe constitutes a link between the friends. Linking to Weiner's discussion of the inalienable, where items cannot be separated from the giver, in this example, as the item is not given away personally, the self is not diminished. Unlike the case of mothers dressing daughters, this is not about creating others as an extended version of oneself, but rather allowing others to dress in one's clothing and therefore reiterate the strength of that bond, which in turn allows the self to be extended through social relationships.

Conclusion

Clothing has been discussed in this chapter as an external form of aspects of a relationship: as the materialization of a mother's love, the 'coolness' of a friend, the continued alliance with a sister or the dependence upon a husband. The wardrobe is the locus of all of these multiple relationships, the partial materializations of which hang in the wardrobe. In choosing what to wear, and what to simply keep, women are not just selecting which styles they like, but are considering the relationships and person these embody. Choosing which items to wear carries implications for the relationship and whether women accept only certain aspects or the relationship in its totality. In Joanna's case, she wanted to accept her mother's love and her role as provisioner, yet she wants her husband to occupy the role of aesthetic judge. Through clothing, women are able to simultaneously accept and reject aspects of relationships. In Macfarlane's sense (1987), women are able to choose which aspects of other people they take on. Clothing is a means through which women are able to manage these relationships and allows contradictions—such as the autonomous woman's dependence upon her mother. At the same time, when a relationship exists in the material form of clothing, it cannot be ignored or merely left unconsidered. It may become a burden as the individual is faced with an aspect of a relationship she did not wish to confront.

When women choose which items to keep and which items to wear, they are considering not only the relationships that items of clothing embody, but also how these same items can be used in the construction of an identity through clothing. In putting on an item bought by a friend, the consideration is not only how important the person is to the wearer, but whether the colour and style form part of an identity the woman wishes to project. Almost all women I interviewed possessed gifted or passed-down items that they did not choose themselves. What this chapter has shown is that women are able to use gifted items, as well as items they choose themselves, in the construction of their identities through clothing. In chapter 4, the wardrobe was discussed as part of the extended self (Gell, 1998), as the various disparate aspects of the self hang in the wardrobe, both in terms of who women are today, who they used to be and who they wish they could be again. Given that women's relationships hang in the wardrobe, it therefore follows that the self is extended through these same relationships. Borrowing a cool friend's clothing allows a woman to try out whether, on wearing this person's clothing, she too can be trendy and cool. By attaching themselves to the relationships that inhere to clothing, women are able to extend the parameters of the self and explore not only 'is this me?', but also 'could this be me?'.

This act of experimentation can be a moment of failure as much as a moment of success. As women try on a cool friend's top, women may look in the mirror at themselves and realize that this is not 'me' at all; this failure is felt all the more poignantly when women go out wearing the same top and fail to live up to the exuberance or coolness of the item of clothing as they realize the limits of who they can be. On other occasions, women may feel compelled to wear the top gifted to them by their mother, which does not correspond to women's sense of who they are. On wearing the top, they are not able to 'express' themselves as they wish, but instead experience the parameters of the self defined by their mother. As has been discussed already, clothing may be a medium through which women's intentions are externalized, as they try to impact upon other people. In the case of clothing bought by someone else, women may be wearing an item of clothing that externalizes the giver's intentions, and, therefore, in wearing the top, women have no sense in which they can construct their own identity through clothing. Clothing can allow women to expand on the possibilities of who they can be, but, as in the case of Joanna, the items her mother bought her fixed and delimited who she could be. On other occasions, when the gifter 'gets it right' and the woman tries it on and realizes it is 'me', the clothing has allowed women to successfully experiment with who they can be. When women wear gifted or borrowed clothing, they are attaching themselves to social relationships in an attempt to explore who they could be through clothing. Discussed in the next chapter is how women do this through experimentation with fashion and styles, as they link themselves to a more general, normative sense of the kind of person who would be associated with that item.

–7–

Fashion
Making and Breaking the Rules

One of the reasons choosing what to wear can become such an anguished moment is the fact that women have to balance so many different concerns, ranging from personal preferences and body shape to wider social norms of what is acceptable wear. This concern over what is acceptable incorporates the norms and sartorial expectations produced by the fashion 'system'. The images in magazines, on television and in advertisements produce an understanding of what is 'in' and what the ideal body is supposed to look like (Gunter and Wykes, 2005). Images of the fashionable ideal are ubiquitous, as they seep outside the domain of fashion and infiltrate television shows, films and, in the era of spin, even politics. Despite its omni-presence, the impact of these images on women's clothing choices cannot be assumed. One of the legacies of cultural studies is that consumers have agency in deciding what to buy (Hall, 1981), as consumption is recognized as a central arena for the construction of identities (Campbell, 1996, du Gay, 1997, Wilson and de la Haye, 1999). This applies to fashion in that what is 'in' or how women should look is not simply dictated; rather, women exercise choice in deciding whether a particular fashion fits their personal aesthetic. Women's ideas of what is fashionable are always refracted through their own social networks: friends, work colleagues and family members. As women worry over whether they have got it right, they are more often than not measuring this against the trendy woman who works in their office or a cooler younger sister than against a de-personalized image in a magazine.

As women choose what to wear, 'fashion' may be experienced as panic (as they worry over whether they have 'got it right') or as a creative possibility for innovation. The current fashion system is characterized not by the succession of homogeneous styles, but by fragmentation and uncertainty. At any one time, there are multiple definitions of what is 'in', and the burden of fashion is shifted to the individual consumer. In such a context, where there are seemingly 'no rules, only choices' (Ewen and Ewen, cited in Muggleton, 2000), post-modern accounts see fashion as offering endless possibilities for individual expression. However, this fails to account for the many experiences of dressing within my ethnography, where fashion is often experienced not as a free choice, but as an expectation placed upon the individual. In these instances, the lack of clearly defined homogeneous fashions for many women is not experienced as liberating, but as a constraint. The choices made in such moments of anxiety tend to be extremely conformist as women fall back on items they 'know' how to wear. As already discussed in chapter 4, women have their own rules of which items go together which govern how dressing takes place. To be introduced here is how women use the external guidance of fashion magazines, television programmes and books to facilitate the creation of outfits from the wardrobe.

This chapter focuses on how women mediate potential panics through such 'rules' and how fashion may be seen as a creative potential for individuals. The innovation and creativity of fashion coexists with, and is dependent upon, conformist and rule-bound choices made on the majority of occasions. As Simmel (1971) pointed out, a key characteristic of fashion is the perpetual and unresolved tension between individuality and conformity. Fashion requires innovators who create new looks, which, in order to be defined as 'fashion', must be taken up by the wider population. However, what my ethnography shows is that the relationship between innovation and conformity is a concern for the innovator as much as it is for those who choose to play it safe. Therefore, the tension Simmel identified as being the basis for fashion change is experienced as a tension played out by individual women in the act of dressing.

Fashion and the Wardrobe

The ephemeral nature of fashion would appear at first glance to be at odds with the long-term relationship to clothing that women have to many of the items of clothing in their wardrobes. This chapter looks at how women balance their desire to be fashionable with their often entrenched personal aesthetics as they connect the fleeting with the grounded. The ways in which a long-term relationship to clothing is inextricably linked to fashion are evidenced in the links between personal biographies and fashion. Almost all women I worked with were able to trace their lives in terms of a series of fashions or 'looks' in which they participated or remembered others wearing. The temporal specificity of fashion and its capacity to define a moment in time—or even more widely, a decade—mean that women use it to anchor their understanding of the past and as a measure of the passage of time. Common to almost all of the life stories I collected was the tendency of women to narrate the 'looks' they wore as a chronological sequence of separate, entirely distinct fashions. Telling a life through a chronology of styles is both a product of how individual life stories are told (Giddens, 1991) and how the narratives of fashion history are similarly constructed. Even if sub-cultural styles by definition do cohere around shared clothing, music and lifestyle, the history of sub-cultures as a series of defined groups (Polhemus, 1994) belies the actual diversity and ambiguity of practice. So, too, when women told their lives through clothing, they did so in terms of a series of styles, with little recognition of the gradual phasing out or the purchases that were out of synch with this.

Running through the narratives was a clear tendency for women to characterize their teenage years as ones of experimentation and a series of fashions. These coherences around clothing are therefore also constructed by women as a product of youth, as conformist participation and subsequent rejections come to stand for the fickle preferences of children and teenagers. With one exception, all of the women I interviewed were over the age of twenty and distance themselves from their teenage sartorial selves. They see themselves as now being sufficiently mature in their clothing choices to reject absolute adherence to the current fashion. For example, Rosanna, now in her late twenties, gasps with horror as she recalls the looks of her teenage years, when she participated in a fleeting series of fashions and other explicit counter-cultural looks. Such repudiation of the mainstream that inheres within subcultural looks coincides with teenage rebellion, fickleness and lack of permanence of identity. Now, whilst she still maintains an interest in fashion and always knows what is happening on the catwalks, she would never buy into one whole look. Referring to the 1980s revival, she stated, 'I don't like strong trends ... I like some aspects of it, but I think it's nice to take bits of it and integrate it into what you like, but when you see people who've got the whole look—it's like being a teenager when you haven't got your own identity so you just use someone else's'. Such a disavowal of complete adherence to a look here forms a signifier of Rosanna's claims to maturity, the capacity to compromise and recombine diverse facets of clothing.

This example characterizes the attitude many women I interviewed had to fashion: they were not driven by a desire to keep up with every single trend, nor did they wish to appear 'unfashionable'. In Rosanna's case, the introduction of some new items that fit with what she already owns shows a negotiated participation whereby fashion is a means to allow her to be innovative and fashionable, yet—as she still wears the items she already owns—there is no radical stylistic break from her 'safe', usual clothing. This partial relationship to fashion is enabled by, and mirrored in, the current fashion context. Despite the existence of bi-annual fashion shows in New York, London, Milan and Paris, fashions are far more rapidly changing and ephemeral than a twice-yearly shift. As many high street retail outlets, such as Zara, Top Shop and H and M, acquire new stock every six weeks, the shelf life of items of clothing becomes even briefer as the quantities of goods escalate. The speeding up of new fashion means that there is no expectation of a complete update of the wardrobe bi-annually, but rather individual items are introduced by Rosanna (and many other women) on an almost monthly basis to update her look.

In addition to allowing innovation and creativity, the speeding up of fashion also was experienced by the women I worked with as a source of anxiety. The examples of women who have wardrobes spilling over with clothes yet are still unable to make a selection are too numerous to delineate here. This process applies to how women choose from their wardrobes and how they choose what to buy from the shops. In both cases, this indecision can be seen to occur not in spite of the quantity of clothing on offer, but because of it. This is exemplified in the case of Louise and the occasion discussed in chapter 5 when she had to choose what to wear for a party with a group of friends she had not seen for a long time. On this occasion, she felt unable to wear anything in her wardrobe and ultimately came to feel alienated from the contents of her own wardrobe. She wanted to look funky and fashionable on this occasion, yet the clothing in her wardrobe appeared drab and disappointing. She felt equally alienated from the clothing she saw in the shops, partly because she was struggling financially at the time. More than this, though, she cannot connect with what she sees in the shops; each shop she goes into seems to present so many choices, yet these apparent choices mask a startling sameness in what she can buy. Empirical research into the fashions presented in the British high street has pointed to the uniformity in styles presented across a range of retail outlets (FashionMap archive, 2001–2006). In any given season, almost all high street shops carry similar items and styles; even though stock is replenished regularly, the replacement styles are distinguished from each other through what could be characterized as 'marginal differentiation' (Lipovetsky, 1994: 131). This sameness of the merchandise often leads to buying decisions becoming even more difficult, as Louise does not want to spend her precious money on getting it *almost* right. In the end, she is inspired by someone she sees on the street; she is so taken with the jeans (that she has already seen in a shop) when she sees them on the person that she opens up a store credit account and buys them. Louise is now able to connect the familiar safeness of her own wardrobe with the constantly changing clothing in the shops through seeing the fashion worn on an actual person. The girl in question was wearing jeans (a staple item for Louise), yet they are in the current fashionable style that Louise has seen in the shops. She therefore recognizes the style as 'in' and also as something that fits her personal aesthetic. Louise is therefore able to 'do' fashion through attaching herself to someone else; this allows her to be both safe and sufficiently fashionable in her choices.

For Louise, the possibilities of fashion are a cause of anxiety, but in the end it is through wearing the fashionable item that she is able to make a creative assemblage. When she sees the cropped jeans worn by someone on the street, she pauses to wonder whether they 'could be me' as she connects her own personal aesthetic with fashion as enacted by the passer-by. More commonly this process of linking the individual sense of style with the external sense of fashion is mediated through someone a woman knows. In the last chapter, this happens in the case of the four women who live together, where three of the women are able to introduce a new look into their wardrobes by using the clothes of Lizzie, the fashion pioneer of the house. For Jane, who has a very clear sense of herself through clothing, her only forays into new styles are when she borrows Lizzie's clothes. Unlike the other women in the house, Jane never attempts to replicate the look by buying the same or a similar item in the shops. The ways in which new looks generate within this shared house form a working out of the tension that Simmel (1971) identified as the core of fashion innovations—the tension between individuality and conformity. When Lizzie introduces a new look into the house, it is sometimes reproduced by the other girls in the house. The girls do not just unthinkingly emulate the styles of their friend, but—like Louise—they consider the fashionable item as they try to imagine themselves in the item, wondering 'could that be me?'. The 'individual', innovative or fashionable look is one which women do not want to feel is external, but rather that the fashion fits a woman's sense of her self.

What these examples show, as does my ethnography more widely, is that women are more able to make connections between themselves and fashionable clothing when they see fashion on people they know. When fashion is considered through the multiple domains of fashion—such as magazines, retail outlets and television programmes—women are not considering it in terms of the material items of clothing on actual bodies they can see. Fashion is reduced to a glossy image, presented on someone with whom women have no personal connection. It is furthermore extremely difficult to talk with any certainty about what 'fashion' is in light of the multiple and often contradictory sources of fashion information. These domains of fashion are also sites for the production of knowledge about fashion, as they exist as overlapping discursive arenas (Foucault, 1980). Within these sites are multiple agents (Entwistle, 2000), as the fashion 'expert' ranges from buyers to journalists to celebrities. As fashion seeps into so many arenas of contemporary life, with every media event becoming a fashion event, fashion is no longer a separate domain. For example, David Beckham's sartorial habits make the front page of the tabloids, eliding the worlds of sport, celebrity and fashion. In the context of such a range of media presentations of what is fashionable, it is hardly surprising that on many occasions in my ethnography women felt alienated from fashion as it exists in the shops and in magazines. When women cannot connect with what is in the shops, they appropriate fashion through people they know: friends, families and work colleagues. When clothing is seen on a friend—or even on a stranger, in Louise's case—it is at least embodied, material and so comes to appear possible.

Using 'the Rules'

As much as fashion media produce possibilities and uncertainties surrounding fashion, these same media outlets can offer a sense of stability to women through establishing 'rules' of fashion. The fashion media range from magazines with an explicit fashion focus to celebrity magazines which are permeated with fashion 'dos' and 'don'ts'. These magazines include statements about what the current fashions are and advice on what to wear. Most fashion magazines describe what is in, with the guidance over what not to wear hinted at in the sections of celebrities who have 'got it wrong'. Two examples that were popular amongst several of my informants were *In Style* magazine and the television programme 'What Not To Wear' (which is based on a best-selling fashion advice book of the same name. These will be considered here both in terms of the 'safety' they present and as they were used by women I worked with as an assurance that they had got it right.

In Style is a monthly women's magazine which focuses almost exclusively upon clothes and fashion (most other magazines also have sections on celebrities, relationships and sex), and the sub-title of the magazine is '*your own personal stylist*'. Despite being a mass-produced, generic style magazine, there is an attempt to individualize the magazine for readers by categorizing women's body shapes. Advertisements for the magazine are present on the London Underground trains, thus forming part of the everyday visual landscape for many thousands of women. The advert is separated into blocks of colour or patterns, under each of which is a corresponding clothing rule, such as 'vertical stripes elongate short legs' or 'turquoise compliments a tan'. The premise is that, if you stick to the 'rules', you will end up wearing clothing that suits you, making you look and feel fantastic. These principles also are manifest in the actual magazine. For example, there is a regular feature entitled 'Style file: Assessment management', which, in one edition (IPC Media, March 2004: 51–4), focuses upon the skirt. The article discusses three types of skirt (pencil, mini and circle) and offers guidance on which body shapes are able to wear them and how they should be worn. Taking the specific example of the pencil skirt, three possible outfits are pictured. There is an outline of who should wear it ('fuller frames') and who shouldn't wear it ('narrow, straight up-and-down frames'). The article also contains advice on how to wear a pencil skirt which corresponds not only to body shapes but is also linked to particular fashions or styles. For a 1940s look, readers are advised to team the skirt with 'chiffon or satin camisole tops' and a heel that adds 'definition to the leg'.

The rules here centre upon how the different shapes and styles of one item flatter different body shapes. Women are expected to be able to interpret what to wear by correlating their body shape with those described. Whilst women can identify their 'actual' body type in the magazine, the premise of these magazines is that, by dressing appropriately, you can manipulate your body to look more like the 'ideal' body. This magazine, therefore, forms part of the wider media representations of female beauty (Thesander, 1997: 55); despite the multiple images of women's bodies in various media, the parameters of what is beautiful are incredibly narrow. Gunter and Wykes (2005: 5) have argued that fashion advertisements construct feminine beauty as white, thin and always sexually alluring. Because magazines present women with an ideal and explain how to achieve it, women are both constructed as deficient and lacking and are then offered advice on how to manipulate their body shape so that it comes closer to the normative. The promise of the fashion media is that this beauty can be bought (Thesander, 1997: 32), as even for the 'apple-shaped' or 'flat-chested' woman, the right body shape is attainable.

Similar 'rules' of clothing, which always seem to centre upon women's body shape, are also present in the immensely popular television programme 'What Not To Wear', presented by two fashion journalists-turned-stylists, Trinny and Suzannah.

With only a couple of exceptions, all the women I worked with were familiar with the programme, many also possessing the accompanying book. Unlike *In Style* magazine, however, the stance taken by this programme is quite anti-fashion. On the television programme each week, a member of the public, having been secretly nominated by their friends or relatives for having terrible dress sense, has Trinny and Suzannah sprung upon them and are offered £2,000 to buy a new wardrobe. The condition of this is that they obey Trinny and Suzannah's fashion 'rules'. The process begins with the woman having to encounter her almost-naked reflection in a mirrored room, whilst the two women highlight the woman's good points and prod and poke at her flabby bits. The person then has to try on one of her favourite outfits, which invariably the stylists hate because it accentuates the woman's 'problem area'. Participants are then cheered up by being told what rules they should follow to flatter their shape, and are sent off to spend £2,000 with various interventions from Trinny and Suzannah. The end result is inevitably a delighted transformation, as the woman becomes a convert to the rules.

The book involves a delineation of these rules; the overall principle being to educate women to dress to 'show off what you love and hiding what you loathe about your body' (Constantine and Woodall, 2002: 7). Dressing is presented as an act of 'disguise' (2002: 8), as women choose clothes to suit their body shape. The book contains ten main chapters, each of which focuses upon a particular physical defect, such as 'big tits', 'no waist' or 'short legs'. Each chapter follows the same structure; for example, the 'big arms' section (40–51) opens with a photo of Suzannah naked frowning at her allegedly huge arms, facing the dilemma of what is 'the owner of plucked chicken wings supposed to wear in the summer?' The rest of the chapter depicts a selection of items of clothing with photos of her wearing the 'worst' example and beaming wearing the 'best item'. Under the example of each is given a reason, such as cap sleeves are bad because 'on big arms these look like a stretched swimming cap atop a mountain of flesh' (42). Following these is a list of outlets at which to shop if you are cursed with large arms and a list of the 'golden rules for big arms', including 'small prints cover a multitude of flabby flesh' (51). Similar to *In Style,* the focus is upon how body defects may be concealed, as dressing becomes an act of deception. In each case, the starting point is a deficient and faulty body which can be rectified by following the rules. Whilst these rules are adapted to different categories of body shapes, and perhaps ages, there is little recognition that women choose clothing according to idiosyncrasies of personal preferences.

In the context of the multiple possibilities for what is in and the accompanying expectation that women will get it right, these rules clearly have a strong appeal. Many women had clear rules of their own which centred upon similar issues, such as how to make their stomach look flatter. To be considered here are two sisters, Patsy and Theresa, who both bought the magazine *In Style,* and Patsy possesses the *What Not To Wear* book. These two women form an interesting example of how 'the rules' are a means through which they find security in their clothing choices, yet are always used in relation to women's own sense of style. Patsy is in her early thirties, currently lives alone and is passionate about clothing, popping into the shops several times a week for a brief familiarization with available stock. She works in public relations for a large corporate agency, where there is no formal dress code, yet, for regular meetings with important clients, there are certain expectations regarding what is suitable attire. Patsy tends to favour knee-high fabric black or brown boots, a knee-length A-line skirt in denim or perhaps black and a white shirt or pale pink or blue polo-neck. Patsy confesses that many of the styles of clothing she chooses do relate to her perception of her body shape; she is very slim, yet she feels she is disproportionately large around the hips. Like all women I interviewed, Patsy has a sense of what her 'problem area' is, yet she is also aware of how to redress the perceived fault. She usually chooses to wear A-line skirts because they cling to the hips, yet—as the skirt lengthens and the shape triangulates out—also balance the size of her hips. There is a greater circumference of material around her knees, making her hips look correspondingly smaller. Similarly, she usually pairs darker skirts with paler tops, as the eye is drawn to the lightness of the top, and the skirt and her hips visually recede. Patsy owns very few pairs of trousers or jeans. She talks with despondent longing of finding a perfect pair of jeans, loving the style, yet feeling too self-conscious to wear them, as they delineate the precise size and shape of her legs. She does wear her parallel-line black trousers when meeting her friends for drinks, because the fabric hangs vertically from the hips rather than following the contours of her legs, and therefore minimizes the appearance of the upper legs. Patsy is rigid about what shapes she can and cannot wear.

Theresa, Patsy's elder sister, also has a clear sense of what she can and can't wear, although her concerns are less with body image, and more that she has less confidence than Patsy about buying a new style which is different from clothing she already owns. Her concerns therefore centre more explicitly upon the 'fashion' element of choosing what to wear. Spending most days at home with her two young children, the salient sartorial division of her day is between her practically oriented day-wear and the clothing she wears for dinner with her husband when he returns from work. Theresa possesses vast amounts of jeans and uses them both as day-wear and combined with a smarter top in the evening. As discussed in the last chapter, the vast majority of Theresa's clothes are gifts; when an item is bought for her or given to her, she no longer has to make a choice. Her primary concern when dressing is to look good, yet she also wants to wear slightly fashionable clothing. She is confident in her usual aesthetic and, as such, is quite apprehensive about buying items outside her usual style. When Theresa was invited to a ball with her husband, she bought a new dress for the occasion: a black cap-sleeved dress, which, having two layers of fabric, clings to the outline of her body, reaching her ankles. Her main cause for concern was what shoes to wear. When I first spoke to her about it, she had decided she was going to wear a pair of shoes she had had since she was eighteen; the shoes were court shoes (closed heel and toe, with no buckles or straps) made of black velvet, with a one-and-a-half-inch heel rounded like a cone. The colour and lack of adornment seems to set them outside of the parameters of being fashion shoes and leads Theresa to define them as a 'classic', feeling that they would compliment the traditional style of the dress. They are also a 'classic' in the sense that they are a characteristic shoe style for Theresa.

On a shopping trip prior to the ball, Theresa chances to be shopping in Top Shop, including a brief perusal in the shoe section, which at the time was dominated by shoes with extremely pointy toes. As the shoes had been around in the shops for a few seasons now, Theresa had had time to get used to seeing them and decided that she would quite like some 'trendy' shoes. She is cajoled by the assistant into trying on a black pair; they have a covered toe, are perched on a two-and-a-half-inch stiletto heel and have an ankle strap. When Theresa first tried them on and looked down at her feet, she was struck by how pointy her toes looked, exclaiming she looked like a 'witch'. However, on looking sideways in the mirror, and in discussion with the shop assistant, Theresa conceded, with surprise, how nice they looked, tailoring the shape of her foot. Having purchased the shoes, she tries them on with the dress at home in front of the mirror and feels reassured as she becomes accustomed to the novel style; she also feels slightly fashionable in them, having modernized her look. Her primary concern then becomes whether she will be able to stand in the shoes, as her children shriek with perversely amused delight: 'mummy you'll fall over when you dance!' Her concerns proved unfounded, and she now plans to wear the shoes to another event.

Theresa still wants to play safe, wearing classic clothes that she considers stylish, yet she simultaneously wants to have fun with clothing and have a slightly more fashionable edge. On this occasion, she successfully managed to balance the two: the shoes fit her pre-existing aesthetic, and, in being slightly more fashionable and different, she is able to play with this secure sense of self. What Theresa's and Patsy's examples make clear is that they use the 'rules' in order to give them a sense of security, in both their body shape and in their sense that they have got the style right. However, they do not simply passively follow the rules; instead, they use them to engender a feeling of confidence. Indeed, both women bought an item of clothing on occasion because they loved it and not because of their body shape or what they 'ought' to wear. For example, Patsy often wears pale pink, not only as it suits her complexion, but because it makes her feel feminine, and the lightness of the colour is agentic in lifting her mood and making her feel happy.

Using the rules presented by the fashion media is also a way for women to situate themselves in the 'external' world of fashion and the media. Whereas Louise, and indeed Jane, on occasion (certainly not on every occasion they shop) find fashion in retail outlets to be an external and alien world, Theresa is able to navigate it effectively through the rules. She uses the rules in conjunction with advice from friends and family. When she still lived near her sister in London, she would often meet Patsy in a shop at lunchtime to get her opinion on whether an outfit was suitable for her. Theresa also gets ideas from magazines such as *In Style* and uses them as an explicit guide to how she may make her purchases. When she sees an item she likes, she rings up the retail outlet to see if the item is in stock, then makes a trip to the shop to try it on. The magazines thus explicitly mediate Theresa's wardrobe and the outside world of fashion, giving her guidance on what to wear and what is fashionable. This is always located in her already existing sense of style, as she uses the magazines to see if she can connect the internal aesthetics of her wardrobe with the externally defined fashions. In turn, this process is mediated through the advice of people she knows.

Breaking of Rules: Making of Fashions

Rules are helpful when women shop for and choose an outfit, yet they are also conversely important in accounting for how innovation may arise, as women deliberately break these rules. The individuals described in this section have their own clothing rules of what goes with what, yet, in creating new looks, they break these very rules as well as official style rules. Helen is an aspiring fashion designer, having just finished an MA in fashion design in Nottingham. Originally she is from a small town in Scotland, where the shopping landscape consists of a sparse collection of high street shops. She comments that, 'fashions catch on there about nine months after you get them here in Nottingham'. She moved to Nottingham four years ago, and, feeling the pressures of being a fashion student in a new city, she started adopting a new 'funky, street' look. As a recent graduate and newlywed, working in an exclusive designer boutique in Nottingham, she has adopted a more 'settled, stylish' look. One of her key concerns when dressing is not to look like a 'fashion victim'. For example, before she moved to Nottingham, she bought a plaid knee-length skirt with a beige background and green and red lines. Whilst this was bought in an anonymous shop in Edinburgh, the pattern is one which at a glance looks like the trademark Burberry print. This particular fabric and style has become omni-present in the last few years, in particular on handbags, and has become a signifier of the mindless fashion victim and the 'chav'. Helen no longer wears her skirt, dreading the thought that, if she did, everyone would think she was a 'Burberry wannabe'.

However, simultaneously, she pays heed to and wants to coincide with what is in fashion. During one wardrobe interview, in a pile of clothes at the bottom of her wardrobe, Helen unearthed a short fitted dress with spaghetti straps, the under-layer consisting of black and white swirls and a thin black gauze layer on top. Purchased by her then boyfriend (now her husband) to wear to a party, she has not worn it recently. In light of the incipient trend towards monochrome on the high street at the moment of the interview, Helen reconsiders the dress and moves it back to the upper part of her wardrobe. She plans to wear it over a pair of trousers, recognizing the particular fashion yet adding her own interpretation to it. She is keen to look slightly different, but within the parameters of her own aesthetic. Helen is extremely logical, methodical and practical in creating new looks. When selecting outfits to wear, she professes to 'wear pieces that everyone else might have in their wardrobe but I like to wear them in a different way'. The innovative look is created through the way in which items are put together or the manner in which they are worn.

Every woman I worked with had her own sense of 'what goes'. This knowledge is a source of certainty when women know which items don't go together, but sometimes it is causes uncertainty as women try on a new outfit and ask 'does this go?'. In moments of uncertainty, women fall back on items they know they can wear, determined by both their own rules and the wider rules of what is acceptable. Women who use the rules of fashion to mediate panic are more typical of those I interviewed than Helen. Women like Helen are atypical, but they signify an important group of innovators who by definition have to be the minority. McCracken (1988) refers to the 'complementarity of goods', whereby the colours, textures and styles of the clothing are perceived to determine which combinations can be made. This sense of aesthetic order equally entails which items cannot be combined; it is through breaking away from preordained 'rules' that innovation is generated. Helen's innovations are generated by her own personal aesthetic. She has a clearly defined sense of what goes, which is extremely sensitive at times, and—like Patsy and Theresa—she possesses many key 'safe' items which go with most things.

Despite having clearly defined aesthetic rules, Helen is keen to make herself look slightly different. One of the ways in which she manages this is through the purchase of 'multi-purpose tops'. For example, on a recent visit to the Liberty sale shop, one of the items she bought was a three-quarter-length shirt dress in a typical Liberty print of bold swirls of contrasting colours—in this instance, fuchsia, red, pale blue and beige. Whilst the print is recognizable as Liberty's, it moves beyond a more standard bold floral print to a more edgy psychedelic look. Helen wore the dress fastened up and belted to a friend's housewarming party with a pair of turquoise sandals and her favourite Girbaud jeans. Girbaud is a French label that specializes in unusually styled denim and is a particular favourite of Helen's. These jeans are demarcated as different through the absence of a waistband, deep pockets at either side, and, in the lower half of each leg, there is a pleat at the front which conceals a fold of extra fabric. When Helen walks, the pleats open, liberating the excess of fabric which envelopes her ankles.

The funky couture look of the jeans challenges the traditional floral Liberty look; rather than combining the Liberty-print dress with a smart pair of shoes and matching handbag, Helen draws upon the more subversive aspects of the fabric, such as the substitutability of vibrant colours. The look is further enhanced by the baggy jeans, which, instead of having a hem at the bottom, are torn into shreds and have white threads hanging from them. She does not feel tyrannized by the dress and the combinations this seems to compel, but she has the confidence to assert her own combinations as she adjusts it to her personal tastes. The dress speaks to multiple orders dependent upon how it is combined: the settled staid look, but equally it has within it the potential for mild subversion. The latter element is matched by an item from the funky order of Helen's wardrobes, creating a new aesthetic logic. The combination creates an innovative look which flouts the expected way in which the dress would be worn. As is typical of many items Helen buys, the dress is a multi-purpose item, as it can be worn over jeans and as a conventional dress. When buying it, she was attracted by these potentials, as she envisioned also wearing it opened, like a coat, over a top and trousers. Alternatively, she may shorten it to make it more like a long shirt, or she might sew in elastic along one side so the material is gathered up on one side. Buying items which she feels she will be able to wear in many ways is typical of Helen's style, and she possesses many tops which double as dresses which can be worn off the shoulder for a sexier look or buttoned up for a more 'settled' look. She loves the possibilities of items like the dress.

Eclecticism as the Generation of Fashions

Helen creates new looks through wearing and combining her clothing in a slightly unusual manner. The next example, Alice, is also in her early twenties; she is a former fashion student living in Nottingham. Like Helen, Alice is conscious of the standard combinations that are made and seeks to move slightly beyond this; however, in Alice's case, the attempt is more marked, as her acts of assemblage and the generation of innovatory looks can be seen in part as the demolition of pre-existing clothing 'rules'. Such a position arises out of her socialization into particular clothing taxonomies and an adamant desire to look different. Alice's wardrobe is unlike any other I saw; the colours of the clothing are kaleidoscopic, with barely any black items. Alice has always loved colour and dramatic prints and grew up in a family of eccentric dressers. In particular, her elder sister has a similar style to Alice. As a young girl, Alice was given her elder sister's hand-me-downs and was therefore materially incorporated into this aesthetic. Even now the two sisters regularly swap clothing, as Alice's wardrobe extends to her parents' home in London, where her sister still lives. Throughout her childhood and into her early adulthood, Alice and her sister appear to pay little heed to the conventional rules of what colours ought to be worn together. Unlike any other woman I worked with, Alice sees all the clothing in her wardrobe as possible items to be combined.

Alice still has a sense of what goes together, yet it is extremely unlike that of any other woman I interviewed. When discussing what she wears with her only black dress, she points at her red shoes, or green and gold shoes, stating that she couldn't wear black shoes as 'black doesn't go with black. It'd near enough kill me!' She also possesses staples in her wardrobe, which are seen to go with anything: denim jacket, smart trousers, jeans, denim skirt, white shirt, white t-shirt, solid-coloured tube tops. Similarly, she has fall-back items: clothing which, no matter how many failed items are tried on, will always work. For most women I interviewed, such items are a pair of jeans or something relatively plain. Alice's fail-safe item is a knee-length, short-sleeved jersey dress which is low-cut at the back. It is covered with bold horizontal turquoise, black, blue and white stripes. The closeness, thickness and positioning of the different coloured stripes is not uniform, giving the pattern a haphazard quality. When worn, the dress hangs loosely from the body and lacks any shape definition. In fact, the structure of the dress is created through the pattern; for example, around the middle, there is a thick band of diagonal stripes which form a contrast to the predominantly horizontal stripes of the rest of the dress. Through this pattern, a waist is created and defined.

Whilst this item is eye-catching in itself, just as important is how Alice wears it. One evening, she wore it with her 'tacky silver sandals' from a cheap high street shop, luminous pink nail varnish and her hair in a mullet style (encouraged into this by her elder sister); 'it looked so trashy, a little bit crazy'. She thinks of it as one of her sexiest outfits. Many of her friends have tried it on and find the dress too baggy and unflattering, yet the way in which form is created through pattern and the subtle revealing of the back forms part of Alice's alternative understanding of sexuality. Given that Alice actively wants to look different and unlike anyone else, is on a limited budget and lives in Nottingham, where there is not an extensive range of alternative clothes outlets, she has to combine clothing in unexpected ways in order to generate quirky and innovative looks.

In selecting outfits, Alice explicitly aims to wear clothing that will make her stand out and look different; yet the peculiar combinations she makes are also naturalized, as part of her personal aesthetic. It is often when she is explicitly trying to look 'different' that she deliberately tries to break the rules. Last summer she was invited to a ball; not really being a 'ball-y person', Alice did not own any suitable dresses. She was clearly aware of the convention of such occasions when women are expected to buy a new dress, tending towards the excessive and glamorous. For the ball, she wore a rigidly structured A-line floor-length skirt, which skimmed the hips and then formed a hoop around her ankles. The style is similar to that of a traditional ball gown. However, the skirt was made of denim. Here the 'rule' being broken is that of the social conventions of place and occasion. With the skirt she wore a 'raunchy' backless shimmery gold top. Although denim is becoming increasingly acceptable for non-casual occasions, its use for a ballgown is quite unexpected. Alice did not select to wear something totally unacceptable, such as a pair of ripped, fraying denim jeans. The shape and form of her skirt was conventional; it was the fabric that was so shocking. Here the innovative is created not by an utter discarding of conventions or fashion rules, but rather from within these very parameters, as the conventional becomes subversive.

One of the standard rules championed by Trinny and Suzannah on 'What Not To Wear' is to never mix patterns (such as stripes and spots). Never one to abide by the rules, when Alice wears one of her many patterned items, she often mixes different patterns within one outfit. For example, on a recent trip back to London, when she was getting ready with her sisters, she wore a knee-length fitted pencil skirt in a pale, shimmery pink fabric. It is covered with delicate horizontal stripes. The soft feminine effect of the colour is enhanced by the presence of two embroidered butterflies on the front of the skirt. At times Alice wears the skirt as a top, winding it around her body and tying it up with ribbon in order to give her look a slight edge. On this occasion, she wore the skirt with a top in a brighter pink than the skirt. The top is covered with a mauve and green bold floral print. Despite being floral, the print is not feminine in a conventional sense, as the flowers are extremely bold, with as much emphasis being given to the stalks as to the flowers. The femininity in the top is present in a gathered ruffle around the neck and its delicate mesh fabric. In this outfit, Alice brings together the delicate shimmering and simple embroidery of the skirt with the bold, more unconventional femininity of the top. She decided to wear this outfit, anticipating that the colours of the two items would match by visualizing the successful outfit in her mind. She knew the colours were right and she felt confident to combine patterns that others might consider a little risqué. Although Alice actively cultivates an eye-catching look, here it is evident that, to her, the colours of the top and skirt did go together. She asserts that she 'has a good understanding of colour, that's why I make those sorts of decisions'. Alice's eclecticism is a combination of an active effort to look different and something she has acquired and cultivated throughout her life.

Not surprisingly, Alice faced a dilemma over what shoes to wear with such a bold combination, and she ended up wearing bright red wedge strappy shoes. The new aesthetic logic created by the combination of the skirt and shirt seemed to demand an equally bold and clashing choice of shoes. On seeing the outfit, Alice's younger sister exclaimed, 'what have you got on! What have you come as?' However, her elder sister reinforced Alice's decision, telling her she looked 'really cool'. Alice states that once the clothes were all on and she looked in the mirror, she felt it really matched as an outfit. It was the fact that this outfit was 'unusual and risky' that excited her about it. Alice is aware of what other people's perceptions would be and, when talking about, it refers to Trinny and Suzannah, who would see such an outfit as an abomination. Alice's exasperated response would be, 'but why can't you? You can't have rules, until you put items on you just never know ... things start working in different sorts of ways'. Here Alice makes explicit that, through making an unlikely combination, a new logic of clothing and 'what goes' is created. Interestingly, the main constraint Alice experiences in her clothing choices relates to her body shape: 'if I thought I looked too chunky I wouldn't wear it'. So intrusive and pervasive is the presentation of a homogeneous feminine ideal through media representations that Alice is unable to step outside of them. The pervasiveness of such images needs to be seen in the wider cultural context of normative ideas over gender roles, where women are associated inextricably with their bodies (Bordo, 2003). For women, 'culture's grip on the body is a constant, intimate fact of everyday life'

(Bordo, 2003: 17), seen in the micro-practices of how women walk, eat, talk, carry themselves and, of course, in how they clothe themselves. Alice is confident enough to overturn the rules of fashion, yet she is unable to overturn her sense of not being slim enough.

Conclusion

This chapter has focused upon the dual influence of fashion on women's clothing choices: it can create a fear in women of getting it wrong or allow them to be creative in assembling a new look. Very rarely did any of the women I interviewed buy a new look in its entirety from the shops; the ways in which women dress fashionably is always in relationship to the clothing they already own. As a consequence, the key relationship that women consider is how to reconcile their long-term relationship to clothing and the acquired preferences they already have with the supposedly ephemeral and shifting world of fashion. This is a concern for almost every woman I worked with. Even if they are not constantly debating over whether to look fashionable, women still have to negotiate how to incorporate new items within their wardrobe and how to change or update their look. In constructing a look that is 'now' and 'in', women are also considering whether this connects with their sense of themselves through clothing. In my ethnography, women's participation in fashion was always rooted in women's existing clothing, friendship groups and relationships.

This chapter outlined three ways in which women were innovative in the styles they created. First, in many instances, women were innovative by combining their existing clothing in new outfits. Such decisions may be influenced by women's knowledge of what is in fashion at the moment, but the actual ways in which they are innovative is by playing with their own sartorial codes and their sense of what goes. The knowledge garnered from the wider fashion media and from seeing the clothes that friends are wearing affects how women reinterpret the possibilities of their own wardrobes. This raises the second way women can be innovative, which is by connecting the clothing in their wardrobe to fashion as it is presented in the shops through seeing their friends or other people wearing fashion. As such, externally defined fashions are made accessible to women as they see them on real people. Women are able to connect their own sense of style with the official face of fashion through the mediation of friends and family.

Third, women sometimes explicitly used the external media of fashion to guide them on what to wear. Using 'rules' of dressing or following what a magazine states is 'in' at the moment allows women to navigate what to wear in the sea of multiple possibilities. Even when these rules help women alleviate the panic of dressing, they are always negotiating wearing something that makes them look and feel like themselves. The external influence of the fashion media is used by women as a guide and arises out of the basic anxieties that women have over what to wear. These rules give a sense of security but are never seen as an absolute to be copied; if they are followed religiously, they can be incredibly restrictive in terms of how women can construct themselves through clothing. In actual practice, in giving women security and confidence that they have not 'got it wrong', the rules can allow women to expand upon the possibilities of being fashionable or trying new looks.

Rather than hampering creativity, following fashion rules is often the very domain for the generation of innovatory looks. These rules cover the whole spectrum of fashion practice and are a crucial pivot in the shifting balance between individuality and conformity. This balance between creativity and constraint is a dilemma for the individual as she chooses what to wear. These rules are therefore crucial both for the woman who wants to fit in yet still be up to date, and also for the fashion innovators, who still know the rules of what should be worn together. This is the very basis of innovation—the rules are there to be broken. The women who are able to effectively manipulate the rules to be fashion innovators must, by definition, be in the minority. The fashion artist negates the fashion conformist, as the former is the vanguard of change.

–8–

Dressing Up and Dressing Down
Can You Wear Jeans?

On a daily basis, as women rush out to work or to pick up their children, they have neither the time nor the desire for dressing to be an existential crisis; as one woman stated to me, she just wanted to be able to 'be'. She wanted to look and feel like herself, without spending hours in the process. The women I interviewed managed dressing quickly through having a core group of items that are worn on a regular basis and require no thought or planning—women 'know' these items of clothing look good. This habitual relationship to clothing is how most women routinely choose what to wear, yet sometimes these safe choices can seem drab and boring, leading women to self-consciously engage with their clothing. As women try on their clothing in new combinations, they are considering whether the new outfit 'could be me', a process which more often than not ends up with women not enacting a new identity through clothing, but with women falling back on the same 'habitual' items. This dynamic between the creative possibilities of who women could be, seen in the array of items in the wardrobe, and this 'safe' self, seen in the items women end up wearing all the time, is pivotal in understanding women's clothing choices and forms the basis for this chapter.

Habitual clothing requires no extensive deliberation, as women 'know' it works; this knowledge is part of an embodied, practiced cultural competence (Mauss, 1973). This also incorporates the knowledge that the clothing is right for the social occasion, as clothing worn to the office is both appropriate for the normative codes of work, yet still fits a woman's personal aesthetic. Having different sets of clothing allows women to enact social roles. Goffman defines a role as a person's specialized capacities (1974: 128), which become a 'social role' when attached to a particular status or position (1971a: 27). Habitual clothing helps women to draw out these specialized capacities. Such roles emerge out of a more constant personal identity, which is 'perduring over time ... has a biography' (Goffman, 1974: 128–9). The implication of Goffman's theory is that women have a constant personal identity, and social roles are drawn out situationally. However, when women's identities are considered through clothing, it does not follow that when women are home alone, and thus freed from social constraints, that this is when they enact their core identity through clothing. In fact, when women are in the unseen domain of the home, they are often extremely conformist in their clothing choices. Wearing habitual clothing allows women to not have to think about their sartorial self and to conform to the norm of 'being ordinary'.

The paradox this chapter presents is that the more possibilities of the self one is offered, the more habitual and conformist it becomes. The many potential outfits in the wardrobe are often experienced as a burden of choice, as women arrive at the conclusion that they have 'nothing to wear'. As the previous chapter highlighted, the apparently infinite choice offered by late-modern consumer culture (Hyland-Eriksen, 2001) and the range of identities these offer can be experienced as a cause of anxiety, where anxiety is the 'possibility of freedom' (Kirkegaard, 1944, cited in Giddens, 1991). The freedom to construct an outfit is what often makes dressing such an anxious act, as women I worked with rarely exercised this freedom of choice, but often fell back on their core items. This anxiety is exacerbated in the context of contemporary Britain, where there is an expectation to dress 'individually'. As has been argued as far back as Durkheim, individualism is a core societal and cosmological value, as the 'religion ... of the modern individualized collectivity' (Thompson, 1998: 98). As cosmologies are defined as an idealized version of how society ought to be, they are not necessarily representative of practice (Bloch, 1989, Bloch and Parry, 1982, Lan, 1989). When seen in a British context, cosmological notions such as individualism can, by the same token, be understood as hortative rather than descriptive; we are all expected to have an individual self to express through a medium such as clothing. The 'idea of culture' (Douglas, 1991: 134) becomes the 'idea of the self' (213), as unitary and unique. Yet what women actually wear falls in clear contrast to the discourse of individual expression, as most women do not have the time, or even the inclination, to externalize a unique self all the time, and they fall back on habitual clothing.

Being Yourself, Changing Yourself

Irrespective of women's backgrounds, how much money they have or what their background is, all women I worked with had some items they wear all of the time and some items they wear rarely. On average, the range of items that women are selecting from on a daily basis—their 'active' wardrobe—is less than 38 per cent. Most women sub-divide their clothing into 'home', 'work' and 'going-out' clothing, which makes very small the actual number of items that women are choosing from to go to work or to go out. One of the defining features of habitual clothing is that women are comfortable wearing it, as items women have lived in and which soften with the body. Items that are worn rarely do not permit the same 'comfort', as the unfamiliarity of the item on the body engenders a self-conscious awareness of wearing the item of clothing. All women I interviewed owned both types of clothing, yet the degree to which women relied on habitual clothing varied. Clare is an example of someone whose relationship to her clothing is extremely habitual. She is in her late twenties and doing an MA in fine art. She was born in the South of England and now lives in Nottingham in a terraced house with her boyfriend, who works as a night porter for a security firm. She spends most days working from home, going in to university a couple of days a week; every day she wears a pair of jeans or black cords with a loose t-shirt and a jumper for cooler weather. Her act of getting ready in the morning is rapid, selecting whichever t-shirt is on top of the pile in her chest of drawers, and similarly the pair of jeans or trousers that are easiest to access. If she is going in to university, she often dresses in a smarter manner, and so puts on one of her fitted black shirts (she has six of them).

When she is getting ready to go out in the evenings, she spends more time deliberating over what to wear. On most occasions, she ends up falling back on her pair of embroidered jeans and one of her smarter black shirts. She says, 'I can always wear my black shirts, they go with everything'. The black shirts and the jeans which define her habitual wear are worn all the time as they go with everything, alleviating the burden of assemblage. Although she has one wardrobe in which she hangs her clothes and two chests of drawers (each with four drawers), this range of items does not make dressing easier for her; rather, it causes her to fall back on 'reliable' items. Like many other women I interviewed, Clare does not even consider the majority of her clothes when choosing an outfit. Simmel (1971) has argued that, in modern society, the sheer quantity of consumer goods leads to our incapacity to appropriate these items of 'objective culture' in the development of subjective culture. In the case of the wardrobe, women are faced with a personal collection—and, as such, an appropriated form of objective culture. Even when women are faced with this 'subjective culture' of their clothing, they are often so overwhelmed with this choice that they end up falling back on tried and trusted combinations.

Because her black shirts have been worn routinely, they become something she knows she can rely on. Habitual clothing therefore forms part of Goffman's discussion of how everyday appearance (1971a), along with actions and gestures, is a way in which social stability is established. When Clare wears her black shirts, she knows they look good, she feels right in them and wearing them is a way of establishing 'ontological security' (Giddens, 1991)—that is, a sense of security in who she is, as she knows these shirts are 'me'. She feels physically comfortable wearing the shirt, as the fabric does not make her feel too hot, and she is able to move her body in it. Comfort arises out of the materiality of the fabric and the style of the clothing; yet, as she has worn it so many times, she also 'knows' how to wear it. Dressing is an acquired competence and skill, as part of wider bodily self-management. Goffman (1971b: 248) notes that any gesture or activity will have been awkward or difficult when first tried, even activities so taken for granted such as walking and tying one's shoes. It is only through doing something repetitively over a period of time that a practice becomes naturalized. This routine relationship is also embodied and material, as habitual clothing is no longer awkward or worn in a self-conscious manner.

Clare feels comfortable in the shirt as it fits her sense of herself; equally important is the need to 'fit in' on particular social occasions. Ordinarily, Clare goes out to the pub with her boyfriend and his friends; however, her ordinary confidence was disturbed on the occasion of her new work friends inviting her out for the first time on a 'girls' night out'. She was used to going out with the same group of people, and, as most of these were men, she had not been out with a group of women for several years. The anxiety increased as she perceived all the women to be much slimmer than she was and as dressing up in a very 'glamorous, girly' way. Clare describes them as the 'kind of people that get their nails done every week and go to the hairdressers every other week'. Clare comes from a relatively poor background and never had many clothes purchased for her; she is the first person in her family to go to university and funded it all herself with loans and part-time jobs. Clare has always bought things from designer discount stores or cheap mail-order catalogues. Now that she works in a high street shop, she buys things for work from there as her 'uniform' but sees it as 'very middle-class and older'. She has a definite sense of herself as being different from these women in terms of their style, personalities and ideals of femininity. Before the night out, the women at work discuss what they will be wearing and new items they have bought. Ordinarily, Clare would have worn a black shirt and jeans to go out in. However, listening to their gossip and plans of outfits, she starts to think maybe she should try something new. Resolved to wear her jeans, she considers buying a 'dressy' top from the shop she works in with her discount. She considers a few sleeveless tops—one with silver glitter on it, another pink with flowers on it—all items she considers appropriate for a night out 'with the girls'. In the end, everything she tries on 'was what they would wear, not me. I'm not that kind of girl'. In trying on the items in the shop, Clare is all too aware that she cannot just 'buy' an identity in the shops, as post-modern theorizing would suggest (Featherstone, 1991). Instead, as Skeggs (2004) has argued, what matters is not just the item itself but also having the appropriate embodied cultural competences to wear it. Barnes and Eicher have argued that dress is something which helps to create a communal identity, as it 'includes and excludes' (1993: 1). For Clare, being 'included' does not just entail wearing the right assemblage of clothing; 'getting it right' is also a matter of demeanour and having the right body to wear the outfit.

As she considered the various tops, it emphasized Clare's sense of otherness from the women at work; she feels herself to be an outsider not only from the group of women but also from the femininity they embody. Skeggs (1997) has argued that the ideal of femininity has been constructed historically as middle-class and white. In her ethnography, she found that, when working-class women 'try on femininity they often feel it is the wrong size. It was designed for someone with a different bodily shape' (1997: 100). Clare experiences this in terms of her actual body, as she perceives a discrepancy between her reflected image and the slim silhouette of the other women. She also feels femininity does not fit her sense of herself as a woman. Skeggs's research cites examples of women 'trying it out' on a night out, as 'fun', or in order to make them feel good about themselves, as they distance themselves from the sexual and bring themselves closer to 'being respectable'. However, for Clare, she was not going out with women in a similar position of 'trying it on'. For the other women, this is the femininity they routinely performed on a night out.

Her sense of being an outsider to the group became even more marked on the actual night out, as she felt uncomfortable in the situation. Instead of her jeans bought from work marking her as an insider who shops at the right places, when she told the other women the jeans were from the shop they worked in, she felt that they looked down on her: 'they obviously thought "she can't afford anything else, she has to get it on discount"'. Whilst Clare felt uncomfortable on this occasion, the discomfort arose not from feeling she had got it wrong, but rather that she did not fit in to the social group. Clare briefly considered conforming to her perception of what the others thought she 'ought to wear'. However, she has such an entrenched sense of her self through clothing and what she knows she can wear, that, in the end, she falls back on her most habitual items: a black shirt and a pair of jeans. The clothing fits her sense of her self, but not the occasion.

Whenever possible, Clare wears clothing that she feels comfortable in. The only occasions when she breaks out of this routinized relationship to clothing is when particular events have explicit dress codes to which she knows she has to conform, such as a ball or a wedding. Within her wardrobe she has five outfits that have only been worn once; each of the dresses were bought with a specific occasion in mind, and, whilst they are all items that mark a contrast to her usual clothing, they are all items she felt good wearing. For example, the outfit she wore to her graduation ball forms an example of a particularly cherished outfit, consisting of a matching halter-neck top and skirt, made of bronze-coloured silk. The top is fitted and covered with bronze sequins; the result is a sparkling and detailed contouring of her body. The skirt fits tightly around the waist and hips and then falls in an A-line shape to the floor. The skirt is made of silk with a thin gauze layer on top, and so when the material folds it has the appearance of an oil slick, the folds appearing like a dash of white lightning. When worn, the rigid folds of the plentiful skirt brush against the legs, and the raw silk rustles with every step. Having been worn only once, the outfit encapsulates the memory of this one event, the first ball Clare had ever been to, which she still talks about with animated excitement. Wearing a formal skirt and the skimpy top that glitters and sparkles, a consciousness of the outfit was engendered in her when she wore it. Thurgood Haynes (1998), writing on debutantes' dresses, discusses how the ornate jeweled and beaded corseted robes enables a physical and psychological transformation in the wearer. Similarly, the sequins on Clare's dress dazzle in the lights, and the rigidity of the fabric materialize a transformation in Clare, who self-consciously engages with her image through an outfit that makes her look and feel very different. Ordinarily, she wears the same clothes all the time, yet here Clare dresses to conform to particular conventions; her embodied relationship to the physical item of clothing is such that she not only looks but also feels different.

I'm a Woman Now! Conforming to the Normative

Clare's ball dress is a classic example of non-habitual clothing; as she is not used to wearing it, it falls in contrast to her ordinary self through clothing. In conforming to the expectations of the event, the material relationship she has to the clothing allows different facets of herself to be materialized: she felt 'elegant, glamorous'. As I found with other women I interviewed, women often use normative dress codes not to repress who they 'really' are, but as a means to expand upon themselves. Marie, a twenty-eight-year-old who lives with a male friend and works in a book store, owns hardly any event or going-out clothing. She has a range of trousers and shirts that she wears to work and a selection of casual t-shirts and jeans that she wears at home or out to the pub. As she goes to the pub with her flat-mate or with a few close friends or her sisters, it is not an occasion for her to dress up. She has just one special outfit which she bought especially for a formal charity dinner to which she was invited. She had contemplated wearing some black clothes she already had, but a couple of friends insisted that she had to buy a dress, and they managed to cajole her into it. The purchase she eventually made was a knee-length strappy black dress. The straps and the top part of the dress—which is cut into a bra-cup shape—are made of satin. The rest of the dress hangs loosely and is made of black polyester. As she owned no other dresses, buying the dress was 'a bit of an ordeal, I mean it was nice to buy but I didn't really know what I was doing. Also I had to buy the shoes, a pair of stockings, and a strapless bra. It's like everything that goes with this dress, not just the dress!'

She jokes about the dress that now she is 'turning into a real woman'. She has never owned such a dress, and she had to stand and walk in a different way when she wore it (because she was wearing heels and not wearing trousers). Moreover, she admits she felt different, more 'feminine'. The outfit is, in fact, extremely conventional in its femininity and what many women would consider an 'easy', comfortable outfit to wear. In his discussion of modern family life in the West, Gillis points to the discrepancy between the idealized model family as perpetuated through myths and rituals and the actual families we live with (1996: xv). The former becomes an idealized model, as a reference point for the actual everyday practices of family life (also discussed in Miller, 2001). Similarly here, Marie has never done 'being a woman' or 'feminine' before and attempts it by utilizing the normative model of conventional femininity, which is not how most women dress most of the time. For many women, 'being a woman' is not something self-consciously engaged with, and it becomes part of their everyday practice. Iris Marion Young (2005) makes a distinction between being 'female' and being 'feminine'. Marie had always been female in the sense of her lived embodied relationship to her gender, yet she was not explicitly feminine (2005: 6) in the sense of adhering to the social conventions and constraints of femininity. On this occasion, she adheres to these conventions of 'making herself pretty'; as she is attempting it for the first time, she selects her outfit in reference to the most normative femininity in order to transform herself. This example, in common with all of the others, shows that characteristic of clothing that will 'transform' the wearer is that it falls in distinction to the rest of the wardrobe. Marie is able to transform herself through the most normative clothing, as she opens up new possibilities for her feminine self.

Conforming Individuality

In Marie's case, the rarely worn event wear allows her to try out a new identity through clothing; for other women, event wear, and the corresponding dress codes, can activate aspects of the self that are not present normally. Kaiser (2003: 186) has defined identity as the 'organised set of characteristics an individual perceives as representing or defining the self in a given social situation'. Dressing involves situating the self in a social context, and so the clothing codes of social occasions allow the enactment of particular identities. Sonya is a British Asian woman in her early thirties and lives with her partner, who works as an accountant, in a home that they own in South London. When she is at home writing up her doctoral thesis, she wears the same clothes day in and day out, tending to wear baggy trousers and fitted high-neck tops (she never reveals any flesh, often not even wearing sleeveless tops) in dark colours. Occasions when she is called upon to wear something different are moments for intense deliberation and trying on of outfits in front of the wardrobe. On such social occasions, she has to consider herself in a 'seen' context. Usually when she is at home, she does not concern herself with looking 'individual'. It is the social occasion that means she is called upon to be an individual, with the ensuing normative expectations that she will dress in a unique manner that best expresses her self. The relationship between conformity and individuality is therefore necessarily oppositional. In his discussion of the development of modern life, Simmel (1971) raises this tension between looking the same and looking different as he identifies two forms of individualism. First, individualism is defined as equality, when people are freed from social constraints and hierarchies and therefore free to dress in the same manner. The second form characterizes modern life, and here individuality is equated with being unique and looking different from everyone else. For Simmel, these two forms of individuality are subsequent historical developments. However, when they are taken together, they raise the possibility that there is a cultural expectation to look 'individual', in this case meaning unique. Yet when this expectation is considered at the level of practice, how people actually dress is often extremely similar to one another and therefore relates to the other notion of individualism, where everyone is free to dress the same. People both conform to what others are wearing and the expectations of an event, and, even when they are striving to look 'unique', this is still an act of conforming to the discourse of individuality.

The ways in which people attempt to dress individually will be interrogated further through considering Sonya's event wear, most of which are what she calls 'pieces' bought from an antique clothing shop, such as a 1940s jacket, a 1950s Chinese jacket or a 1930s embroidered waistcoat. The waistcoat is made of black heavy wool, with a wide band of gold embroidery and beading around the neck. It is, in fact, a men's item (Sonya is very small and svelte), which means that it hangs straight down off her shoulders. Sonya does not wear anything under it, and wears a pair of navy or grey cropped trousers with it—making it 'funky' rather than staid. She has worn it to a twenty-first birthday party and to an engagement party. As she rarely has a chance to wear it, she states that she wishes she had a display cabinet to put it in. The item of clothing is valued through aesthetic distance, even when it is worn. The body beneath is neither revealed nor the focus of attention. As discussed in the chapter on personal aesthetics, Rosie's experiences of the failed outfit make her conscious of the heaviness of the leather skirt. In her case, the feeling of the externality of the item is experienced as a negative, as the item was meant to be an 'easy' one she could rely on to make her feel good. In Sonya's case—and indeed characteristic of event wear' more widely—is that such items are supposed to make the wearer conscious of wearing them. Once they become 'comfortable' and fused with the wearer, they are by definition then habitual wear.

Such items compose a large part of Sonya's event wear, yet another major constituent of this type of clothing is her 'Indian' clothing. She was born in a suburb of London, having only lived in India for a while when she was at school, yet both her parents are Indian. Having refused to wear such clothing when she was younger, now in her early thirties, she recently went to India for the first time without her parents and has now started to wear more Indian clothing, much to the delight of her mother. She would never wear such items as casual wear and only wears them on smarter occasions. In fact this relationship to her Indian clothing is the same as one of my other main informants, Mumtaz, whose parents are originally from India. Mumtaz has a vast selection of Indian clothing, which she wore habitually in India; now living in London again, she only wears them to weddings or other formal occasions. The formal occasion involves an evocation of traditional wear, and equally in a context where most people do not wear such clothing, the wearing of what appears to be traditional clothes that conform is in fact 'individual'. For Sonya, such Indian clothing has never been her habitual wear as it was for Mumtaz, and she bought several outfits on her recent trip to India with her partner. She is already planning to wear one of the outfits she bought to a wedding. The top is made of gold silk, with bronze and navy blue floral embroidery; the loose, long skirt and scarf are made of navy blue chiffon silk with gold embroidered flowers. She loves the 'old, vintage, antique-y look' of the top; rather than this solely being conceptualized as an 'Indian' top, the aesthetic of it is something which fits with Sonya's ordinary event wear style, typically purchased from the antique shop.

Event wear is only worn at social occasions in the presence of other people, not at home alone. It is on such social occasions, when subject to the gaze of others, that a unique look is forced by the occasion. Sonya professes that what she loves about her 1930s waistcoat is that it excites a great deal of comment for being so unusual. The paradox being that, in looking unique, she is conforming to this reified notion of the 'individual'. One of the ways in which Sonya makes herself appear individual is through wearing her Indian clothing. On a daily basis, in her habitual clothing, her ethnicity is not made visible through her clothing. As Stuart Hall has argued (2005: 94), whilst everyone is situated in terms of ethnicity, this is not something that is always given explicit recognition. On some occasions, ethnicity may form part of the self-conscious creation of an identity position. So too here, Sonya's ethnicity is not something which she makes visible through clothing on an everyday basis. However, in wearing such outfits, she is able to use her ethnicity as a resource; the clothing mobilizes facets of her self and family past that she chooses not to emphasise ordinarily. She is simultaneously able to look different, yet still be herself. She manages to conform to the generalized and abstract ideal of having a unique self, through her particular resources and enactment of her ethnicity.

Work, Home and Play: Where is the Real Me?

Habitual clothing and non-habitual clothing both answer and address different concerns with identity that women have. Women know that habitual clothing is 'safe', whereas non-habitual clothing that women rarely wear speaks to concerns over whether this 'could' be me. Usually non-habitual clothing is items worn to particular events, and as such it has been discussed so far in terms of the normative expectations of events. Women often wear such items to conform to particular social occasions; often the dress codes become a means through which women can 'try out' particular identities. Inasmuch as event wear involves situating the self in a particular social situation, so too habitual clothing, such as work clothing, involves similar sartorial codes. Even though habitual clothing is characterized as something women know 'is me', when they wear the same favourite shift dress to work, they are still dressing to fit in to a particular social role. As women occupy several social roles, they also have several corresponding sets of habitual clothing. Like almost every woman I interviewed, Margaret, a married primary school teacher in her early thirties living in North London, has three main domains of habitual clothing: work, home and going-out clothing. Her work clothing is worn daily and all conforms to a particular type: a fitted shirt with grey or black loose-fitting trousers. All of her tops and shirts worn to work have collars, something which serves to adequately formalize the item. Her central concern at work is how to remain both comfortable and also to be taken seriously as a woman at work. She berates the headmistress at her school for wearing a puffer jacket and a bum-bag: 'why didn't she just get a handbag, like any other woman?' Margaret rarely wears skirts to work, finding them a 'hassle'; yet she manages her femininity through the carrying of a handbag and wearing fitted shirts in colours such as lilac.

Margaret uses her work clothing to draw out aspects of her personality, or 'capacities' in Goffman's sense, which are appropriate for particular social roles. She also uses clothing to submerge aspects of the self that are not pertinent to that role—for example, a shirt that is too low-cut or tight would be considered inappropriate as her sexuality is not an aspect of her work self. Putting on her work clothing is also part of how she 'frames' the situation as work (Goffman, 1974). When she puts on her work trousers and shirt at home, she is already preparing herself for the work environment; this involves both how she is supposed to appear and how she should behave. This act of 'framing' work is also an act of 'bracketing out' (Garfinkel, 1984)—that is, defining the work context as separate from and different than other domains. She does this through her clothing as she divides her clothing into three main sections: her work, home and going-out clothing. She does this to the extent that her work clothing is never worn out, even though many of her home trousers and going-out trousers are very similar in style (loose, baggy with a drawstring waist in dark colours). Not mixing work and home clothing enables Margaret to draw a boundary between the two aspects of her life; she admits she finds it very 'useful ... makes life easier' to keep these clothes separate. As soon as she returns home from work, she always changes into jeans or casual trousers, a t-shirt and her grey Timberland fleece. As Nippert-Eng (1996) points out, people, through material means, attempt to draw boundaries between different domains as 'territories of the self'.

This act of separating out becomes important as women often consider one of these to be the 'real' me. Most women I interviewed tended to see their authentic self in their home clothing or, more often for younger women, their going-out clothing. Even though no women I interviewed saw work as where the 'real me' resided, women did still personalize their work outfits—seen, for example, in the colours Margaret picks for her work shirts. Women are able to manage the 'role-distance' (Goffman, 1974) through incorporating both social expectations and personal preferences; even if the clothing was still separated out as being for work, by incorporating a sense of a woman's own style, it was not worn as a uniform. Interestingly, women often saw work as not being a place where they could enact a core identity, as one woman stated to me you are very 'restricted' in terms of how you can behave and, indeed, what you can wear. The implication is that the social expectations that are part of the work environment produce a conformity that impedes women's ability to freely express themselves. In light of this, it would follow, then, that, when women are home alone and completely unrestricted by social codes, they would wear their most expressive or individual clothing. However, when we actually consider what women wear when they are alone in the house, it is amazing how similar the styles of clothing are: tracksuit bottoms, jeans, hoodies. On one level, this is due to practicalities, but it also raises the possibility that rather than the 'real me' being an individual, in fact it is extremely conformist. It is not that the outside world forces women to conform, but rather that in many instances it places the burden of individuality on women, a burden women can alleviate when they are home alone.

This raises an interesting issue between how often women wear clothing and what kind of identities this constructs. Habitual clothing, by being worn all of the time, externalizes a routinized, safe and comfortable self. Yet for a couple of women I interviewed, the clothing that they saw as the most closely aligned with their core identity was their 'fantasy' items of clothing—clothing they never wore except when trying it on in the bedroom. Such items included the glittery ball gown when the woman has no occasion to wear it or a 'fairy skirt' the woman sees herself as too old to wear. In seeing these as the 'real' me, these women are recognizing, albeit implicitly, that the items of clothing they actually wear on a day-to-day basis is extremely conforming. Instead these items women never wear are separated from social conventions and the expectations of others. These examples, although vastly the minority, demonstrate that an understanding of identity through clothing needs to be considered through clothing women wear all the time and through the clothing women rarely wear. These fantasy items, by definition, externalize a completely different self to the safe self that is embedded in their routine clothing.

Changing the Real Me

Habitual clothing is useful for allowing women to just 'be', to carry on in an un-self-conscious routinized relationship to their clothing. However, choosing what to wear is not just the perpetuation of habitual selves. On numerous occasions within my fieldwork, women told me they were bored of their clothing and tired of wearing the same 'easy' things all the time. The occasion for a new outfit often arises from such moments of boredom, from a change in the work situation, a new love interest, the desire for promotion or the arrival of a new and funky colleague. Through combining 'safe' items with new ones, women are able to adapt or redefine these habitual selves. Patsy, a single woman in her early thirties, is someone for whom the process of deciding what to wear in the morning is at times agonizing, often making her late for work. Every weekend, she plans what she will wear on Monday and Tuesday, and the process of getting ready is easy and quick. As she becomes more exhausted by the rigours of the working week and the inevitable socializing that follows her working day, towards the end of the week the process of decision making becomes more agonizing and elongated. On such occasions, Patsy often ends up wearing her knee-high fabric black boots, a denim skirt and a black belted cardigan.

The boots are by far the most foundational item in her winter wardrobe, which she admits to 'living in', wearing them almost daily, only changing into shoes on the rare occasions she can force herself out of her boots, for fear of them becoming ruined. The boots are an assumed starting point for her selection of an outfit, as is the cardigan, which is a key style for Patsy, seen in its omni-presence in both her summer and winter wardrobes, in a variety of colours. Because these items are pretty much a 'given' if she cannot decide what to wear, the first item she actively decides upon is whether to wear one of her denim skirts or one of her other A-line skirts she often falls back on. The final item she decides upon is the top, which, in the winter, is usually either a polo-neck or a long-sleeved t-shirt style fitted top. Getting ready for work inevitably involves such a trajectory, from the boots and cardigan that she knows she can absolutely rely on, to the active choice of one of her habitual skirts, and finally the top which is selected in reference to the skirt as the whole outfit is pieced together.

She dresses like this most days and is someone who adores clothing, seen in her vast wardrobe; yet there are occasions when she forces herself out of this routine. On one particular occasion in late February, feeling she needed a mid-week perk and deadened by wearing black and dull colours all winter, she decided to wear a new lime green ribbed, fitted polo-neck. As the item is new, there was no pre-determined outfit. On this occasion, instead of pre-assuming the most habitual item she owns, the boots, she started off with the most exciting: the new green jumper. She decided that, as the jumper was so vibrant, she should wear one of her denim skirts. However, since she had six denim skirts, choosing the right one proved problematic. She initially concluded that an A-line knee-length one was appropriate, as she knows this shape goes with the boots; her 'usual' work one was in the wash, which left her with a choice of two. One she professes to be her 'favourite', but more as an evening or summer skirt; she decided to try on anyway. It is indigo denim, with a front slit to the top of the thighs. Thinking it would be fine with black opaque tights, not showing excess leg, she tried it on, but just 'didn't feel like that today. It's not right'. Disheartened, she looks at the other one and remembers that it makes her look 'hip-y'. Although initially appearing to be identical to the first one she tried on—knee length, dark inky denim, yet with a smaller slit—in fact across the front there is a horizontal seam (just below the front pockets, which goes all around the front of the skirt). On the body, this seam sits at the widest part of the hips, which Patsy feels draws attention to them. She did not even try this one on. Still adamant she will wear the green jumper, she rummages through her cupboard and encounters an ankle-length, A-line denim skirt, with a slit at the back; this is the item she ends up wearing. 'I can always rely on this one!' The 'easiness' and reliability of the item is based upon its fabric and shape, and the A-line style of the skirt means that width is created by the fabric, serving to minimize her hips. Furthermore, this is one that is 'tried and trusted'—worn so often it is known to work and assimilated into habitual wear.

On this occasion the ordinary trajectory is inverted, as the most exciting item is the first one chosen, and the most habitual ones are tried on last. This sequence is in fact quite common for women when they want to break out of their normal patterns. They enforce a change by selecting a single new or special item from which subsequent habitual items must be matched. The 'special' item is then made wearable and comfortable by being teamed with safe habitual items. The only way in which Patsy is able to lift her mood is by forcing the habitual to take second place, to get out of what she perceives as the drabness of selections. Patsy is able to perk up her mood and be noticed in a slightly different outfit, yet still feel comfortable in her 'classic items'. Importantly, this also enables her to transform the unseen context of work into a seen one. Ordinarily, as she dresses the same every day, she does not dress to be noticed as she falls back on 'safe' clothing, which in effect may diminish the self through such conforming acts. On this occasion, she does not make herself noticed by disrupting the normative and dressing inappropriately for work. Instead, she self-consciously engages with her habitual clothing, which is usually defined by being un-thought-out. In the act of dressing, she temporarily makes her habitual clothing non-habitual.

Denim: Fitting in, Feeling Like Me

In dressing, women have to negotiate a series of often opposing factors: the expectation to conform, yet still looking like themselves; to be seen, yet to still feel comfortable; to wear clothing that is safe and fits normative expectations, yet is still interesting and exciting. Often in the face of such burdens and expectations women fall back on the habitual, yet the very routine nature of habitual wear serves to perpetuate the feelings of drabness and dullness. Patsy deals with this through combining the 'safe' and the new; this tactic ensures that she feels comfortable in her clothing yet is able to enact a small change in her habitual clothing. The fact that Patsy chooses a denim skirt as her 'safe' item is not surprising given the dominance of denim in almost all of the wardrobes I looked at, as many women 'live' in jeans. Because denim is seen to go with everything, it is often used as a way to introduce new items into women's active wardrobes, and indeed of resolving panicked moments of dressing.

Denim is a heavy twill fabric, woven with tightly twisted cotton yarns. As a result of such tight twisting of the cotton yarns, the density of the fibres results in an extremely strong, hardy and structured fabric (popularized first in the eighteenth and nineteenth centuries by manual labourers). The fabric is able to maintain its shape and is therefore capable of structuring the body beneath. Many women I worked with talked of their search for the perfect pair of jeans; a search which seems incredible given the quantity of pairs of jeans owned by these women. Patsy has four pairs of jeans, only one of which she wears regularly. None of these jeans are designer label or particularly expensive, but she confides that she tries on jeans in almost all retail outlets she visits. If she found this 'perfect' pair, she says she would spend 'anything'. She has the exact mental image: 'in my mind everything would fit really nicely. As I'm quite pear shaped, I need ones that minimize my hips. Low cut are the best. They have to be boot-legs, they make me look so much more proportioned. And my legs look longer!' She pictures not only the jeans, but the body they would give her. One of the pivotal concerns women have when they are assessing an outfit in the mirror is the body that the clothing gives them. Gunter and Wykes have argued that, to varying degrees, the majority of women at some point suffer from body image dissatisfaction, which they define as the 'discrepancy between the perceived self and the ideal self' (Gunter and Wykes, 2005: 4). Patsy knows what her actual body shape is, yet she also knows what her ideal body shape is (her mental picture of her body, Kaiser, 2003: 98), and moreover sees it as achievable in the right pair of jeans. She feels that her hips are out of proportion to the rest of her body, and the perfect jeans would give her the perfect silhouette through the positioning of the back pocket. Furthermore, through denim's structuring effect, the fabric would hold in the flesh of her bottom. The fantasy of jeans for Patsy, and many other women I interviewed, entails the fantasy of altering the shape of the body.

Jeans are not only cherished for their ability to structure the body, but also because of their ability to soften and age with the wearer. When the cotton fibres are spun into yarns to make denim, the yarns are so tightly wound that when the fibres are dyed with indigo, only the surface fibres are dyed (Corbman, 1985, Hatch, 1993). Therefore, as jeans are worn, the darkened surface of the fibres is gradually eroded to reveal the white core of the fabric. The more the surface is abraded through wearing, the more the jeans lose their colour, making the embodied act of wearing evident as soft white cotton strings appear across the knees and the bottom. As the cotton yarns are so tightly wound, when denim is first worn it is coarse and rough to the touch, yet the nature of denim changes as it is worn, as the soft white cotton emerges, softening the fabric. Not surprisingly, a number of women I interviewed cited their most comfortable item of clothing as an aging pair of jeans. As the wearer changes, so to do the jeans, softening with age. They hold the body shape, the sweat and the smell of the wearer. Herein lies part of the endless appeal of jeans: they are widespread as a style, yet the generic is simultaneously personalized through this material propensity to age. Through this process of softening as the person wears them, the jeans have a shared biography with the wearer. So important is this process of aging that now many jeans are enzyme washed, an industrial process that, through chemical abrasion of the surface, artificially replicates the long-term processes of wear and tear.

Denim therefore allows women to feel they fit in by being a generic, widely accepted type of clothing and also the item that is the most personalized. Denim's capacity to do this arises out of its being worn on the body and how it is manufactured and designed. Since the arrival of denim jeans in the late nineteenth century, denim's core identity has remained constant: the distinctive fabric, manufactured in a particular way to achieve structured degradation and the colour (despite the odd fashion for other coloured jeans, blue remains a constant). Irrespective of the vagaries of fashion, denim remains a permanent fixture in the worn wardrobe. Denim is also a fabric amenable to many processes and finishes. Finishes such as stone washing and enzyme washing, both of which produce a distinctive worn finish, enable fashions to be incorporated within the constant of the denim jeans. Now the sole constituent of denim is not only cotton but also polyamide or elastane (Lycra®), which can be integrated into the fibres to give the fabric elasticity, adding further dimensions to its material capacities. The safety and the reliability of jeans are maintained, yet through the details of the processes or practices such as embroidery, they can still be funky and cutting-edge. Through the styling and the processes and details, jeans are able to be exciting, yet still safe. For many women, jeans are a staple of the practical day wardrobe—being hardy, easy to wash and having high combinational potential—and they are also a key item of evening wear.

Jeans resolve one of the fundamental contradictions involved in choosing what to wear: to be able to conform to social categories of acceptability, yet still to be yourself. In the protean shifts of fashion and the multiplicity of items that magazines claim to be 'in fashion' at any given time, denim is stability and certainty. As something that almost everyone wears regularly, most women 'know' how to wear denim jeans. It is therefore 'comfortable'. Moreover, although denim has a stable, core identity which is historically unshaken, the variety of cuts, processes and detailing available allow the wearer to feel individual in her selection. As the item, once chosen, becomes worn all the time, the wearer and jeans age symbiotically. As the body becomes less taut and softer, so too jeans unwind as the fabric relaxes and softens to the touch. Jeans are therefore personalized and differentiated through the individual acts of wearing.

Conclusions

This chapter has argued that the core dynamic of getting dressed is between the habitual clothing women wear all of the time and clothing that is worn rarely and allows women to transform themselves. This discussion sheds light on why women wear denim all the time. Denim allows women to fit in, given that it is so widely worn and is not restricted to any particular sub-culture or group. At the same time, it fits women's sense of self; worn regularly, women are comfortable wearing it. As it is worn on the body, it is no longer just a generic normative code of acceptability, but the very act of wearing is an act of personalization. Denim jeans are therefore 'comfortable' as they age with the wearer and carry the imprint of the person's body. Further, because denim is seen to go with everything, through acts of combination, women are able to combine it creatively with new items. The wearing of denim therefore allows contradictions in the self through clothing.

Contradictions are allowed in the wardrobe through the presence of habitual and non-habitual clothing. Having the full range of clothing in the wardrobe helps women to consider fundamental identity questions, such as the self they are confident they can be, the 'safe' self and the self they aspire to being. Habitual clothing, as something which women know they can wear, is by definition un-self-conscious and therefore enables women to not have to engage with any active questioning of identity. When faced with the potentially disorienting potentials of who they could be, they fall back on what they know. As habitual items have been worn often and become personalized through wearing, a symbiotic relationship between body and clothing develops. Habitual items often have been worn so many times that they have softened and become fitted to the body shape. In contrast, the relationship between body and wearer that event wear engenders actively encourages women to engage with questions of identity. As these items are rarely worn and are often more rigid and materially elaborate, the items remain external to the wearer, as women are conscious of the items. This division impacts upon the moment of dressing. The wearing of non-habitual items involves a self-conscious engagement with the question 'is this me?', as women deliberate over the potentialities of themselves in the external form of clothing. Non-habitual clothing forces a reflective engagement with the clothed body. With habitual items, women just assume it is 'me', unless this is disrupted by a particular event.

Through looking at habitual and non-habitual clothing and the interplay between the two, this chapter has challenged the widespread cultural discourse that conformity is in opposition to individuality. Rather than individuality being oppressed by social expectations, two important points have emerged from this ethnography. First, individuality itself is a social expectation; on particular occasions, women have to conform to the cultural norm of 'being an individual'. Therefore, individuality is an aspect of the self, rather than the self in its entirety. Inasmuch as Goffman argues that being a mother can be a social role, what I have argued in this chapter is that so too is 'being ordinary' or 'being an individual'. Second, women are almost always dressing for social occasions, and, as such, I found that conforming to social expectations can allow women to expand upon themselves. However, on other occasions, just as women expand on themselves through social relationships, they also do this through normative expectations of the sort of person they think they could be.

In considering the coexistence of issues such as individuality and conformity, safety and creativity, it is necessary to situate what women actually choose to wear in the context of the whole range of items women have in their wardrobe. Dressing crucially involves the tension between the un-thought-out embodied self that women enact daily and the possibilities and potentials of who they think they could be. The wardrobe has hanging within it a range of items—some forgotten about, some rarely worn but that women wish they could wear and others that are worn all the time. The clothing in the wardrobe therefore consists of all parameters of the self: being an individual, fitting in, the person one is all the time, who one was, who one wishes she could be. The self through all of the clothing in the wardrobe is full of many contradictory attributes which may or may not be present on particular occasions. This is perhaps why clothing is so central and apt in attempts to create and externalize the self, as it is able to make present and submerge aspects of the self. Clothing, as a material form, gives women the sensation of having a self, including a self with agency. Through clothing, women attempt to create themselves; when successful, women have a sense that this is 'me'. This 'me' is present by virtue of being materialized, and indeed partially created, through the clothing. A crucial part of this process of self-creation involves a creative interplay between habitual and non-habitual clothing; women may be both conformist and regress to safety, yet simultaneously creatively inject themselves into this interplay as they may critique their conformist selves through clothing.

Conclusions

Why do women wear what they wear? The common-sense answer might be that this is determined by what is in fashion, what is present in high street shops or what is being worn by celebrities. This book, however, offers an alternative explanation, which is based upon the original approach of looking not at what is on sale in the shops, but at how women choose what to wear on an everyday basis in their bedrooms. This ethnography of a seemingly mundane, daily practice demonstrates the multiple and overlapping factors that women negotiate in constructing their appearances. This complexity and uncertainty is often not apparent from women's publicly presented selves, and so this book argues that the answer to the question why women wear what they wear lies in the process of how women make clothing choices. The wardrobe itself is characterized by contradiction, as women see all of the different aspects of their social selves hanging before them. The wardrobe presents women with both the possibilities and also the limitations of who they are and who they wish they could be. On a daily basis, women attempt to actualize these diverse possibilities in an outfit that is suitable for the occasion of dressing; once items of clothing are taken from the wardrobe, they are held against the body or tried on as women deliberate over their mirror image. When a woman's idealized image of who she could be gives way to uncertainty when she sees her actual image, this questioning of the self continues, and the woman goes back to the wardrobe to reimagine herself, and the process continues. Through looking at these equivocations, ambivalences, ambiguities and the ways women change their minds about their clothes, it is possible to understand the complex process through which women decide what to wear. In as much as women's clothing choices are not determined by what is in the shops, nor are they determined by what is hanging in the wardrobe, as women have agency in balancing the possibilities and constraints of their individual and social identities.

Women's sense of who they are is not derived from the glamorous world of celebrity or high fashion, but is enacted through the routine and everyday acts of getting dressed. Women perform, reiterate and question this sense of themselves through the minutiae of the everyday, as they move between the wardrobe and the mirror and try on different outfits. To access the complexity of this process, it was necessary to carry out an ethnography which emphasized detail and depth rather than attempting to be representative of all women. The emphasis was not only on what women choose to wear, but also how they choose items and reject others. Through looking at the practice of getting dressed, and the process of identity construction, my argument is that underpinning all of these seemingly diverse concerns women negotiate when dressing is the pivotal dynamic between the clothing women wear all the time and clothing women rarely wear. This dynamic is so central to women's clothing choices that it is common to all of the women I worked with, irrespective of their social background or position. They all negotiate this tension between anxiety and possibility and between safety and creativity. Differences in women's social positions, such as their ethnicity, are, on occasion, very important to women. Such factors impact upon the way in which these tensions are experienced and which particular item of clothing women choose to wear. A woman may be debating whether she will fit in or whether she will still stand out by wearing a sari as much as a pair of jeans. Differences in ethnicity or social class may be very significant to women's sense of themselves and how they dress, yet the argument put forward here is that the underlying logic in terms of how women make clothing choices arises out of the ambivalences I have discussed. This was given explicit attention in the final chapter and will be revisited here by way of a conclusion in order to illuminate the key issues of this book.

Rethinking Fashion, Rethinking Body Image

The centrality of this dialectic between safe, easy acts of dressing and the desire to be different and creative means that the act of constructing an identity through clothing is an ambivalent one. This notion resonates with discussions over fashion more broadly, as the constant fluctuations in styles have led to it being characterized as ambiguous in its shifts between innovation and conformity (Simmel, 1971), revealing and concealing the self (Sennett, 1971), sexuality and modesty, androgyny and femininity. There is clearly a relationship between an individual's experience of choosing what to wear and the wider fashion context. It would be easy to argue that the current fashion climate, with the rapid turnover of styles and lack of certainty over who the 'experts' are, produces women's uncertainty as they stand in front of their wardrobes. However, because women negotiate so many different factors when they choose what to wear, the wardrobe panic cannot be reduced to a single consideration such as fashion. When women are deliberating over whether to look funky or dress timelessly, they may also be debating whether the same skirt makes them look respectable or overly sexualized. This act of balancing is central to getting dressed, as dressing is neither the quest for individuality nor the retreat to conformity. The coexistence of many contradictory factors is central to 'getting it right'.

The argument put forward in this book is that women's actual relationship to fashion cannot be reduced to the workings of the high street, celebrity magazines or what designers put on the catwalk. As women deal with looking fashionable through clothing they put on their bodies, that they wear to go out with their partner or maybe wear to work, women's participation in fashion is always situated in their lives, relationships and biographies. Moreover, women's sense of what is 'in' is always seen in relation to what is 'me', as no two women have exactly the same relationship to fashion. The act of wearing what is fashionable involves women connecting what they like and what they know with what is new and present in the external arenas of the high street shops. Therefore, concerns over fashion tie in to women's considerations of their habitual selves and how they can comment upon this same 'safe' self. Women are often able to make this connection between the clothing they already wear and the fashion seen in the shops through seeing people they know wearing a new style or asking the advice of a friend.

These same issues that are raised in terms of how women relate to fashion can also be applied to an understanding of women's body images. Just as we cannot understand how fashion changes or why particular fashions get widespread acceptance by solely looking at the official face of fashion, nor do women's body images derive solely from the media construction of an ideal body. The current moral frenzy surrounding the media reiteration of an unrealistic model of beauty centres on a condemnation the skinniness of catwalk models and speculations on the negative impact these images may have. When this same issue is considered through my ethnography, none of the women I interviewed were in a constant state of feeling inadequate about their body size and shape. Almost everyone admitted to having been on a diet at some point, and many dieted at some point during the time that I worked with them; yet this was not their sole concern as they chose their clothing or looked in the mirror. I am not generalizing from the women I worked with to state that no women see their bodies as inadequate on a regular basis; rather, I contend that, based on the experiences of women I worked with, it cannot be assumed that to be a woman living in contemporary Britain means to feel constantly inadequate. To suggest that simply because there is a proliferation of increasingly slim women in the media means that women are constantly dieting in order to achieve this positions women as dupes who see their own bodies in relation to a distorted magazine image. These debates may be more applicable to younger women, as these unrealistic ideals feed into the inevitable insecurities and uncertainties of adolescence; however, the women I worked with were all nineteen or older.

More often than not, the body images of the women I interviewed were influenced by the bodies of people they saw around them or compliments about their bodies received from partners or friends. Women's relationship to their body image is incredibly complex and shifting and is dependent upon the occasion and whether women are considering the opinions of a man or of a group of friends. Even when women were dressing for a date with their partner, they were not simply dressing for what they thought that man would like to see them wearing; as women project their concerns over their favourite shoes or make-up onto the unsuspecting man, women are also dressing for themselves. When getting ready, a woman may spend ages deliberating over what shoes to wear, but usually the man the woman was supposedly dressing for will not remember what shoes she was wearing. On many occasions, women get ready with friends, and this female sociality was crucial to how women constructed their appearance: they were not dressing 'for' other women but with friends. This was a relationship of not competitiveness but solidarity. I was often present when women chose what to wear, and so I entered into this relationship, commenting on outfits and what suited the woman or what was appropriate for the occasion. I was also able to see how women's relationships to their clothing and body image shifts throughout the year. Even if women have a routinized relationship to their bodies, this may be disrupted or questioned on particular occasions, such as buying a new skirt or putting on some weight. It is on occasions like this when uncertainties and insecurities come to the fore. For some women, seeing their body as inadequate is a more frequent occurrence; for other women, it only occurs rarely.

Part of the 'safety' that habitual clothing offers is that women know how to wear these items, and they know the outfit looks good on their body. In specific instances of dressing when women's sartorial sense of themselves is disrupted, women have to consciously engage with their image, body and who they can be through clothing. The first visit to a new restaurant or meeting a new boyfriend's parents for the first time may result in a woman panicking that she cannot put the right outfit together. On these occasions, women feel unable to fit themselves into the specific occasion; this crisis over what to wear is linked to novelty of occasion, of people or even of a new item of clothing or a new 'look'. This sense of disruption may be experienced as a disruption in how women see their body shape. They may question whether they are fashionable enough or whether they look chic and mature enough. At such times, questions over body image may become paramount, but these always intersect with other concerns women have. Because clothing forms an extension of the self and thus women know what clothing they like, they have a sense of who they are through clothing. On certain occasions when this sense of self is questioned, women may come to see not only their bodies but also their sense of self as inadequate.

Women's sense of confidence engendered through wearing clothing all the time is therefore not absolute because it is subject to change. The change can be caused by an external change—such as a new boyfriend—or by an internal change—such as a woman becoming bored by her wardrobe. Habitual clothing is comfortable and easy, yet what my research has shown is that no women want to be reduced to being this same habitual self all the time. As women become tired of who they are through clothing, they either make a new purchase or combine their old clothes in a new way. Shifts in women's tastes always involve this dialogue between the woman they know they are habitually and the possibility of who they can be. Changes are not just imposed from an external fashion shift, but rather the constant novelty fashion offers is a means through which women can extend themselves through clothing.

Clothing as a Way of Being

My conclusions arise out of the integrity of my data. I observed the minutiae of getting dressed, what women were questioning as they moved from one outfit to another, and how they constructed who they are through clothing as they commented, 'this is so me', 'this could be me', 'I can't wear it, it's just not me'. Given how many instances I can recount of women failing to 'be' the person they thought they could through clothing, it is apparent that clothing does not simply reflect the self or identity. Instead, by virtue of being a material form that women can look at, hold and put on their bodies, clothing gives women a sense that they have a self and indeed that they can change it. These questions are ones these women would not perhaps sit and debate, but it is through clothing that they are engaging with these profound questions of daily existence. The clothing in their wardrobe is the means through which women engage with their sense of who they are and their place in the world. It also gives them a sense of the sort of person they can be in that world. This idea echoes Wilson's assertion that, 'for the individual to lay claim to a particular style may be ... a proof that one does at least exist' (Wilson, 1985: 122). This assertion is given even more weight when personal style is seen as materialized in items of clothing. Because clothing is an object women can touch and feel, it gives women a material and substantial sense of having a self. Clothing quite literally does the ontology of the self, where this self is a material practice that women are engaging with. Women always negotiate these issues of self-construction through specific items of clothing as they look at, touch and try items on their bodies. They consider being cozy and secure through the softness of a cashmere pashmina or whether they could be a different person by wearing a leather skirt. Even when they are asking 'is this me?', the act of questioning the self is not a metaphysical, abstract one; instead, women ask this question through the specific items of clothing in their wardrobe.

Even for women who do not see themselves as engaging with these big issues all the time, by virtue of wearing the same items of clothing habitually, clothing can effectively come to externalize women's sense of who they are. Even women who did not wish their clothing to define who they were were faced with occasions when they had to deliberate over this, as they 'fit' self to place and to people and chose to make particular aspects of themselves matter on this occasion. Women use clothing as a material means through which, in Strathern's sense, they can draw out traits from 'within' (1979: 249). When assembling outfits from their wardrobes, women are draping around their bodies aspects of themselves, such as personality traits or ethnicity. As aspects of the self exist in the material form of clothing, in choosing what to wear, dressing is an act of 'surfacing' particular aspects of the self. Goffman (1971a, 1974) has defined personal identity as persisting over time, consisting of multiple capacities, which are activated dependent upon particular social situations. The wardrobe can be seen as everything women 'are', yet the selection of a particular outfit is when women draw together certain traits from the multiple attributes and capabilities that women have. As the wardrobe is accumulated over time, dressing is also an act of making present aspects of a former self, as a woman may wear an item of clothing from her past in a new combination. Choosing what to wear is, therefore, an act both of 'surfacing' and also of 'presenting' disparate aspects of the self; it is also an act of 'drawing in' relationships, as women wear gifted or borrowed items and extend themselves through relationships.

If one considers the wardrobe to be an extension of all the diverse former and current aspects of the self, then it is apparent that the self is extremely contradic-tory: simultaneously conformist and individual, un-thought out and reflexive. The interplay between these factors is the underlying logic to the act of getting dressed, as women strive to both be themselves and to make choices they 'know' are them, yet to still be creative. This interplay between the need for security and a desire to be changing and dynamic recapitulates the dynamic between individuality and conformity that Simmel (1971) identified as the core dynamic of fashion. What my ethnography demonstrates is that this is also women's fundamental relationship to clothing and is a key tension within the self. When women wear an outfit, they have to commit to one 'look', and therefore these contradictions and ambivalences are not always apparent in the self that is presented in public. This dialectic of dressing the self is only accessible through observing how women choose what to wear.

Bibliography

Anthias, F. (2005), 'Social Stratification and Social Inequality: Models of Intersectionality and Identity', in F. Devine, M. Savage, J. Scott and R. Crompton (eds), *Rethinking Class: Culture, Identities and Lifestyle,* Basingstoke: Palgrave Macmillan.

Arnold, R. (2001), *Fashion, Desire and Anxiety: Image and Morality in the Twentieth Century,* London: Taurus.

Auslander, L. (1996), 'The Gendering of Consumption Practices in 19th Century France', in V. De Grazia and E. Furlough (eds), *The Sex of Things: Gender and Consumption in Historical Perspective,* London: University of California Press.

Banerjee, M. and Miller, D. (2003), *The Sari,* Oxford: Berg.

Banim, M. and Guy, A. (2001), 'Dis/continued Selves: Why Do Women Keep Clothes They No Longer Wear?' in A. Guy, E. Green and M. Banim (eds), *Through the Wardrobe: Women's Relationships with Their Clothes,* Oxford: Berg.

Barnes, R. and Eicher, J. (eds) (1993), *Dress and Gender: Making and Meaning,* Oxford: Berg.

Barthes, R. (1985), *The Fashion System,* London: Cape.

Bartky, S. (1982), 'Narcissism, Femininity and Alienation', *Social Theory and Practice,* 8(2): 127–43.

Baudrillard, J. (1981), *For a Political Economy of the Sign,* St Louis: Telos.

Bayly, C. (1986), 'The Origins of Swadeshi: Cloth and Indian Society, 1700–1930', in A. Appadurai (ed.), *The Social Life of Things,* Cambridge: Cambridge University Press.

Bean, S. (1989), 'Ghandi and Khadi, the Fabric of Indian Independence', in A. Weiner and J. Schneider (eds), *Cloth and the Human Experience,* London: Smithsonian Institution Press.

Bedeski, R. (1994), *The Transformation of South Korea,* New York: Routledge.

Belk, R. (1995), *Collecting in a Consumer Society,* London: Routledge.

Bell, D. (1998), 'Wealth Transfers Occasioned by Marriage: A Comparative Reconsideration', in T. Schweizer and D. White (eds), *Kinship, Network and Exchange,* Cambridge: Cambridge University Press.

Berger, J. (1972), *Ways of Seeing,* London: Penguin.

Bloch, M. (1989), 'The Symbolism of Money in Imerina', in M. Bloch and J. Parry (eds), *Money and the Morality of Exchange,* Cambridge: Cambridge University Press.

Bloch, M. and Parry, J. (1982), *Death and the Regeneration of Life,* Cambridge: Cambridge University Press.

Bonner, F., Goodman, L., Allen, R., Janes, L. and King, C. (eds) (1992), *Imagining Women: Cultural Representations and Gender,* London: Routledge.

Bordo, S. (2003), *Unbearable Weight: Feminism, Western Culture and the Body,* Berkeley: University of Calfornia Press.

Boucher, F. (1967), *History of Costume in the West,* London: Thames and Hudson.

Bourdieu, P. (1977), *Outline of a Theory of Practice,* Cambridge: Cambridge University Press.

Bourdieu, P. (1990), *Photography—A Middle-Brow Art,* Cambridge: Polity.

Breward, C. (2000), *Cultures, Identities, Histories: Fashioning a Cultural Approach to Dress,* in N. White and I. Griffiths (eds), *The Fashion Business: Theory, Practice, Image,* Oxford: Berg.

Breward, C. (2003), *Fashion,* Oxford: Oxford University Press.

Breward, C., Conekin, B. and Cox, C. (eds) (2002), *The Englishness of English Dress,* Oxford: Berg.

Breward, C. and Evans, C. (eds) (2005), *Fashion and Modernity,* Oxford: Berg.

Breward, C., and Gilbert, D. (2006), *Fashion's World Cities,* Oxford: Berg.

Brilliant, R. (1991), *Portraiture,* London: Reaktion Books.

Brydon, A. and Niessen, S. (1998), *Consuming Fashion: Adorning the Transnational Body,* Oxford: Berg.

Buckley, R. and Gundle, S. (2000), 'Fashion and Glamour', in N. White and I. Griffiths (eds), *The Fashion Business: Theory, Practice, Image,* Oxford: Berg.

Butler, J. (1990), *Gender Trouble: Feminism and the Subversion of Identity,* London: Routledge.

Butler, J. (1993), *Bodies that Matter,* London: Routledge.

Campbell, C. (1996), 'Shopping, Pleasure and the Sex War', in P. Falk and C. Campbell (eds), *The Shopping Experience,* London: Sage.

Campbell, S. (1983), 'Attaining Rank: A Classification of Kula Shell Valuables', in E. Leach and J. Leach (eds), *The Kula,* Cambridge: Cambridge University Press.

Carrithers, M. (1985), 'An Alternative Social History of the Self', in M. Carrithers, S. Collins and S. Lukes (eds), *The Category of the Person: Anthropology, Philosophy, History,* Cambridge: Cambridge University Press.

Chalfen, R. (1987), *Snapshot Versions of Life,* Bowling Green, Ohio: Bowling Green State University Popular Press.

Cho, H-J. (1995), 'Children in the Examination War in South Korea: A Cultural Analysis', in S. Stephens (ed.), *Children and the Politics of Culture,* Princeton: Princeton University Press.

Cho, H-J. (1998), 'Korean Women and Their Experiences in the Traditional World', in Research Institute of Asian Women (ed.), *Korean Women and Culture,* Seoul, Korea: Research Institute of Asian Women.

Clarke, A. (2000), '"Mother Swapping": The Trafficking of Nearly New Children's Wear', in P. Jackson, M. Lowe, D. Miller and F. Mort (eds), *Commercial Cultures,* Oxford: Berg.

Clarke, A. and Miller, D. (2002), 'Fashion and Anxiety', *Fashion Theory,* 6(2): 191–214.

Clifford, J. and Marcus, G. E. (eds) (1986), *Writing Culture: The Poetics and Politics of Ethnography,* Berkeley: University of California Press.

Cohn, B. (1989), 'Cloth, Clothes and Colonialism: India in the Nineteenth Century', in A. Weiner and J. Schneider (eds), *Cloth and the Human Experience,* London: Smithsonian Institution Press.

Colchester, C. (ed.) (2003), *Clothing the Pacific,* Oxford: Berg.

Cole, S. (2000), *'Don We Now Our Gay Apparel': Gay Men's Dress in the Twentieth Century,* Oxford: Berg.

Constantine, S. and Woodall, T. (2002), *What Not To Wear,* London: Weidenfeld and Nicolson.

Corbman, B. (1985), *Textiles: Fiber to Fabrics,* New York: McGraw-Hill.

Corrigan, P. (1995), 'Gender and the Gift: The Case of the Family Clothing Economy', in S. Jackson and S. Moores (eds), *The Politics of Domestic Consumption,* London: Prentice Hall.

Craik, J. (1993), *The Face of Fashion: Cultural Studies in Fashion,* London: Routledge.

Cwerner, S. (2001), 'Clothes at Rest: Elements for a Sociology of the Wardrobe', *Fashion Theory,* 5(1), 79–92.

Daly, M. (1979), *Gyn/Ecology: The Metaethics of Radical Feminism,* London: Routledge.

De Beauvoir, S. (1997/1949), *The Second Sex,* London: Vintage.

De Certeau, M. (1984), *The Practice of Everyday Life,* Berkeley: University of California Press.

De Grazia, V. and Furlough, E. (eds) (1996), *The Sex of Things: Gender and Consumption in Historical Perspective,* London: University of California Press.

Delphy, C. (1995), 'Sharing the Same Table: Consumption and the Family', in S. Jackson and S. Moores (eds), *The Politics of Domestic Consumption,* London: Prentice Hall.

Denzin, N. (1989), *Interpretive Biography,* London: Sage.

DeVault, M. (1991), *Feeding the Family: The Social Organization of Caring as Gendered Work,* Chicago: University of Chicago Press.

Devine, F., Savage, M., Scott, J. and Crompton, R. (eds) (2005), *Rethinking Class: Culture, Identities and Lifestyle,* Basingstoke: Palgrave Macmillan.

Douglas, M. (1991), *Risk and Blame: Essays in Cultural Theory,* London: Routledge.

du Gay, P. (1997), *Production of Culture: Cultures of Production,* London: Sage.

Duneier, M. (1992), *Slim's Table: Race, Respectability and Masculinity,* Chicago: University of Chicago Press.

Dworkin, A. (1974), *Woman-Hating,* New York: Dalton.

Edholm, F. (1992), 'Beyond the Mirror: Women's Self-Portraits', in F. Bonner, L. Goodman, R. Allen, L. Janes and C. King (eds), *Imagining Women: Cultural Representations and Gender,* London: Routledge.

Eicher, J. (2001), 'The Cultural Significance of Dress and Textiles', in *Reviews in Anthropology,* 30: 309–23.

Entwistle, J. (1997), 'Power Dressing and the Fashioning of the Career Woman', in M. Nava, A. Blake and B. Richards and I. MacRury (eds), *Buy This Book: Studies in Advertising and Consumption,* London: Routledge.

Entwistle, J. (2000), *The Fashioned Body,* Oxford: Polity.

Entwistle, J. (2001), 'The Dressed Body', in J. Entwistle and E. Wilson (eds), *Body Dressing,* Oxford: Berg.

Entwistle, J. and Wilson, E. (eds) (2001), *Body Dressing,* Oxford: Berg.

Evans, C. (2000), 'John Galliano: Modernity and Spectacle', in N. White and I. Griffiths (eds), *The Fashion Business: Theory, Practice, Image,* Oxford: Berg.

Evans, C. and Thornton, M. (1989), *Women and Fashion: A New Look.* London: Quartet Books.

Evans-Pritchard, E. E. (1940), *The Nuer,* Oxford: Clarendon.

FashionMap archive (2001–2006), Nottingham Trent University.

Featherstone, M. (1991), *Consumer Culture and Post-Modernism,* London: Sage.

Femenias, B. (2004), *Gender and the Boundaries of Dress in Contemporary Peru,* Austin: University of Texas Press.

Fine, B. and Leopold, E. (1993), *The World of Consumption,* London: Routledge.

Forty, A. (1999), 'Introduction', in A. Forty and S. Kuchler (eds), *The Art of Forgetting,* Oxford: Berg.

Forty, A. and Kuchler, S. (eds) (1999), *The Art of Forgetting,* Oxford: Berg.

Foucault, M. (1970), *The Order of Things: An Archaeology of the Human Science,* London: Tavistock.

Foucault, M. (1980), 'Truth and Power', in C. Gordon (ed.), *Power/Knowledge: Selected Interviews and Other Writings 1972–77,* New York: Pantheon Books.

Gage, J. (1993), *Colour and Culture: Practice and Meaning from Antiquity to Abstraction,* London: Thames & Hudson.

Garfinkel, H. (1984), *Studies in Ethnomethodology,* Cambridge: Polity.

Gell, A. (1998), *Art and Agency: Towards an Anthropological Theory.* Oxford: Clarendon Press.

Giddens, A. (1991), *Modernity and Self-Identity: Self and Society in the Late Modern Age,* Cambridge: Polity.

Gillis, J. (1996), *A World of Their Own Making: A History of Myth and Ritual in Family Life,* Oxford: Oxford University Press.

Ginzburg, C. (1988), 'Morelli, Freud and Sherlock Holmes: Clues and Scientific Method', in U. Eco and T. Sebeok (eds), *The Sign of Three: Dupin, Holmes, Peirce,* Bloomington: Indiana University Press.

Godelier, M. (1999), *The Enigma of the Gift,* Chicago: University of Chicago Press.

Goffman, E. (1971a), *The Presentation of Self in Everyday Life,* London: Penguin.

Goffman, E. (1971b), *Relations in Public: Microstudies of the Public Order,* London: Allen Lane.

Goffman, E. (1974), *Frame Analysis: An Essay on the Organization of Experience,* Harmondsworth: Penguin.

Gregson, N., Brooks, K. and Crewe, L. (2001), 'Bjorn Again? Rethinking 70s Revivalism through the Reappropriation of 70s Clothing', *Fashion Theory,* 5: 3–28.

Gregson, N. and Crewe, L. (2003), *Second-Hand Cultures,* Oxford: Berg.

Gregson, N. and Beale, V. (2004), 'Wardrobe Matter: The Sorting, Circulation and Displacement of Women's Clothes', *Geoforum,* 35(6): 689–700.

Gullestad, M. (1996), *Everyday Life Philosophies: Modernity, Morality and Autobiography in Norway,* Oslo: Scandinavian University Press.

Gunter, B. and Wykes, M. (2005), *Media and Body Image: If Looks Could Kill,* London: Sage.

Hall, S. (1981), 'Notes on Deconstructing "The Popular"', in R. Samuel (ed.), *People's History and Socialist Thought,* London: Routledge.

Hall, S. (ed.) (1997), *Representation: Cultural Representations and Signifying Practices,* London: Sage.

Hall, S. (2000), 'Conclusion: The Multicultural Question', in B. Hesse (ed.), *Un/settled Multiculturalisms: Diasporas, Entanglements, Transruptures,* London: Zed Books.

Hall, S. (2005), 'New Ethnicities', in L. Martin Alcott and E. Mendietta (eds), *Race, Class, Gender and Nationality,* Oxford: Blackwell.

Hammersley, M. and Atkinson, P. (1995), *Ethnography: Principles in Practice,* London: Routledge.

Hansen, K. T. (2000), *Salaula: The World of Second-Hand Clothing and Zambia,* Chicago: University of Chicago Press.

Hansen, K. T. (2004a), 'Dressing Dangerously: Miniskirts, Gender Relations and Sexuality in Zambia', in J. Allman (ed.), *Fashioning Power: Clothing, Politics and African Identities,* Bloomington: Indiana University Press.

Hansen, K. T. (2004b), 'The World in Dress: Anthropological Perspectives on Clothing, Fashion and Culture', *Annual Review of Anthropology,* 3: 369–92.

Hatch, K. (1993), *Textile Science,* Minneapolis: West Publishing.

Hebdige, D. (1987), *Subculture:Tthe Meaning of Style,* London: Routledge.

Hendrikson, C. (1995), *Weaving Identities: Constructions of Dress and Self in a Highland Guatemalan Town,* Austin: University of Texas Press.

Hodkinson, P. (2002), *Goth: Identity, Style and Sub-culture,* Oxford: Berg.

Holland, J. and Adkins, L. (eds) (1996), *Sex, Sensibility and the Gendered Body,* London: Macmillan.

Holland, S. (2004), *Alternative Femininities: Body, Image, Identity,* Oxford: Berg.

Hollander, A. (1993), *Seeing Through Clothes,* London: University of California Press.

Holliday, R. (2001), 'Fashioning the Queer Self', in J. Entwistle and E. Wilson (eds), *Body Dressing,* Oxford: Berg.

Hollows, J. (2000), *Feminism, Femininity and Popular Culture,* Manchester: Manchester University Press.

Hoskins, J. (1989), 'Why Do Ladies Sing the Blues? Indigo Dyeing, Cloth Production, and Gender Symbolism in Kodi', in A. Weiner and J. Schneider (eds), *Cloth and the Human Experience,* London: Smithsonian Institution Press.

Hoskins, J. (1998), *Biographical Objects: How Things Tell the Stories of People's Lives,* London: Routledge.

Hyland-Eriksen, T. (2001), *Tyranny of the Moment: Fast and Slow Time in the Information Age,* London: Pluto.

IPC Media (March 2004), *In Style: Your Own Personal Stylist,* St. Ives: Caerphilly.

Jackson, S. and Moores, S. (1995), *The Politics of Domestic Consumption,* London: Prentice Hall.

Johnson, K. and Lennon, S. (eds) (1999), *Appearance and Power,* Oxford: Berg.

Kahn, N. (1993), 'Asian Women's Dress: From Borquah to Bloggs—Changing Clothes for Changing Times', in J. Ash and E. Wilson (eds), *Chic Thrills: A Fashion Reader,* London: Pandora Press.

Kaiser, S. (2003), *The Social Psychology of Clothing,* New York: Fairchild Publications.

Keenan, W. (ed.) (2001), *Dressed to Impress: Looking the Part.* Oxford: Berg.

Kibria, N. (2002), *Becoming Asian American: 2nd Generation Chinese and Korean American Identities,* London: Johns Hopkins University Press.

King, C. (1992), 'The Politics of Representation: A Democracy of the Gaze', in F. Bonner, L. Goodman, R. Allen, L. Janes and C. King (eds), *Imagining Women: Cultural Representations and Gender,* London: Routledge.

Kopytoff, I. (1986), 'The Cultural Biography of Things: Commoditisation as a Process', in A. Appadurai (ed.), *The Social Life of Things,* Cambridge: Cambridge University Press.

Kuechler, S. (1999), 'The Place of Memory', in A. Forty and S. Kuchler (eds), *The Art of Forgetting,* Oxford: Berg.

Kuechler, S. and Miller, D. (eds) (2005), *Clothing as Material Culture,* Oxford: Berg.

Kuechler, S. and Were, G. (eds) (2004), *The Art of Clothing: A Pacific Experience,* London: University College London Press.

Kvale, S. (1996), *InterViews: An Introduction to Qualitative Research Interviewing,* London: Sage.

La Fontaine, J. (1985), 'Person and Individual: Some Anthropological Reflections', in M. Carrithers, S. Collins and S. Lukes (eds), *The Category of the Person: Anthropology, Philosophy, History,* Cambridge: Cambridge University Press.

Lan, D. (1989), 'Resistance to the Present by the Past: Mediums and Money in Zimbabwe', in M. Bloch and J. Parry (eds), *Money and the Morality of Exchange,* Cambridge: Cambridge University Press.

Laver, J. (1995), *A Concise History of Costume,* London: Thames and Hudson.

Lawler, S. (2000), *Mothering the Self: Mother's Daughters, Subjects,* London: Routledge.

Leach, E. (1970), *Political Systems of Highland Burma: A Study of Kachin Social Structure,* London: Athlone.

Lefebvre, H. (1991/1974), *The Production of Space,* Oxford: Blackwell.

Levi-Strauss, C. (1966), *The Savage Mind,* London: Weidenfeld and Nicholson.

Levi-Strauss, C. (1969), *The Elementary Structures of Kinship,* Boston: Beacon.

Levy, A. (2005), *Female Chauvinist Pigs: Women and the Rise of Raunch Culture,* New York: Free Press.

Lipovetsky, G. (1994), *The Empire of Fashion: Dressing Modern Democracy,* Princeton: Princeton University Press.

Lurie, A. (1992), *The Language of Clothes,* New York: Random House.

Lyotard, J. F. (1984), *The Post-Modern Condition: A Report on Knowledge,* Manchester: Manchester University Press.

Macfarlane, A. (1987), *The Culture of Capitalism,* Oxford: Basil Blackwell.

McCracken, G. (1988), *Culture and Consumption: New Approaches to the Symbolic Character of Consumer Goods and Activities,* Bloomington: Indiana University Press.

McRobbie, A. (1994), *Post-Modernism and Popular Culture,* London: Routledge.

Malinowski, B. (1922), *Argonauts of the Western Pacific,* London: Routledge and Kegan Paul.

Mann, C. (1996), 'Girls' Own Story: The Search for a Sexual Identity in Times of Family Change', in J. Holland and L. Adkins (eds), *Sex, Sensibility and the Gendered Body,* London: Macmillan.

Mauss, M. (1973), 'Techniques of the Body', *Economy and Society,* 2(1): 70–89.

Mauss, M. (1985), 'A Category of the Human Mind: The Notion of Person, the Notion of Self', in M. Carrithers, S. Collins and S. Lukes (eds), *The Category of the Person: Anthropology, Philosophy, History,* Cambridge: Cambridge University Press.

Mauss, M. (1992), *The Gift,* London: Routledge.

Mead, G. H. (1982), *The Individual and the Social Self: Unpublished Work of G. H. Mead,* London: University of Chicago Press.

Melchior-Bonnett, S. (2002), *The Mirror: A History,* London: Routledge.

Mercer, K. and Julien, I. (1994), 'Black Masculinity and the Sexual Politics of Race', in K. Mercer (ed.), *Welcome to the Jungle: New Positions in Black Cultural Studies,* London: Routledge.

Merleau-Ponty, M. (1974), *Phenomenology, Language and Sociology. Selected Essays of Merleau-Ponty* edited by J. O'Neill, London: Heineman Educational.

Miller, D. (1987), *Material Culture and Mass Consumption,* Oxford: Basil Blackwell.

Miller, D. (1997), 'How Infants Grow Mothers in North London', *Theory, Culture and Society,* 14(4): 67–88. London: Sage.

Miller, D. (1998), *A Theory of Shopping,* Cambridge: Polity Press.

Miller, D. (ed.) (2001), *Home Possessions,* Oxford: Berg.

Moi, T. (2002), *Sexual/Textual Politics,* London: Routledge.

Moi, T. (2005), *Sex, Gender and the Body: The Student Edition of What Is a Woman,* Oxford: Oxford University Press.

Muggleton, D. (2000), *Inside Sub-culture: The Post-Modern Meaning of Style,* Oxford: Berg.

Mulvey, L. (1975), 'Visual Pleasure and Narrative Cinema', *Screen,* 16(3): 6–18.

Munt, S. (2001), 'The Butch Body', in R. Holliday and J. Hassard (eds), *Contested Bodies,* London: Routledge.

Napier, D. (1985), *Masks, Transformation, and Paradox,* Berkeley: University of California Press.

Niessen, S., Leshkowich, A. and Jones, C. (eds) (2003), *Re-orienting Fashion: The Globalisation of Asian Dress,* Oxford: Berg.

Nippert-Eng, C. (1996), *Home and Work: Negotiating Boundaries through Everyday Life,* London: University of Chicago Press.

Oakley, A. (1976), *Housewife,* Harmondsworth: Penguin.

O'Connor, K. (2005), 'The Other Half: The Material Culture of New Fibres', in S. Kuchler and D. Miller (eds), *Clothing as Material Culture,* Oxford: Berg.

Osteen, M. (ed.) (2002), *The Question of the Gift,* London: Routledge.

Paul, P. (2005), *Pornified: How Pornography Is Transforming Our Lives, Our Relationships, and Our Families,* New York: Times Books.

Peiss, K. (1996), 'Making Up, Making Over: Cosmetics, Consumer Culture and Women's Identity', in V. De Grazia and E. Furlough (eds), *The Sex of Things: Gender and Consumption in Historical Perspective,* London: University of California Press.

Polhemus, T. (1994), *Streetstyle: From Sidewalk to Catwalk,* London: Thames and Hudson.

Rabine, L. (2002), *The Global Circulation of African Fashion,* Oxford: Berg.

Rapport, N. (ed.) (2002), *British Subjects: An Anthropology of Britain,* Oxford: Berg.

Renne, E. (1995), *Cloth that Does Not Die: The Meaning of Cloth in Bunu Social Life,* Seattle: University of Washington Press.

Riegl, A. (1982), 'The Modern Cult of Monuments: Its Character and Its Origin', trans. K. Forster and D. Ghirado, *Oppositions,* 25: 21–51.

Sahlins, M. (1972), *Stone Age Economics,* Chicago: Aldine-Atherton.

Sahlins, M. (1976), *Culture and Practical Reason,* London: University of Chicago Press.

Sennett, R. (1971), *The Fall of Public Man,* Cambridge: Cambridge University Press.

Shields, R. (1991), *Places on the Margin: Alternative Geographies of Modernity,* London: Routledge.

Silverman, D. (ed.) (1997), *Qualitative Research: Theory, Method and Practice,* London: Sage.

Simmel, G. (1971), *On Individuality and Social Forms,* Chicago: University of Chicago Press.

Skeggs, B. (1997), *Formations of Class and Gender: Becoming Respectable,* London: Sage.

Skeggs, B. (2004), *Class, Self, Culture,* London: Routledge.

Sontag, S. (1979), *On Photography,* Harmondsworth: Penguin.

Stanley, L. (1992), *The Auto-Biographical I,* Manchester: Manchester University Press.

Stanley, L. and Wise, S. (1993), *Breaking out Again: Feminist Ontology and Epistemology,* London: Routledge.

Strathern, M. (1979), 'The Self in Self-Decoration', *Oceania,* 49(June): 4.

Strathern, M. (1992), *After Nature English Kinship in the Late Twentieth Century,* Cambridge: Cambridge University Press.

Summers, L. (2001), *Bound To Please: A History of the Victorian Corset,* Oxford: Berg.

Tarlo, E. (1996), *Clothing Matters,* Chicago: University of Chicago Press.

Tarrant, N. (1994), *The Development of Costume,* London: Routledge.

Taylor, L. (2002), *The Study of Dress History,* Manchester: Manchester University Press.

Taylor, L. (2004), *Establishing Dress History,* Manchester: Manchester University Press.

Thesander, M. (1997), *The Feminine Ideal,* London: Reaktion Books.

Thompson, K. (1998), 'Durkheim and Sacred Identity', in N. Allen, W. Pickering and W. Watts Miller (eds), *On Durkheim's Elementary Forms of Religious Life,* London: Routledge.

Thurgood Haynes, M. (1998), *Dressing up Debutantes: Pageantry and Glitz in Texas,* Oxford: Berg.

Turner, B. (1984), *The Body and Society: Explorations in Social Theory,* Oxford: Blackwell.

Veblen, T. (1899), *The Theory of the Leisure Class: An Economic Study of Institutions,* New York: Mentor.

Vickery, A. (1998), 'Women and the World of Goods: A Lancashire Consumer and Her Possessions, 1751–81', in J. Brewer and R. Porter (eds), *Consumption and the World of Goods,* London: Routledge.

Vinken, B. (2004), *Fashion Zeitgeist,* Oxford: Berg.

Wallman, S. (1984), *Eight London Households,* London: Tavistock.

Warwick, A. and Cavallero, D. (1998), *Fashioning the Frame: Boundaries, Dress and the Body,* Oxford: Berg.

Weiner, A. (1989), 'Why Cloth? Wealth Gender, and Power in Oceania', in A. Weiner and J. Schneider (eds), *Cloth and the Human Experience,* London: Smithsonian Institution Press.

Weiner, A. (1992), *Inalienable Possessions,* Berkeley: University of California Press.

Weiner, A. and Schneider, J. (eds) (1989), *Cloth and the Human Experience,* London: Smithsonian Institution Press.

White, N. and Griffiths, I. (2000), *The Fashion Business: Theory, Practice, Image,* Oxford: Berg.

Wigley, M. (1995), *White Walls, Designer Dresses: The Fashioning of Modern Architecture,* Cambridge, Mass.: MIT Press.

Wilson, E. (1985), *Adorned in Dreams: Fashion and Modernity,* London: Virago.

Wilson, E. and de la Haye, A. (eds) (1999), *Defining Dress. Dress as Object, Meaning and Identity,* Manchester: Manchester University Press.

Wilson, G. (1995), 'Money: Patterns of Responsibility and Irresponsibility in Marriage', in S. Jackson and S. Moores (eds), *The Politics of Domestic Consumption,* London: Prentice Hall.

Winship, J. (1987), *Inside Women's Magazines,* London: Pandora Press.

Wolf, N. (1990), *The Beauty Myth,* London: Vintage.

Young, D. (2001), *The Colours of Things, Memory, Mentality & an Anthropology of the Senses in North West South Australia,* unpublished PhD thesis, University College London.

Young, I. M. (2005), *On Female Body Experience: 'Throwing Like a Girl' and Other Essays,* Oxford: Oxford University Press.

Index

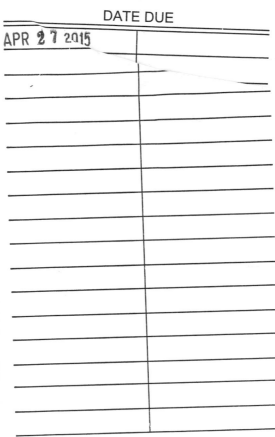

DATE DUE

APR 27 2015

DEMCO, INC. 38-2931